# CIVIL SERVICES OF THE UNITED KINGDOM

## 1855-1970

*By the Same Author*

'Civil Service Staff Relationships' (Hodge, 1943)
'The Civil Service: Its Problems and Future' (Staples, *2nd edn.,* 1948)
'An Introduction to Public Administration' (Staples, *4th edn.,* 1966)
'The Essentials of Public Administration' (Staples, *3rd edn.,* 1964)
'Civil Service or Bureaucracy?' (Staples, 1956)
'British Public Service Administration' (Staples, 1961)
'Approach to Public Administration' (Staples, 1966)

*

'The Failure of the Left' (Staples, 1947)
   *A political study by 'Norman Mansfield'*

*

'Ypres, 1917' (Kimber, 1967)
   *Autobiographical*

# CIVIL SERVICES
## OF THE
# UNITED KINGDOM
## 1855-1970

## E. N. GLADDEN
M.Sc.(Econ.), Ph.D.(Public Admin.)

FRANK CASS & CO. LTD.
1967

First published in 1967 by

FRANK CASS AND COMPANY LIMITED

67 Great Russell Street, London, WC1

Printed in Northern Ireland
by W. & G. Baird, Ltd., Belfast

# CONTENTS

# vi

# *Contents*

## TABLES

## FORMS

## DIAGRAMS

## ACKNOWLEDGEMENTS

In writing a book on such a subject as the Civil Service it is necessary to consult numerous official and semi-official bodies and persons whose titles or names it would be invidious to associate with my personal views. I must, however, remark upon the unfailing helpfulness with which my, often inconvenient, applications for information have been met and to express my sincere thanks to all who have aided me in this way.

Special mention is due of the Clarendon Press, Oxford, for kindly agreeing to the reprinting of the quotation on page 197 from H. E. Dale's *The Higher Civil Service of Great Britain,* first published by them in 1941, and to the Controller of Her Majesty's Stationery Office for information quoted from various official publications.

E. N. GLADDEN

New Barnet, March 1967

# INTRODUCTION

At a time when the Civil Service is on the eve of changes that may well prove as radical as those of 1853/70 and 1919/20 it should be useful to have a study of the Civil Service as it is today, with some indication of how the present situation has come about. *Civil Services of the United Kingdom* aims at providing just such a study. It does not presume to offer a blueprint for the future, a task that is at this very moment in much more competent hands.

This new work is a development of the same author's *Civil Service or Bureaucracy?* (Staples Press, 1956) which appeared shortly after the Report of the Priestley Commission on the Civil Service (1953/5). Much of the basic descriptive matter of the former book has been retained and brought up to date, but whereas the original work was written intimately from the inside with the aim of providing a critical appreciation of the working of the Civil Service at that time, the present work is designed to look at the Civil Service from a rather broader viewpoint. To this end information is included, specifically in Chapters XI and XII, of certain other civil service and quasi-civil service fields not usually covered in surveys of this kind.

The author, as a retired civil servant and active teacher of public administration, is not merely concerned with the Civil Service's participation in policy making, in questions of constitutional propriety, or in the sources of bureaucratic power, but particularly in the day-to-day working of the system as the institution of government personnel management. We should not be content to look down from the top but also attempt to see the machine from the level of middle management, as well as of the office counter where the most constant liaison with the public is made.

It needs to be emphasized that the book is about the Civil Service as a whole and not about specific groups and classes, to each of which a complete study could well be devoted. It does not even concentrate upon the Administrative Class which, largely because of its importance and a general interest in its activities as the leadership group, is the chief concern of most works on the Civil Service. Naturally the place and activities of such a leadership class must figure prominently in any book on this topic, and in addition the

Clerical – Executive – Administrative classes, as the Civil Service group devoted *par excellence* to government administration as a vocation, must receive major consideration. But this should not be interpreted as minimizing the contribution of the varied Professional, Technical and Industrial groups which provide the skills of a widening range of non-administrative occupations that are vital to the development of the modern industrial and welfare state. Their great diversity and manifest differences are authoritatively illustrated by H.M. Treasury's *Introductory Factual Memorandum on the Civil Service*,[1] submitted to the Fulton Committee, which devotes separate chapters to as many as forty-three distinct staff groups, each of which covers a separate class and in some cases two or three. Clearly any attempt even to summarize their basic characteristics and activities would be out of the question in a work of the present dimensions! As practitioners in other professions and occupations, whose bounds usually transcend those of the Civil Service, they are not our concern here, but as officials of the Central Departments their problems are the problems of the Civil Service in general, and with these we are certainly concerned.

The 'Contents' should tell the reader clearly enough what the book is all about, and it is proposed to devote the rest of this 'Preface' to a brief resumé of some of the changes that are already taking place.

## Coping with a Rapidly Changing Environment

While the search for the political ideal goes on, the tasks and shape of the administrative machine are changing almost daily. One of the major problems of the student of political science in its broader aspects, and of public administration in particular, is to keep up with the flow of events. Old established institutions disappear and are replaced by new ones almost overnight: new methods and procedures are introduced before morning. Thus the notes on the Chart facing page 10 have had to be supplemented with information about structural changes in the departmental system that have taken place since 1965.

The process continues and the situation must be considered dynamically. Fortunately we have been concerned with the Civil Service as a professional staffing institution and only incidentally with the Central Departments as part of the machinery of government, but it is not possible to discuss personnel matters out of relation with the purposes the staffs are appointed to serve. Change, though inevitable, is not a virtue in itself. Certainly static administration is indicative of institutional decline, but there are losses

[1] Official document only.

inevitably associated with administrative changes that need to be offset by clear advantages to render them worthwhile.

Since 1960, under governments of both the leading parties, administrative changes have been hectic, to say the least. Much of this has followed logically upon the normal requirements of politics: much has therefore been unavoidable and indeed welcome, but not all. When we note, for example, (1) the hiving off from the Treasury of functions which are evidently so closely associated with the finance function that complete divorcement is bound to generate organizational difficulties of its own, (2) the introduction of new Departments such as the Ministry of Land and Natural Resources, whose functions cut across those of a number of Departments, creating additional complexities that seemed better avoided, and (3) the establishment of a brand-new Ministry of Technology to act as a sort of administrative cannibal to digest the existing not-so-old Ministry of Aviation and parts of other established Departments, one is bound to wonder whether, insofar as they were administrative, the changes could have been more economically contrived. Old Departments may well need a shake up at times – all human institutions do – but it may well be asked whether these were the best ways to administer the medicine. It must be realized that a new Department, however, brilliantly it may be staffed – usually at the expense of other sectors of the Administration – takes time to settle down into an administrative team capable of working at even normal efficiency. In the meantime the system has to bear exceptional costs of staff ineffectiveness. What this may have amounted to in recent years is impossible to assess, and the paucity of serious criticism of the administrative changes, even in Parliament, is probably due to the existence of so few outside people who are really knowledgeable, or indeed sufficiently interested, in administrative matters. This is a costly national weakness in our particular brand of Administrative Society. One thing can be said that is relevant to our subject: the British Civil Service, with all its shortcomings, some real and many imagined, again and again demonstrates its capacity to deal effectively with such administrative eruptions, which need to be all in the day's work.

## Recruitment Trends

The most recent Report from the Civil Service Commissioners, covering the year 1965,[1] shows certain modifications in the trends indicated in our text. Thus there was an increase in the successful

[1] *Report of Her Majesty's Civil Service Commissioners, for the period 1st January to 31st December, 1965, Ninety-ninth Report (HMSO 1966).*

candidates for the Administrative Class, coming from universities other than Oxford and Cambridge, of from 16 per cent in 1964 to 24 per cent in 1965. For the same group more mature recruits from outside amounted to 70 between the ages of 30 and 52 for Principal Posts and 3 from persons with suitable specialized experience for Assistant Secretary posts.

In the competitions for the Special Departmental Classes, for which the number of suitable candidates continued to fail to meet the full needs of the Departments concerned, an improvement brought about by the holding of a separate competition without written examination for Inspectors of Taxes in the Inland Revenue led to the adoption of the same arrangement for the Ministry of Labour and Post Office posts, which, with those of the Inland Revenue, constitute this particular field.

General expansion in the work of the Departments led to an increased demand for Executive Class recruits and although there were about 2,500 successful candidates in 1965 (compared with approximately 1,800 in 1964 and 1,500 in 1963) this left five hundred vacancies still unfilled.

Recruitment for the Clerical Class was characterized by increased delegation of recruitment to the individual Departments and regionally, by means of the G.C.E. method, and by the extension of similar arrangements to other comparable classes. The trend away from true competition continues.

## A New Full-Scale Review of the Civil Service

Following the recommendations of the Estimates Committee in their Report of 1965 reviewing Civil Service recruitment, which is examined in the text,[1] the Government decided to set up a special committee, under the chairmanship of Lord Fulton, to take a comprehensive look into the structure and working of the Civil Service, the first review on such a scale since that of the Royal Commission's (Tomlin) inquiry of 1929/31. This new committee has a massive and highly important job on hand, for the consensus is that so considerable have been the developments in the scope of government, as well as in both general and government administration, during these last two decades that radical readjustments in the Civil Service are long overdue. Evidence from the various interested organizations and individuals is in course of submission to the Committee but the absence of officially printed evidence (whose publication is apparently left to the discretion of the bodies concerned) means that the public is not being adequately informed as the investigation

[1] See page 79.

develops. No doubt there are advantages in this particular mode of approach – which is of course not new and is well in line with tendencies to invest official proceedings with an air of exaggerated secrecy. While there are manifest disadvantages in the normal procedures of Royal Commissions, which usually suffer from a lack of research facilities and are too dependent upon *ex-parte* statements, it must be emphasized how much students and researchers today are dependent upon the voluminous information papers, or blue books, of previous inquiries for what we know about the Civil Service. We all – or nearly all – are proud of belonging to a Democracy, but it is as well to remember that the retention of a maximum of freedom may well in the future depend upon the emergence of an Informed Democracy, and it is by no means certain that we are maintaining our ground here.

Let us now look at a few representative examples of proposals which are emerging from this national dialogue on the Civil Service.

## H.M. Treasury's Proposals

Among the submissions that, understandably, have had a good deal of publicity, are those of the Treasury,[1] who have come out in favour of an amalgamation of the Administrative and Executive Classes to form a new management structure. For those who have observed at first-hand the typical inside attitudes of the Higher Civil Service in the past this recognition of the obvious, really does emphasize the radical nature of the changes that are taking place around us. Our leaders, political and administrative, if by nature slow in recognizing new developments at the stage of incubation do have the virtue of recognizing a dead horse when it gets in their way. The empiricist, fortunately for us all, stops the flogging and aims to get rid of the carcase without delay!

The proposed amalgamation of the two classes amounts to little more than a superimposing of the present Administrative gradings on the top of the present Executive gradings, but with the overlapping grades eliminated. As a result the new structure would consist of eight grades from Grade I (Permanent Secretary) down to Grade VIII (Executive Officer). There would be 18 year old recruitment at G.C.E. A level into Grade VIII, with normal prospects of rising to Grade VI and a widened graduate entry, also into Grade VIII at an appropriate point, but with starring of those with sufficiently high academic qualifications and performance at the selection stage. Recruitment would extend to provide opportunities of

---

[1] See *Whitley Bulletin* (Civil Service National Whitley Council Staff Side), Vol. XLVI pp. 120–23 (Aug, 1966).

promotion from the Clerical Class at the base, and to the selection of suitable Professional and Technical officials in the higher ranges. These proposals have much to be said in their favour but it is to be observed that present attitudes towards the cultivation of an elite solely upon normal school performance are not to be completely discarded.

## The Professional and Technical Groups React

H.M. Treasury's proposals have had a good press inside as well as outside the Civil Service. Naturally the Executive groups have welcomed the acceptance of a doctrine which they have been supporting on the basis of hard experience. It is equally understandable that the Clerical group is highly critical at not being brought into the scheme of reorganization. It is, however, in the evidence of the Institution of Professional Civil Servants[1] that possibly the most interesting reaction is to be discerned. They stigmatize the Treasury's proposals as 'inadequate and unreal'. While they agree with the abolition of the distinction between Administrative and Executive work they consider that the amalgamation should include the Professional and Technical groups and that the Higher Civil Service, including all these categories, should be consolidated into a number of grades, appointment to and progress within which should depend entirely upon capacity and ability. The Institution promises to submit further details on how their proposals should be implemented. They have also, with commendable enterprise, put in hand an inquiry into Civil Service practices in a number of other countries which they propose to submit to the Fulton Committee in due course.

But their ideas about the exchangeability of professional and administrative posts point to some real difficulties. While it is generally conceded that the senior posts in the Civil Service should be open to transfer or promotion from all groups within the Service – and in fact professional people have for long been promoted in those Departments where their specialist knowledge is of particular value in the performance of the Department's administrative duties, such persons are bound to be at a disadvantage in competition for those more general administrative positions requiring the experience of a profession they have not originally chosen as a career and to which others have devoted their full-time energies. As administration becomes more and more accepted as a profession in its own right this

[1] See *State Service* Vol. XLVI pp. 366–9 (Dec., 1966). This is the journal of the Institution of Professional Civil Servants, which represents the many senior Professional, Scientific and Technical classes in the Civil Service.

position will become more and more generally recognized. While there must always be avenues for exceptional persons to enter a profession for which they can demonstrate a special aptitude – and in any case there can be no question of government administration becoming a closed profession – it would be wrong for the State to accept the assumption that top administrative posts are suitable resting places for persons who have served well in other capacities and deserve a respite from their labours. Such an idea is by no means a new ingredient of the public image of the State Service, but under modern conditions it needs to be exorcised like the Devil! Certainly one can go all the way with the Institution's claim that members of other professions who show a flair for administration should be given every opportunity to acquire the necessary skills and qualifications, but it is not everybody who has the ability to excel in several diverse lines of activity, and when all is said and done administration has quite a peculiar taste that does not appeal to everyone!

## The Labour Party's Views

Having looked at selected inside views on Civil Service reform we should now consider what is being said outside and, since everybody appears to be saying something, often without a lot of evidence that they know what they are talking about, there is a sound case for paying attention to the submissions of the government party, than which surely none is likely to prove more influential. In a well-argued document[1] the Labour Party make a number of proposals, some of which are also widely advocated in other quarters and are therefore of particular interest.

They support the integration of the Administrative, Executive and Professional classes and advocate a much wider flow of experienced persons into the Civil Service, not only from other branches of public service but also from industry and elsewhere. It is considered particularly desirable for a Minister to be able to appoint a small group of qualified outsiders to form a sort of personal cabinet somewhat on Continental lines. Their main task would be to find out what was going on in the Department, to act as liaison between Minister and staffs and to transmit from the Minister a political impulse to the Department. This would be one of the ways of countering an alleged tendency of senior civil servants to keep their Minister in the dark as to what was going on in his parish. It must

[1] *The Fulton Committee on the Civil Service*: *Labour Party Evidence* (The Labour party, Transport House, 1967).

be said straight away that neither the disease nor the proposed cure appear to be true assessments of the actual situation.

The Labour Party's evidence recognizes the growing specialistic nature of public administration and the expanding need for improved in-service training, but does not apply these conclusions to the existing facts. Public administration has long ceased to be an amateur's province. To understand what goes on inside the administrative branches the outsider must equip himself with the essential knowledge. Too many politicians, including some newly appointed Ministers, are sadly ignorant of the subject and seem quite happy to go on making highfalutin schemes without taking their administrative requirements into account, with disastrous results when it comes to putting them into operation. Only philosophers can afford to be so unpractical! Is it to be wondered therefore if some of them, so ill-equipped when they come face to face with their administrative advisers, are as children in their hands – as we all tend to be when dealing with experts in any field of which we have little knowledge. If we are wise we accept the doctor's diagnosis, but the politician ought not to be in such a position *vis-a-vis* the administrator. He must be able to understand the administrative assumptions and be in a position to put his advisers straight, for *inter alia* administration is also his business. In the light of this situation it is very unlikely that the proposed outside aides would be sufficiently knowledgeable for some time, perhaps not during the whole of the Minister's normally brief period in the particular office, and in practice the services he receives from his permanent officials through his official staff would invariably prove more helpful. The aides' position could be unenviable! The situation could of course change quite a lot if there were more people about who were knowledgeable on public administration, namely if its study were carried forward as seriously in this country as it is almost everywhere else in the world that matters.

Both in the Labour Party's statement and elsewhere attention is rightly given to the need for improved training of civil servants, but it is difficult to resist the impression that usually the reformers have in mind only the top graduate ranges and that little attention is being given to the many, out of whom more of the leaders could undoubtedly be recruited. Very laudably the Labour Party propose that the recently established Centre of Administrative Studies[1] should be expanded into a Graduate School of Government, but adds that they support the Fabian Society's plan that such a school should stress the new function of the Civil Service in planning

[1] See page 95.

ahead the development not only of the economy but the social structure generally: also that it should encourage in students constructive thinking on the forward planning of transport, housing, the social services, and so on.[1] That civil servants should be trained to take a greater interest in such matters goes without saying, but the statement contains more than a whiff of Webbsian bureaucracy, and is certainly not consistent with earlier admonitions on the evil of civil servants working out plans behind the Minister's backs, and the plan to bring in outsiders to keep an eye on them. Any such school should surely emphasize that the Civil Service's planning contribution must be confined to the development of their own administrative techniques and of the existing parliament-authorized services for which they are responsible under their Minister. The real improvement to be achieved here is surely in the liaison between inside administrators and outside planners: both elements need to understand better the limitations of the one and the objectives of the other. Too often they work at cross-purposes, and it can be hazarded that the fault is attributable more to the inadequacies of the politicians than to the incompetence and machiavellian designs of the public officials.

Another important topic considered is the organization of the Civil Service's management and control. The Labour Party come down decisively in favour of drawing the establishment function away from the Treasury and placing it in the hands of a strengthened Civil Service Commission. This is a very widely supported proposal, although it has its several variations: e.g. that the conjunction of the two services should be effected inside a separated Prime Minister's Office. This is one of those tidy solutions that become less and less acceptable the more they are examined. In the first place such a change involves the basic structure of government and is therefore a constitutional matter. We first need to ask why Civil Service direction is centred in the Treasury, and to answer this the whole history of the Exchequer and the Prime Ministership would be at issue. Today the important fact surely is that the Prime Minister's executive position to a large extent depends upon his membership of the Treasury Board. This could be altered, but not just to make Civil Service management a little tidier. If a Prime Minister's Office were to be set up, on the analogy of certain overseas systems, it could well be argued that this could further strengthen the Prime Minister's position, which is already strong enough, and it could be suggested that a better plan would be to place the central management functions in a much reinforced

---

[1] *Op cit.*, para. 89, p. 17.

Cabinet Office, which would bring such management under the Cabinet as a whole. But this is not the place to pursue such revolutionary ideas.

We still have the question whether it would be a sensible idea to transfer the management, or establishment, function outside of the central executive office (whatever its title) and place it in the hands of an independent commission. Despite the existence of such arrangements overseas, the idea seems quite unpractical if responsible management is to be maintained. Some advocates of the change recognize this and favour the opposite process of bringing the Civil Service Commission into the central executive office. One of the assumptions here is that there is no longer any reason for the selection of persons for the public service to be carried out impartially be an independent body as a quasi-judicial operation. This is a dangerous assumption, and anyone who has been involved in appointments of any sort knows that this is so. Even if strict impartiality were achievable under such an arrangement it would still be desirable to leave the selection process with a quasi-judicial body, on the grounds that such choosing should not only be above suspicion but be seen to be so. What a boon the proposed arrangement would be to the special correspondents of the Press! Even if none of these arguments applied and in practice the work of the present Civil Service Commission and the Treasury Establishments side had grown up under one control, surely by the very process of the division of labour and the great advantages to be obtained by specialization in the field of staff selection would have meant that the Fulton Committee would be seriously considering what sort of division had now become necessary!

From the three documents of evidence to the Fulton Committee referred to in the preceding sections only certain points of particular interest to our study have been selected for brief consideration. Many other matters of considerable importance are dealt with in the several texts.

### Strengthening Parliamentary Influence upon the Administration

Two current constitutional developments are of special importance to the present study. The first is the acceptance of the idea that Parliament needs to be better informed about what is going on inside the Departments, and that improvements in this direction would strengthen its control of the Executive which has been weakening for some time past. Despite the consistent rejection by Ministers of proposals that parliamentary select committees should

be given increased authority to examine the running of the Administration, similar in some ways to the functions of the investigatory
committees set up, albeit for rather different constitutional reasons,
by the United States and French legislatures, the Government has
now made significant initial steps in this direction. In the first place,
with the nomination of a new Select Committee on Estimates on 6th
May 1966[1] it was decreed that of the seven sub-committees thereby
established five should be allocated to specific groups of Departments – namely (1) Technological and Scientific Affairs, (2) Economic Affairs, (3) Social Affairs, (4) Defence and Overseas Affairs, and
(5) Building and Natural Resources – to each of which the Select
Committee assigned specific estimates for examination during the
current session. In addition it was decided that of the other two
Sub-committees – Steering and Supplementary Estimates – the
latter would have time to deal with the Meteorological Services, in
so far as they were covered by the Defence Estimates.

The foregoing change was merely a development of a process that
had been going on within that particular Committee's functioning
for some time, but this was only a beginning. Before the end of the
year the Prime Minister had proposed and the House of Commons
had agreed to the setting up of two specialist Select Committees to
deal with specific subjects: the first with Science and Technology;
the second with Agriculture, both with power to hold public sittings.
These developments, which are only in their infancy, could have
interesting effects both upon the legislature's and the public's image
of the Civil Service, not necessarily to the latter's disadvantage.

### *The Post Office's Proposed Metamorphosis*

The second proposal, which will have a radical impact upon the
Civil Service, reducing its size by half, is the Government's plan to
convert the Post Office into a public corporation, a decision about
which there seems to be a strangely unanimous consensus, even
before the explanatory White Paper has been published. The relative lack of interest in, and apparent approval with which this
proposal is being received is a little frightening. It seems that, despite the General Post Office's remarkable record in the past, and
the revolutionary mechanical changes it is sponsoring under Civil
Service leadership, it is accepted that the Civil Service is quite un-
fitted to continue the running of an undertaking with substantial
commercial elements. With equal insouciance it is also being
assumed that only a Public Corporation can cope effectively with

[1] *First Special Report from the Estimates Committee*, Session 1966–67
(HMSO 1966).

such activities on behalf of the State. There is very little in the history of the public corporations since the war to substantiate this assumption. With the problem of the proper accountability of this particular form still a subject of heated controversy, not to mention the widely held impression that in the great corporations of today, and even more so of tomorrow, the top officials are the inevitable masters interested more in maintaining the corporation's continuity than its highest productivity,[1] one is left with little confidence in either deduction.

While there is certainly a strong case for making the Civil Service more enterprising and in minimizing in every possible way the elements of bureaucracy there is a good case for extending its spirit and principles much more widely throughout the public services, not be it said by creating a more gargantuan Civil Service but by its reorganization, possibly in conjunction with the Local Government and Public Corporation branches, into a series of specialist civil services, each constituting a career within which the development of better methods would be encouraged. Properly to deploy such an organization, or rather series of organizations, we should need a greatly more skilled political executive, probably divided into a policy-making and a managerial section, supported by a more knowledgeable and better serviced Parliament. Is it likely that any enlightened solution will ensue, except tardily under the inexorable pressure of events – a process of which we are at present (in 1966/7) having a most conspicuous experience – unless the Democracy itself decides to take a much greater interest in how the machine works and how it should be worked, namely in Public Administration in its broadest sense, than it does at present?

\*        \*        \*

It is too soon to prognosticate on the trend of the evidence that is flowing towards the Fulton Committee, but it is difficult, from the comments so far being made, to suppress a fear that too much concern is being shown for the problems of the elite – with interested side-glances towards improving the availability of 'plum' jobs so far as they exist – and too little to the problems of maintaining, let alone improving, the morale and efficiency of the vast masses of the 'other ranks' of the Civil Service, an objective made doubly difficult of attainment, but even more necessary, by the expansion of the rat-race mentality in our present society, the generation of special problems by the increasing size of organizations which is of particular impact upon the Civil Service, and the weakening of the Service's

[1] For example, in Prof. J. K. Galbraith's B.B.C. Reith Lectures (1966), on *The New Industrial State*.

own *esprit de corps* following upon the steady erosion of the principle of open competition, the inadequate training provided for
rank and file entrants to the profession, and the poor image of the
Service consistently cultivated by certain sections of the Press, as
well as by smart publicists and superficial theorists.

\*

May I repeat: it is not the object of this work to follow up these
controversial matters, but to provide a reasonably detailed picture
of the Civil Service as it has developed and as it is today, as a basis
upon which the discussion of the problems may be effectively
pursued.

# CHAPTER I

# THE MEANING OF THE CIVIL SERVICE

'Civil Service' has a dual meaning. First as a government institution the term is applied generally to the civilian officials of the Central Government, although its actual scope varies as between one national system and another. Secondly it stands for a spirit of vocational service to the State, of dedication to the service of the community. Historically such a spiritual driving force became necessary, with the advent of democracy, to replace the traditions of aristocratic public service, peculiar to the better types of oligarchic government, which modern developments have to such a great extent rendered ineffectual. Whatever his personal politics a civil servant must be moved by a primary desire to serve the community and by an inclination to place the public weal above natural urges to personal gain.

As an institution the Civil Service in Britain is well understood and highly regarded. Its high professional integrity and relative absence of personal scandal are accepted without question by a nation that rarely stops to consider what it has done to deserve so much. For it is widely recognized that in other climes similar levels of public service prestige and official morality are, even today, too frequently the exception rather than the rule. To the spirit of civil service much less attention has been given. It is taken for granted where it is understood at all. But such a spirit needs understanding and appreciation on the part of those served and unfortunately much misplaced antagonism tends seriously to undermine the confidence that the citizen in his own interest should be eager to conserve. However, it is true that the most critical reactions are against the individual official rather than the institution itself. For even in an age when almost everyone expects to receive some service from the State, the civil servant is habitually regarded as a nuisance, a bureaucrat, or even a drone, employed nonproductively at the instance of some Lord High Inventor of Useless Posts.

No doubt there was a better excuse for such attitudes in the past than in this age of the Social Service or Welfare State which calls for the ministrations of such a large band of public officials. Throughout the ages officials have been reviled as the agents of the strong in oppressing the weak, agents not usually averse from turning the public business to their own advantage. The official was ubiquitous and his services essential from a very early age. On the mountains and the plains, and especially in the river hinterlands, of the Middle East extensive evidence has been unearthed of an advanced administrative system that already existed five thousand years ago. Incised stones, baked clay tablets marked in cuneiform characters, hieroglyphics on temple walls and, later, papyrus rolls, all of which were the stock-in-trade of the recorders of government activities, have as if by a miracle survived in abundance. When it all first began we do not know, but that it has continued since the beginnings of civilization in many forms and continues today, in increasing volume, we are too well aware. Not only in the magnificent realms of Sumer and Babylon, Egypt, China, Greece, Rome and Byzantium, but in every petty realm throughout the world the official has been industriously occupied. As the household of the ruler acquired new public functions the demand for the educated official grew. There has been a regular pattern in this development which has persisted right up to the modern age. From among the growing band of personal servants around the leader, confided with the task of minding the goods and monies, accounting for the supplies, transmitting the ruler's authority, taking care of his authenticating seals, individuals stood out as functionaries with administrative duties. In good periods positions of trust were given to those who were both competent and trustworthy. In Britain this pattern could still be discerned in the times of the Stuarts and the first Hanoverians. It was not indeed till the end of the eighteenth century that the true ideal of civil service began to emerge – a new idea for a new era.

It was in relation to the East India Company that the term 'Civil Service' was first used, mainly to distinguish between the military and civil sectors of the Company's personnel. The Oxford Dictionary gives the date of its emergence as 1785. This was an important distinction at the time, though we are today less bothered by the confusion between the civil and the other branches of government. In all those early empires, which we have just mentioned, the distinction was only occasionally clearly drawn and so long as war was the habitual means of governing this was bound to be so, as indeed it still is today when war supervenes. Civil service, therefore, is a child of peace rather than war, however important its efficiency may be in organizing the State for armed conflict. During the nineteenth century a further differentiation, namely between the politician and the official which had been under way for some time, was considerably accelerated, but it was not until the defeat of patronage and the introduction of impartial selection by means of open competition that the idea of a professional, impartial and devoted service to the State, irrespective of the political colour of the Government, took on its modern shape. A true Civil Service had at last emerged.

There is no accepted definition of Civil Service. Legal definitions are to be found in the Superannuation Acts of 1859 and 1887, depending upon the holding of the Civil Service Commissioners' certificate, but these confined the term 'civil servant' to permanent officials. It would, however, be unrealistic to exclude the large fringe of temporary officials who are at all times to be found in the Central Departments. As good and as authoritative a description as any was provided in the Treasury's submission[1] to the Royal Commission (Tomlin) on the Civil Service of 1929–31, which ran: 'Broadly, therefore, a civil servant may be defined as a servant of the Crown (not being the holder of a political or judicial office) who is employed in a civil capacity and whose remuneration is wholly paid out of monies provided by Parliament.' Even this definition excludes the staffs of certain quasi-civil service organizations such as the Crown Agents for Overseas Governments and Administrations, the Church Commissioners, and Trinity House, whose status and conditions of service are practically indistinguishable from those of the Civil Service, except that these boards do not subsist upon Parliamentary monies. It is also usual to exclude the industrial workers of the dockyards, ordnance factories, Post Office[2] and certain other Departments and to confine the term to the non-industrial grades who deal with the administrative rather than the productive functions of the central departments. The field with which we are concerned is broadly covered by the Civil Service National Whitley Council.

Thus, broadly the Civil Service comprises the civilian employees of the central government. The staffs of the numerous local government authorities and of the public corporations, while sharing both public virtues and public vices with the Civil Service, do not share the label, and by reason of their different constitutional positions may very well be less subject than the central government official to the slings and arrows of public criticism. Even so, the distinction is sometimes very narrow. Local government officials, acting as agents of the Central Departments, may differ very little from, say, the minions of a Central Department sharing a contiguous office. In some countries indeed members of the Civil Service operate in the local government departments. It is a matter of

---

[1] *Introductory Memorandum relating to the Civil Service* (1930), see p. 2.
[2] In 1965 Post Office staffs formerly classified as Industrial were given Non-Industrial status.

c

TABLE I

*Non-Industrial Civil Servants in Britain, 1939, 1947, 1955 and 1965*

| Official classification | 1939 April 1st | 1947[1] April 1st | 1955 April 1st | 1965 January 1st |
|---|---|---|---|---|
| Administrative | 2,100 | 4,200 | 3,500 | 3,500 |
| Executive[2] | 19,300 | 50,600 | 67,300 | 77,800 |
| Clerical and Sub-clerical[2] | 112,900 | 260,500 | 184,800 | 200,500 |
| Typing | 15,300 | 30,400 | 26,800 | 27,400 |
| Inspectorate | 5,800 | 5,600 | 2,800 | 2,900 |
| Professional, scientific and technical[3] | 11,000 | 37,400 | 72,600 | 79,100 |
| Ancillary technical, etc.[3] | 25,900 | 54,600 | 38,600 | 52,600 |
| Minor and Manipulative[3] | 162,600 | 195,100 | 190,600 | 218,500 |
| Messengers, porters, etc. | 19,400 | 45,600 | 29,700 | 34,200 |
| Total whole-time officials | 374,300 | 684,000 | 616,700 | 676,900[4] |
| Add part-time (two counted as one | 13,100 | 21,500 | 19,000 | 20,700 |
| Grand Total | 387,400 | 705,500 | 635,700 | 697,600 |
| Males | 289,000 | 434,400 | 434,000 | 461,600 |
| Females | 98,400 | 271,100 | 201,700 | 236,000 |

[1] 1947 was the peak year for whole-time staff.
[2] General 'Treasury' and Departmental classes.
[3] These groups were re-defined between 1946 and 1947; the other columns are not therefore comparable with the first.
[4] This is not the total of the figures above it, which include part-time officials and are derived from a different source.

history rather than logic whether the railway official is a State servant like his opposite number in the Post Office, and of constitutional custom whether the policeman or the schoolteacher are civil servants. In Britain they are not. But with the growth of socialization the boundaries cannot be defined and it would perhaps be as well to keep an open mind on where precisely the lines of demarcation should be drawn.

Some writers, even in official publications, have used Civil Service as a synonym for the Central Departments in the broadest sense. This may confuse and is to be avoided. It is true that the Central Departments are mainly staffed by the Civil Service, but the wider term must also include the political leaders as well as such non-Civil Service elements as the professional members of the armed forces in the Ministry of Defence. In this book Civil Service refers only to the personnel of the central administration so defined. The departments and their work are a separate consideration, even though the Civil Service is the very essence of their being.

The broad categories of the non-industrial Civil Service are shown in Table I, on page 4.

shown in Table I, on page 4.

### THE WORK OF THE CIVIL SERVICE

Despite certain popular prejudices the civil servant has a considerable job of work to do. He is not employed for the good of his health. The day of the sinecure post has passed and although 'empire building', or the creation of unnecessary posts for prestige purposes, is always a possibility this is one of the dangers that a wider understanding of the Civil Service's true function will help to counter. The tasks of the Civil Service are indeed multifarious and not easy therefore briefly to describe.

Broadly speaking the Civil Service carries out the work of the Executive branch of the Government. The Executive has grown out of the Royal Household and developed since the day when the King himself was the Executive. As his work extended it became necessary to delegate functions to assistants or ministers. Gradually a system of departments emerged, each branch more or less specialising in work of a particular type. The extension of the scope of the Executive has been due partly to the action of Parliament in confiding it with new tasks, and partly to the changing nature of the modern social and economic community for which the Government acts. Today we are confronted by a vast array of immensely powerful and functionally comprehensive Central Departments whose job it is to serve us, although many feel as children in their impressive embrace. Table II on page 6 which classifies the staffs covered by Table I, according to the departmental pattern, will serve to indicate the size of these larger Departments.

It is in the nature of this development of the offices of the State that each minister, the king's specialist in his own particular sphere, is assisted by the permanent members of his Department, who virtually form his collective secretary. The permanent head is still usually known as the Secretary, assisted indeed by a band of

TABLE II

*Non-Industrial Civil Servants Distributed according to Departments, on 1st April, 1965*

| | | |
|---|---:|---:|
| *Post Office* | | 383,800 |
| *Service and Supply* | | |
| Defence (Central) | 2,700 | |
| „ (Air) | 25,000 | |
| „ (Army) | 48,500 | |
| „ (Navy) | 32,000 | |
| Aviation | 24,600 | |
| | | 132,800 |
| *Social Services* | | |
| British Museum | 1,000 | |
| Education and Science | 3,800 | |
| General Register Office | 1,300 | |
| Health | 5,400 | |
| Housing and Local Government | 3,300 | |
| National Assistance Board | 13,900 | |
| Pensions and National Insurance | 40,400 | |
| Smaller Departments[1] | 3,000 | |
| | | 72,100 |
| *Revenue* | | |
| Customs and Excise | 16,200 | |
| Inland Revenue | 57,700 | |
| | | 73,900 |
| *Trade, Industry, Transport* | | |
| Agriculture, Fisheries and Food | 14,600 | |
| Agriculture and Fisheries, Scotland | 2,700 | |
| Export Credits Guarantee | 1,100 | |
| Labour | 20,600 | |
| Power | 1,600 | |
| Technology | 4,300 | |
| Trade | 9,500 | |
| Transport | 6,600 | |
| Smaller Departments[1] | 1,000 | |
| | | 62,000 |
| *Agency Services* | | |
| Central Office of Information | 1,500 | |
| Ordnance Survey | 3,900 | |
| Public Building and Works | 20,800 | |
| Stationery Office | 3,000 | |
| | | 29,200 |
| *Central Government, Home, Legal* | | |
| County Courts | 5,300 | |
| Home Office | 15,400 | |
| Land Registry | 2,800 | |
| Supreme Court | 1,800 | |
| Scottish Home and Health | 3,000 | |
| Treasury | 1,700 | |
| Smaller Departments[1] | 6,700 | |
| | | 36,700 |

*Overseas*

| | |
|---|---:|
| Diplomatic Service | 10,200 |
| Overseas Development | 2,100 |
| Smaller Departments[1] | 600 |
| | 12,900 |

|  |  |
|---:|---:|
| *Grand Total* | 803,400[2] |

[1] These entries cover Departments with less than 1,000 staff.

[2] The difference between this total and the grand total for 1st January 1965 is due to the reclassification of over a hundred thousand Industrials in the Post Office as Non-Industrial on 1st April 1965.

Deputy, Under and Assistant Secretaries. He is in fact the historical descendant of the Minister of the Crown's secretary, whose job it was to keep his master's records and act as his general factotum. Today the Department, with its vast number of civil servants in many grades, is still the minister's administrative factotum, which enables him to carry out the State functions for which he has been made responsible. The Department is the store of administrative experience ever at hand to inform the Minister and assist him in making up his mind or to warn him against attempting the impossible. In other words the Department is the Minister's secretary that keeps his records in their infinite complexity and enables him to render an account of his stewardship almost at a moment's notice; it is also his executive arm, expert in performing his particular specialism in governing, possibly in a merely regulatory way as in the more traditional type of government, possibly by organizing actual services, as the State becomes more and more the nation's Universal Provider.

The Central Departments are no longer confined within the once regal precincts of Whitehall, nor is the individual civil servant of to-day so inevitably a man of the desk. Yet the idea of the Civil Service as an essentially clerical occupation still persists and, despite the recent additions to the vast central administrative structure, it is to be admitted that there is still good logic in this. The Civil Service is predominantly an administrative profession. The one activity that most of its members invariably undertake at one time or another is penmanship and the keeping of records. It is in the very nature of this universal activity, the main means to administering, that the special problems of the Civil Service are to be found.

It might be possible in a book of the present length to provide a reasonably adequate outline of the multifarious tasks of the Civil Service in Britain, but there would be little room for anything else.

Thus we indicate here only a few of the general aspects of this varied field of activity.[1]

As we have seen the most characteristic activity of the civil servant is administration, meaning the whole gamut of office work from mechanical copying and recording of the routine clerk or machinest, through the various shades of clerical work, and office supervision and management, to the higher policy-making tasks of the administrator. It is difficult to draw a line between clerical work and administration, and in fact the best definition will permit the greater to include the lesser. It is true that the leaders will be concerned with policy formulation and decision making, together with organization, direction and control, but in this they do not differ from leaders in other fields of activity, except that their field is administration, not as a by-product, but as a major activity. They, too, are concerned with records, with correspondence and particularly with the manipuation of files, with committee meetings and personal consultations.

The leading civil servants are the administrators whose function is to advise the political Ministers and to run the administrative organization which is essential to the fulfilment of the tasks that Parliament and the Government have delegated to the Ministers. They are the recipients of the store of experience of the Department, able without acting politically to understand the political assumptions of the particular field of activity and to manipulate the administrative means needed to achieve the ends determined by the Minister, as well as to make him aware of the administrative limits within which the policies he may be inclined to choose are workable. Below the administrators are the middle grades responsible for running the administrative machine, often in offices distributed throughout the country: management is one of their important functions. Below them are the clerks in various grades, the machinists, the office-keepers and the messengers who carry out the ordinary routines of the offices. There is indeed a wide variety in this office work and, especially today when the State provides many services directly to the people, these clerks have contacts with the public which call for capacities that were rarely needed by the office worker in the past. There is throughout these various Departments work of a specialized type which is the same in each Department and is carried out by members of the general classes, e.g. personnel (or establishments), finance, instruction, and information work.

These general administrative processes are universal, not only

[1] This task was actually undertaken by the present author in his British Public Service Administration (Staple Press, 1961).

throughout the Departments, but wherever administration goes on. This means almost everywhere in the modern world, which is increasingly becoming an Administrative Society. The main difference is that in the public sphere administration is still usually the major activity and is subject to special rules and conditions that are prescribed by the peculiar nature of State activity.

In addition, the staffs of the several Departments have to be expert in the specialized work of their own Department. Each Minister is at the centre of a specialist world and the functions of the Departments vary considerably. The main Departments are well known, ranging as they do over financial affairs and tax collection, defence measures, oversea relationships, internal domestic affairs, social services, industry, employment and general supplies, but a reference to Table II on page 6 will suffice to refresh the reader's knowledge of the great variety of work of Departments. Some have work of a regulatory nature, others provide services direct to the public. There is a great difference between the work of the Defence Department and that of the revenue and taxation Departments, between trade and communications Departments and the social service Departments. In some cases the civil servants, down to the most junior office grades, need to study the law and regulations on which their work is based: in some cases expert gradings have been introduced or special departmental classes have been recruited instead of the general classes.

Experts of all kinds act sometimes in an advisory capacity, sometimes as executives. They are usually specially recruited. Members of most of the professions are required, particularly legal experts who are needed in all Departments to advise on legal matters and possibly to handle legal proceedings in which the Department is concerned. Medical officers are widely needed, as well as qualified accountants, where the examination of outside accounts is in question. Scientists are widely employed, especially in the defence and supply Departments and scientific research branches. A vast organization like the Post Office not only has a large complement of the ordinary Civil Service grades to carry out the administrative work, but also needs a host of competent engineers to design and service the large communications network on which the Post Office's main activities are based, as well as a number of specialist grades peculiar to its own line of activity, such as postmen, sorters, telegraphists and telephonists, who are usually classified as the manipulative grades. The Stationary Office needs printers; the Ministry of Public Building and Works, architects and builders; the Home Office's Prison Department, warders and governors of prisons. Nor must we overlook the specially appointed inspectors of schools and of factories, and the rest, whose responsible duties are a characteristic of public administration.

The modern state has need of the services of specialists galore and to define the functions of the Civil Service becomes increasingly difficult. If, however, we remember that, despite their legal status as civil servants, members of the professions and other distinct occupations, which have a wider sphere outside the Government Service, are ultimately conditioned by the occupational requirements of their own particular vocations; and if we remember that certain almost purely public activities—such as posts, telecommunications, prison administration—present specialized fields of activity calling for independent study, it will be clear that there remains a reasonably homogenous core of more purely administrative workers about whom the traditional and characteristic problems of the Civil Service arise and to whom the attention of this book can be rationally confined. Moreover, this restriction of focus is justified by the common conception of the Civil Service which does not usually bring to mind the more specialist sectors to which very broad reference has just been made. Our main concern, therefore, is with the office workers with whom more than anyone else the essential characteristics of the Civil Service can correctly be associated. But in adopting this standpoint it would be misleading to overlook the possibility of a radical disturbance of the relative importance of the different groups taking place in the not distant future. The present situation in this respect is certainly dynamic. The increasing importance of technology in the national economy and the advance of automation are portents of change.

## GROWTH OF THE CENTRAL ADMINISTRATION

During the last two hundred years there has been a radical change in the outlook of the official in Britain, a change exemplified by the gradual emergence of the Social Service or Welfare State out of the Aristocratic Police or Regulatory State. In the earlier phase the Government was concerned mainly with preserving the peace, defending the realm from foreign enemies and obtaining the supplies necessary for achieving these objectives, a broadened version of the original function of the ruler and his household. There was, of course, always an element of social service, but it was necessarily limited by the resources available and was usually confined to local operation. Religious and voluntary organizations bore the main burden, while the initiating energies were associated with the free services of the leisured class. It is only during the last hundred years or so that the advances of science and invention have provided the means for administering effectively country-wide services.

The changing nature of the State has involved not only a great expansion in the variety of techniques operated by officials, but also a considerable increase in their numbers. The tasks of administration have become more and more complex. From being a simple secretary and office supervisor the administrator has emerged as a skilled technician in what is virtually a new profession. The chart of the Development of the Central Administration in Britain, 1851–1965, facing page 10 has been designed to illustrate these radical changes in public administration at the centre. In it can be discerned both the steady increase in the variety and number of Government Departments and the growth in numbers of ministers and officials. At the same time the individual Departments have grown substantially in size and complexity, while new ones have sprung up to deal with industrial and social matters, which at the beginning of the period were still left mainly to the private sector, where they were cared for at all.

Dominating this extraordinary administrative development were (i) the tremendous population explosion and the consequent trend towards urbanization, and (ii) the great advances in science, both of which called for increased State intervention and central regulation. New developments in health and sanitation, education, transport and communications, and social matters called for increasing government participation, if minimum standards of service were to be achieved and maintained. Many services originally provided on a voluntary basis had to be supervised, and even taken over, by the Local Authorities or the State, if the requirements of Parliament were to be attained.

Such a movement is much too complicated to be adequately illustrated in flat diagrammatic form. The Chart should not, therefore, be regarded as conveying more than a bird's-eye-view of the background to Civil Service development during the period under review. Yet, unless the reader has such a picture in his mind, he will not be in a position to understand clearly the present situation and problems of the Civil Service.

### THE CIVIL SERVICE OUTLOOK

The concept of a Civil Service, a professional body of non-committed experts in administration dedicated to serve the nation irrespective of their own gain and without reference to party political views or class interests, is thus a modern one. It is interesting to note that during the same period most of the restrictions on office-holding based upon religious belief have disappeared, but sad to relate that in the most recent phase the holding of views of a certain religio-political nature have had to be proscribed to holders of certain posts of trust.[1]

It is characteristic of the idea of civil service that the individual official is known as a 'servant'. This is not a usual designation for the member of a service and it deserves consideration. The truth is that the civil servant, although basically his service is to the Crown whose servant he still is, is habitually conscious of his duty to serve the community, albeit through his master, the Government, which is indeed the people's instrument. In this, the Civil Service differs fundamentally from Bureaucracy, which is self-seeking and self-controlled or the instrument of a narrow oligarchy. There is a tendency to use the term 'bureaucracy' to mean an organization of offices on a large scale, usually with an implication of inefficiency through the use of roundabout or red tape methods, but in truth the mention of Bureaucracy rarely fails to conjure up the vast brute figure of one of the giants with which the ordinary man must ever be prepared to contend. There is nothing of the essence of civil service about this. The Civil Service is the people's service, set up to do nothing more than the people's will.

Much criticism of the Civil Service is misinformed and, it is to be feared, misguided. Even high-minded authorities allow themselves to nod when confusing Civil Service with Bureaucracy. Much of the late Lord Chief Justice, Lord Hewart's famous tirade against the Civil Service represented a natural personal reaction against what he considered to be Parliament's attrition of the Judiciary's historic prerogatives. Lord Hewart, in making his case in *The New Despotism* (1929), accused the Civil Service of grasping for power through the exercise of subordinate legislation and delegated adjudication; developments which were in fact the legislature's way of ensuring the efficient execution of technical matters no longer, for reasons of time and complexity, effectively within its own competence. Such delegation is made according to the conscious sovereign will of Parliament and the criticism, if it was to be made at all, should have been directed to the proper quarter. It is an unfair, as well as misguided, form of attack, not only because the Civil Service is constitutionally incapable of defending itself, but because it panders to the ignorant, if understandable, reactions of many citizens. For this reason it is not likely to cease to be effectively used by publicists who prefer to mask their rooted dislike for all State activity under a more popular cloak. They may be fully justified in their dislike of the policy adopted by the legislature yet

[1] See Chapter VIII.

dishonest in insisting upon beating the wrong horse in the name of justice. Certain, less responsible, members of the press, well aware of the popular dislike of the official even among avowed socialists, take every opportunity to stigmatize the civil servant as 'bureaucrat', and to magnify his every failing while ignoring even the most obvious virtue. Thus one of the most popular dailies rejoiced over an announcement by the Civil Service Commissioners in November 1953 that they were unable to attract sufficient competent clerks to the examinations. They allowed their dislike of the Civil Service to obscure the obvious truth that a loss of official efficiency is to nobody's advantage.

Even a well-wisher such as the late Professor Laski, who knew the Civil Service very well, suggested in his *Democracy in Crisis* (1933) that, with the advent of a leftish government, the Civil Service was likely to show partiality for the *status quo* and obstruct the introduction of necessary social changes. The wrongheadedness of this suggestion, adopted no doubt at the time to add point to the Marxist thesis which the writer supported, was amply proved with the implementation of the radical policies of the post-war Labour Government of 1945. Possibly it is unwise to take such pronouncements too seriously, particularly as Professor Laski himself had earlier[1] made a special point of the essential neutrality of the British Civil Service in serving whatever political party might be chosen by the people. It is a vital characteristic of a Civil Service that it shall be professionally inspired and politically neutral. Its job is to administer and a citizen who is not prepared to serve loyally any government chosen by the people, whatever its political colour, should never think of entering the Civil Service.

Latterly citicism of the Civil Service seems to have been much less savage than during the years immediately following the Second World War. This may be partly due to the rationalization of the process and supervision of delegated legislation and, following the recommendations of the Franks Committee in their Report of 1957,[2] the setting up of the Council on Tribunals to co-ordinate the activities of the several administrative tribunals. Thus the ghosts raised by Lord Hewart appear to have been finally laid as far as Parliament's delegation of legislation and adjudication are concerned. But it would be unwise to be over-confident, for such matters tend to move in cycles.

In the same area a strong movement in favour of the introduction of a Parliamentary Commissioner, on the lines of the

[1] Introduction to Henry Taylor's *The Statesman* (1927 reprint).

[2] *Report of the Committee on Administrative Tribunals and Enquiries,* Cmnd. 218 (1957).

Scandinavian Ombudsman, to deal with complaints from the public against the action of officials, has culminated in the adoption by the Government of a plan[1] to appoint such an authority to deal with complaints against the central administration. At the outset it is proposed that such complaints, subject to certain limitations, must be channelled through Members of Parliament. This arrangement could further strengthen tendencies towards red tape methods, though this is not likely to amount to very much and in the main the Civil Service is not likely to be bothered by steps taken to deal with just complaints. In practice the activities of a British Ombudsman seem more likely to enhance their already high reputation in this direction.

Apart from one poorly substantiated, if rather vituperative, attack by Brian Chapman in his *British Government Observed*,[2] which related only partly to the Civil Service, the real success in this field, also not confined to the central administration, was C. N. Parkinson's *Parkinson's Law* (1955), a high pressure journalistic leg-pull which has had a *succes fou*, and has been taken much too seriously by many who should have known better.[3]

Much current criticism, it must be insisted, rests upon ignorance, not merely of the Civil Service and its function, a sufficiently obscure field of knowledge it must be confessed, but of the very form and scope of our government and of the duties and rights of citizenship. As the attainment and maintenance of democracy itself depends upon the wide dissemination of positive knowledge any excuse for this citizen ignorance is virtually a plea for some form of oligarchy or dictatorship.

All this is not to suggest that the Civil Service is above criticism. This is indeed far from being the case, as later chapters of this book will most certainly show. Our plea is that all criticism should be based upon understanding, for only in this way can the people participate constructively in reshaping their own instrument. The Civil Service itself loses from a lack of understanding and suffers irreparably if it cannot call upon the considered views of those, outside its ranks, whose minds are not biased through being too close to the official grindstone.

[1] *The Parliamentary Commissioner for Administration* Cmnd. 2767 (1965).

[2] (Allen & Unwin, 1964). This criticism should not be allowed to affect appreciation of Brian Chapman's many contributions to the study of public administration, including *The Profession of Government* (Allen & Unwin, 1959), a work of particular interest to readers of the present study, since it provides a comparative account of Civil Service practice in a number of countries.

[3] This first appeared in *The Economist,* in 1955.

### FROM THE WIDER STANDPOINT

It is not an uncommon habit of other administrators piously to pray that they will not act in the roundabout or procrastinating way to which civil servants are supposed to be inherently addicted or of the outside critic to suggest that what the Civil Service needs is an inflow of persons brought up in the school of business. There is both truth and misconception in such attitudes. If, however, the civil servant is habitually non-committal and inclined to get everything down in black and white, with somewhat dilatory results, this is surely attributable to the system he serves and not necessarily to his own ineradicable nature. It is true, of course, that the circumspect and the unenterprising are more likely to feel at home, to settle down as it were, in the Civil Service: it is equally true that lifelong service in the cautious atmosphere of a Government Department is calculated to damp down any inclination to experiment, but it is the public nature of the system itself that moulds the Civil Service and not vice versa. Responsiblity to the political head means that the Civil Service must be anonymous and objective. Responsibility to the public at large through the machinery of parliamentary government means that the civil servant must place on record much that is inessential to the ordinary administrative purposes of his Department. It was widely remarked how many of the wartime entrants, welcomed at first for their naturally free and untrammelled approach, were soon seen to be conforming to the machine they had expected to master even more completely than their established colleagues.

On the other hand it is easy to overemphasize the failings of red tape and 'bureaucracy', so called, in the Civil Service. Critics often speak from hearsay. Some civil servants undoubtedly press caution too far—but these are matters to consider at the end rather than the beginning of this survey. There is certainly a tendency to exaggerate the influence of red tape on the administration of the Central Departments, and to underestimate its effects elsewhere. It will, for example, be a much more important factor in the working of a Department of the older regulatory type than in a technical Department like the Post Office or Ministry of Defence, where much of the detailed day-to-day working of the system will have no shadow of interest to the ordinary citizen, or, at the opposite extreme, in a social service ministry which in its numerous daily contacts with individual citizens carries out many public relations activities that depend upon effective human understanding and not necessarily upon the keeping of records.

There is also, on a somewhat different plane, the suggestion that the State alone is the inspirer of bureaucratic methods, as exemplified by the proliferation of offices, the inordinate use of forms and the lack of the personal touch. It seems, however, that these trends towards technical bureaucracy can be attributed just as much to the large-scale element in State activity as to its governmental aspect. In a world in which the large-scale element tends more and more to abound traits common in the Civil Service are encountered more and more in other spheres of activity. The Organizational Revolution[1] touches all branches of human activity, and it is arguable that the growth of hierarchy which has always characterized governmental organization, both military and civil, and created special problems of relationship within the public structure, is now spreading far and wide, wherever large-scale organization becomes necessary.

The expansion of public administration is a phenomenon that cannot be ignored. Yet it is easy to take it for granted and to evade the problems that the change of emphasis between the private and the public sectors of the economy has been effecting, particularly during the last fifty years. It is easy enough to condemn it out of hand on the lines adopted by the critics already mentioned or of equally stimulating writings exemplified by Ludwig von Mises in *Bureaucracy* (1945), C. K. Allen in *Law and Orders* (1945) and G. W. Keeton in *The Passing of Parliament* (1952), but the cure, if there be one, will be found only in a wider understanding of the basic reasons for these developments. It is certainly unfortunate that democracy, whose success ultimately depends upon such understanding, displays a frightening lack of interest in such matters.

It is as part of this wider sphere of public administration, which encompasses not only the activities of the State, but also those of the numerous local authorities and the growing band of public corporations and other semi-autonomous public bodies, that the Civil Service needs to be understood, unless the people are to wash their hands of all responsibility for its shaping. To be understood the Civil Service must be studied and it is as an aid to such study that this present volume is offered. In the course of generalization much detailed information will have to be omitted, for the pattern is so infinitely varied that only a massive treatise could adequately convey the precise shape and varied essence of the Civil Service as it really is today. Within the vast machine, and despite its general rules, practices vary so infinitely that almost everything that can be generally denied in relation to the Civil Service will be found to be true in relation to some small part of it.

[1] See particularly K. E. Boulding in *The Organizational Revolution* (U.S.A., 1953).

In a democracy the Civil Service belongs to the people, and really to belong a thing must be understood. Such understanding in the present instance depends to a high degree upon an appreciation that the Civil Service differs in no way from other political institutions in being the product of an historical development which is exemplified in its living structure. Accounts that do not recognize this, attempting to describe and analyse the Civil Service as though it were a dead butterfly on a setting board, fail inevitably to convey a true picture of it in its dynamic significance.

The next chapter will explain briefly how the present organization of the British Civil Service has emerged and sketch out its general structure.

# CHAPTER II

# THE MODERN PATTERN EMERGES

The beginnings of the British Civil Service are to be discovered in the courts of the Anglo-Saxon kings, when for the first time administration had emerged as a distinct activity and clerks were beginning to be employed on a whole time basis. An administration profession had been born in Britain for the first time since the Roman withdrawal. We do not know precisely when or at which court this happened, but the distinction of being the first named civil servant appears to belong to a certain Ælfwine, to whom, when making a grant of land in 993, King Æthelred II referred as 'his faithful writer'. Stenton suggests that the history of the Civil Service actually begins in the reign of Æthelstan (A.D. 925–39) when it is known that a staff of clerks was available to accompany the king in his progresses through his realm.[1]

To trace this development for the next thousand years would take more space and, indeed, more research than this present work demands. It is only occasionally, in the interstices of general history, as it were, that the activities can be discerned of these servants, whom we can justly dub, to use a modern expression, the back-room boys of court and government. The whole interesting story would take us along with the struggle of the monarchy with the nobles, the conjuncture of Church and State, the rise of the Tudors, the struggle between Crown and Parliament, and, finally, the achievement of supremacy by the latter in the name of the people. We should watch the Exchequer Court in session; see the tallies being notched, the royal seals being impressed, the Pipe Rolls being laboriously copied. We should note how the Chamber and the Wardrobe gradually gave place to new offices, as the Royal Household became departmentalized, and witness the early emergence of the Treasury, the Secretaryship of State and the Board of Admiralty. We should travel with Chaucer to Canterbury, with Samuel Pepys to Chatham, and with Henry Fielding to the Fleet Prison. On February 11th, 1780, in the House of Commons, we should be listening to an impassioned appeal by Edmund Burke for retrenchment under the submission of 'A plan of reform in the constitution of several parts of the public economy'.

[1] F. M. Stenton *Anglo-Saxon England* (1943), p. 349.

It is not in fact necessary to go back further than the year 1853, which has as good a claim as any to be designated the birth-date of the modern Civil Service. It is true that a good deal had already been done to build up a coherent State administrative service. Sinecures had been considerably reduced, the Treasury had already gained the right to lay down general conditions of service and many of the evils castigated by Burke, if not completely eliminated, had been considerably restricted. But the administrative staffs of the Central Government were still, though legally servants of the Crown, subject to the ministerial heads of the several Departments. They formed a service in their ultimate allegiance, but otherwise were within the patronage of a number of separate political authorities. Only with regard to their superannuation had Parliament claimed the right to lay down the terms to which they should be subjected, for the very good reason that money was involved.

The history of the Civil Service during the next hundred years is most clearly recorded in the reports of the various committees of investigation set up to inquire into its structure and working. Therefore the story may perhaps be most helpfully condensed through a brief review of the most important of these inquiries.

## THE TREVEYLAN-NORTHCOTE PROPOSALS[1], 1853–4

The most notable of these reports, which was signed on November 23rd, 1853, and subsequently published under the title 'Report on the Organization of the Permanent Civil Service', was the work of two outstanding men, Sir Charles Edward Trevelyan and Sir Stafford Northcote. The former was at the time Assistant Secretary at H.M. Treasury, or virtually head of the permanent staff of that Department, a post he held for nineteen years. He had come to this position after a distinguished early career in the Indian Civil Service, to which he was later to return. Northcote had been legal assistant at the Board of Trade, as well as private secretary to

[1] 1854 has recently been officially recognised as the year of the Report but, in so far as the inquiry was authorized by Treasury Minute during 1853 and the Report itself was both drafted and signed during the same year there appears to be little excuse for this post-dating. Further, the proposals are now officially labelled 'Northcote-Trevelyan' but as Trevelyan was undoubtedly the driving force in this matter the previous common practice of using the description 'Trevelyan-Northcote' seems preferable. Already the present author has noted, in a reliable book about the Civil Service, in an article in a Civil Service journal by a noted writer on social topics, and, even more seriously, in a recent Estimates Committee Report, the attribution of the entire reform to Northcote. Even among a galaxy of notables in a brilliant age C. E. Trevelyan's light is excessivly subdued by historians, whose interests are usually not in administration.

Gladstone when the latter was President of that Board: he subsequently transferred his main activities to the political sphere. These
investigators had had the advantage of participating in a series of
inquiries into the public offices which had begun with the Treasury
itself in 1848 and was still in progress. Although the ideas in the
Report were by no means new they amounted to a charter for the
modern Civil Service, of which Trevelyan can justly be singled out
as the father.

The main objective was the destruction of patronage, upon the
evils of which the Report dilated in no unmeasured terms. This was
to be achieved by the introduction of competitive recruitment
through a system of examinations of a literary type, controlled by
an independent board of examiners. Broadly the work of the
Departments was to be classified into two types—mechanical and
intellectual—and performed by two grades of official. These were
to be recruited from candidates, in the case of the former, between
the ages of 17 and 21, in the case of the latter, between the ages of
19 and 25. The higher positions were to be mainly recruited from
inside the Service, by promotion based on merit rather than seniority. An important outcome of this system was to be the welding of
a number of distinct departmental staffs into a real general Service
with a high degree of interchangeability.

The patronage-mongers were immediately up in arms to defend
their perquisites and they were aided by many who honestly felt
that the disadvantages of the new system would outweigh the advantages. Opinion was at first evenly divided. This is clearly demonstrated by the views of the numerous bands of notabilities and administrators to whom the Report was specially circulated by the
Treasury and whose replies were subsequently published, an interesting essay in public relations that speaks well for the authorities
at the time. Opinion in Parliament reflected the general outlook.

In view of this situation the Government decided to hurry slowly.
The proposal to introduce reform by statute was dropped, after
being mooted in the Queen's Speech at the opening of Parliament
early in 1854. The only immediate reform was introduced by the
Order in Council of May 21st, 1855, which authorized the establishment of a Civil Service Commission, with powers 'to examine
young men proposed to be appointed to any of the junior situations
in the Civil Service Establishments'. This enabled a system of pass
examinations to be introduced, but nomination still rested with
Heads of Departments and it was not difficult, by throwing in some
obviously inferior nominees, to ensure the selection of a favoured
candidate. However, some sort of minimum standard was thus introduced and it was no longer possible for nominees who could

hardly read or write to obtain Civil Service posts. The Civil Service Commissioners' first reports disclose clearly the inferior quality of the candidates with whom they had to deal.

## THE SELECT COMMITTEE OF 1860

Although by 1857 opinion in the House of Commons had definitely swayed in favour of open competition, the movement for reform still hung fire. Early in 1860 the House set up a Select Committee to inquire into the existing system of recruitment and its possible improvement. This Committee, under the chairmanship of Lord Stanley, included Sir Stafford Northcote in its distinguished membership. Although it endorsed the principle of open competition the Select Committee's report was disappointing. Recognizing the power of the vested interests and the dangers of retrogression if things were pushed too far too quickly, it concentrated upon improving the existing examination system by radically reducing the scope for evasion. A wider pooling of vacancies was recommended and it was proposed that there should be as many as five and at least three candidates for each vacancy. These proposals were accepted. During the next decade an effective system of limited competitions was built up by the Civil Service Commission. One or two Departments including the Commission itself even introduced open competition on their own.

At last, following the advent of Gladstone's first Ministry in 1868 with Robert Lowe, an avowed reformer, as Chancellor of the Exchequer, an Order in Council dated June 4th, 1870, made open competition obligatory, with certain authorized exceptions. This was a red letter event in the history of the Civil Service. The Civil Service Commissioners could now go ahead, not only with perfecting a system of open competitive examinations of a general educational type similar to those already introduced for the Indian Civil Service, but also under Treasury inspiration with rationalizing the pattern of staff gradings on an all-Service basis: although in practice the varying needs of the work were to prevent the elimination of all departmental gradings. The Order in Council also confirmed and extended the Treasury's powers and responsibilities in staff control.

## THE PLAYFAIR 'COMMISSION', 1874/5

Within a year or two it was found necessary to make a further investigation into the situation and a committee of eight, consisting of Heads of Departments and Members of Parliament was set up in

1874 under the chairmanship of Mr. Lyon Playfair, to inqui
*inter alia,* into recruitment, transfers and general grading. In
three reports the Playfair 'Commission', as it is usually called, p
sented a comprehensive review. It found that the principle of orga
zation proposed by the joint investigators of 1853, based upon
horizontal all-Service general division of labour, had been dis
garded in favour of a vertical division between Departments. T
results had been wasteful and had led to further discontent ins
the Departments. A new structure was recommended.

The Playfair Commission's plan covered four types of post: (i)
a top class of Administrative or Staff Officers, chosen by merit from
inside the Service or from outside if there were no satisfactory
internal candidates; (ii) a small Higher Division, so remunerated as
to attract men of liberal education recruited by a preliminary test
examination at the age of 17, which was to be followed by a
further, but more specialized, competitive examination between the
ages 18 and 23 at the completion of their education: successful
candidates were to remain eligible for appointment by heads of
departments only until their 25th birthday; (iii) a Lower Division
recruited by a competitive examination in 'subjects included in an
ordinary commercial education', from candidates between the ages
of 17 and 20; and (iv) Boy Clerks recruited between the ages of 15
and 17, who would have opportunities to compete for the Lower
Division, but would be discharged at the age of 19 if they failed to
pass a further examination.

The proposals with regard to the Higher Division were retrogressive: in any case they were ignored. A reorganization, covered by
Order in Council of February 12th, 1876, related only to the Lower
Division and the Boy Clerks. As a result the Lower Division began
to emerge as an all-Service class and below it a blind alley grade
of Boy Clerks began to replace the earlier nondescript class of
writers.

## THE RIDLEY COMMISSION, 1886/90

The next comprehensive survey was confided to a Royal Commission under Sir Matthew White Ridley in 1886. It presented four
reports, the last of which appeared in July 1890. On the question of
the division of labour the Ridley Commission were of the opinion
that this was still defective, because the line of demarcation between
the two general levels had been drawn too low. They proposed a
reorganization into First and Second Divisions, the former to be
a small class in three distinct grades recruited between the ages of
20 and 24, by open competitive examination in subjects grouped

similarly to the honours examinations at the universities, and the latter to continue substantially on the lines of the existing Lower Division. Outside these two divisions there was to be provision for special professional appointments and for a class of Boy Clerks or Copyists to carry out the mechanical copying work. The issue of general regulations for the grades covering the whole Service was advocated.

The proposals led to a consolidation of the Second Division as an all-Service class and to a considerable advance in the regulation of the Civil Service as a whole, but again the Upper Division, or Class I posts as they were officially called, was left to develop without formal regulation.

A period of considerable administrative activity lay ahead, during which the State's central administration was to expand in order to cope with the many new functions confided to it by Parliament. The general grades grew and new departmental grades were introduced. Women and girl clerks were employed in increasing numbers, particularly in the Post Office, and typing staff was more widely introduced. Under the policy of segregation these female office workers were separately graded. A new general class began to appear between the Second and First Divisions to deal with work of a higher quality than that of the Second Division, but less important than the policy work of the top class. The new class, which was mainly concerned with accounting, auditing and stores control, was given the appropriate title of 'Intermediate'. At the base of the pyramid, under the Second Division, another general class also appeared; namely, the Assistant Clerks to provide permanent posts for Boy Clerks of a satisfactory standard who could not all be absorbed into the somewhat limited field of the Second Division. They were recruited by competitive examinations of a limited specialized type confined to Boy Clerks.

Thus, many developments, both social and administrative, were occurring to remodel the simple scheme of the 1853 reforms, whose principles, however, were pursued consistently by the Treasury and the Civil Service Commissioners. But these authorities had, at the same time, to contend with a powerful trend in favour of departmental autonomy, reinforced by the principle of ministerial responsibility for administration and the consequent practice of leaving the appointing power in the hands of Heads of Departments. In any case the personnel solution had to be sufficiently flexible to meet the new administrative situations that were emerging with the coming of the twentieth century. A hidebound scheme would have acted as a strait-jacket and led inevitably to breakdown.

As examples of the need for a flexible approach the recruitment of the Labour Exchange[1] Service in 1910 and of the National Insurance Commissions' staffs in 1911 were important. In these instances it was necessary to recruit older staff with appropriate outside experience: only a nucleus of civil servants was transferred from existing Departments. The normal competitions were considered unsuitable for selecting older experienced non-official candidates. To preserve the competitive element and to counter patronage, interview panels were set up, with the Civil Service Commission represented in their membership, and selection by competitive interview was thus introduced. By this means the State obtained the essential services of many highly skilled people of mature age, but not without also absorbing a number of highly individualistic, not to say queer, types who were never to settle down as competent public servants. Some of these left quickly, others lingered on to take their pensions.

## THE MACDONNELL COMMISSION, 1912/15

Obviously, with so many changes going on and in light of the understandable dissatisfaction inside the Service due to chaotic developments, the time was ripe in 1912 for the commissioning of a new full-scale inquiry into the Civil Service. Under the chairmanship of Lord MacDonnell a royal commission was appointed which included Philip Snowden and Graham Wallas among its nineteen members. A thorough survey was ordered and its six reports, published between 1912 and 1915, covered not only the organization of the Departments and working of the Civil Service, but also the specialist branches of the Foreign and Legal Departments. Only the non-clerical officials of the Post Office were left to a select committee, usually known as the Holt Committee, which had been appointed concurrently to investigate this field.

The MacDonnell Commission made a thorough survey and their reports deal with many administrative matters of outstanding importance. They were much concerned to discover lingering pockets of patronage which they wanted to be eliminated. They also found that the general organization had become somewhat confused and in need of reform. Their Fourth Report (1914), which dealt with the administrative-clerical field, contained in addition to Majority proposals, a Minority Report signed by three of the nineteen members.

The Majority, adhering to the principles laid down in 1853, proposed that the general Civil Service should be reorganized into (i) a Junior Clerical Class, recruited from boys of 16 who had

[1] Subsequently renamed 'Employment Exchanges'.

completed the intermediate stage of secondary education (to replace the existing Boy Clerks and Assistant Clerks); (ii) a Senior Clerical Class, recruited at 18 on the completion of a full secondary education (to replace the existing Second Division and Intermediate Classes); and (iii) an Administrative Class, in place of the existing Class I, with conditions standardized throughout the Service. The Minority proposed that the five main existing classes should be similarly reclassified as (i) Second Grade Clerks; (ii) First Grade Clerks and (iii) Junior Secretariat Officers, the main difference being that (ii) was to replace only the existing Intermediate and (i) accordingly to include the Second Division as well as the other two subordinate grades and to be divided into an Upper and a Lower Section, the former being selected from among the latter.

Neither solution was to be adopted, although both were to have an important influence on the future of the Civil Service. In 1914 war came to put a stop to any planned reform for the time being. The war itself, by bringing in experienced temporaries from business and the professions, and inexperienced temporary clerks of all sorts, including many women who had never undertaken paid work before, and by making the Civil Service responsible for many tasks it had never previously undertaken, altered the whole situation overnight, as it were; but in the main only temporarily with regard to the structure and fundamental principles of the Civil Service, as subsequent events were to show.

During the war the shape of things to come was never lost sight of. Our institutions were kept under review and the Civil Service was no exception. In 1917 the Minister of Reconstruction appointed a Machinery of Government Committee under the chairmanship of Viscount Haldane of Cloan. The Haldane Report (Cmd. 9230), which appeared in 1918, is one of the most notable State documents in the field of public administration. It is concerned primarily with the tasks and structure of the Cabinet and the functions of the Departments, and only incidentally with the Civil Service, to which, nevertheless, its findings are of outstanding importance.

An expert committee under Viscount Gladstone, appointed by Treasury Minute of January 2nd, 1918, was given the task of considering the Recruitment of the Civil Service after the war, special reference being made to the MacDonnell proposals with regard to revising the structure of the class covering 'the inferior clerical work in the Public Departments'. In their findings they favoured the solution offered in the MacDonnell Minority Report, emphasizing the importance of leaving it to the individual Departments to decide whether they should employ First Grade or Second Grade Clerks. This committee also made recommendations on recruitment during the reconstruction period, upon which in fact immediate post-war policy was to be based. Another important Committee on Staffs under Sir John Bradbury, appointed by Treasury Minute of February 13th, 1917, issued five reports which contained important proposals on post-war Civil Service organization and working.

### THE REORGANIZATION COMMITTEE, 1919/20

Shortly after the war there occurred the only truly revolutionary change in this field since 1870, namely the application of the system of joint Whitley councils to the Civil Service. Chapter VII is devoted to this development. For the moment it is sufficient to note that the next important report on Civil Service structure was issued by a Reorganization Committee of the new Civil Service National Whitley Council, consisting of representatives of both official and staff interests. It is upon the scheme propounded by this committee of officials that the present organization of the Civil Service is based, and it deserves comment that a plan proposed by the interested parties should have stood up so well to the stresses and buffets of practically a half century. However, it should not be overlooked that this new committee had little research to undertake. Apart from the invaluable working knowledge of its individual members the Reorganization Committee had for its briefing the up-to-date recommendations of committees referred to in the preceding section.

The Reorganization Committee's main Report of February 1920 proposed a new Civil Service structure, which bore the imprint of the recent investigations. The solution can best be conveyed in the Committee's own words:

'The administrative and clerical work of the Civil Service may be said broadly to fall into two main categories. In one category may be placed all such work as either is of a simple mechanical kind or consists in the application of well-defined regulations, decisions and practice to particular cases; in the other category, the work which is concerned with the formation of policy, with the revision of existing practice or current regulations and decisions, and with the organization and direction of the business of Government.

'For work so different in kind it is clearly necessary to secure more than one type of agent. Qualifications adapted to the performance of the simplest kind of work would be unequal to the discharge of the highest kind of work; and it would be impossible to justify the employment on simple mechanical duties of persons capable of performing the highest duties. After the most careful consideration we have agreed that, in order properly to provide for the work falling within two main categories, it will be necessary to employ not less than four different classes, viz.:

(a) A Writing Assistant Class for simple mechanical work.

(b) A Clerical Class for the better sort of work included in the first main category defined above.

(c) An Executive Class; and | for the work included in the
(d) An Administrative Class | second main category defined | above.'

The effect of these proposals was to reclassify the office work of the Departments into three broad types, namely Clerical, Executive and Administrative, each of which was to be performed by a specially recruited class drawn at school-leaving stages from young persons of either sex with an appropriate educational background. Each class was to be divided into grades, recruited successively from the grade below, and it was to be left to the Departments to decide which classes would be most suitable for their work. In theory, if not in practice, the classes were to form separate hierarchies and there was no suggestion that members of each of the three main classes should be employed in every Department.

The Clerical Class, recruited by open competitive written examinations of intermediate secondary standard from boys of 16 to 17 and girls of $16\frac{1}{2}$ to $17\frac{1}{2}$ (subsequently brought into line with the boys) was to have duties which were defined as 'dealing with particular cases in accordance with well-defined regulations, instructions and general practice; scrutinising, checking and cross-checking straightforward accounts, claims, returns, etc., under well-defined instructions; preparation of material for returns, accounts, and statistics in prescribed forms; simple drafting and précis work; collection of material on which judgments can be formed; supervision of the work of Writing Assistants.'

The Writing Assistants, although officially regarded as a separate class were to work inside the clerical sphere in close association with the Clerical Class. They were to be recruited by similar examinations of higher elementary standard from among girls between the ages of 16 and 17, and they were to be employed on the more mechanical clerical practices, including machine operation, but not typewriting, which was to be assigned to a separately recruited class.

The Executive Class was also to be recruited by open competitive written examinations, of full secondary standard, from young persons between the ages of 18 and 19 (except that for the time being special conditions were to apply to the recruitment of young women). The Report states that the work of this class 'covers a wide field, and requires in different degrees qualities of judgment, initiative and resource. In the junior ranks it comprises the critical examination of particular cases of lesser importance not clearly within the scope of approved regulations or general decisions, initial investigations into matters of higher importance, and the immediate direction of small blocks of business. In its upper ranges it is concerned with matters of internal organisation and control, with the settlement of broad questions arising out of business in hand or in contemplation, and with the responsible conduct of important operations.' It was originally intended that the junior grade of this class should be a training grade, but for practical reasons this was a condition that was never to materialise.

The Administrative Class, which for the first time was to become a true all-Service class, was to be recruited between the ages of 22 and 24,[1] by an open competitive examination in subjects embraced by the various honours courses of the universities. Although the examination was to be mainly written it was to include a *viva voce* which was to constitute a test of personality and character, the marks for which were to be added in with those of the written papers. This was an innovation at the time justified because of the class's leadership function. On the duties of this class the Report was brief, but to the point. It said that these duties would comprise 'those concerned with the formation of policy, with the co-ordination and improvement of Government machinery, and with the general administration and control of the Departments of the Public Service.'

Recruits of this class were to form a cadet corps from which selection would be made to higher administrative posts, and this is how the Assistant Principal grade has in fact since been regarded, namely, as a training grade of a purely transitory character whose members have to graduate within a few years to substantive duties.

The Reorganization plan was adopted and gradually applied by the Departments. The new general service, or 'Treasury', classes as they were to be called, were not however adopted by all Departments, some of which regarded it as essential that they should continue to recruit their own special grades; for example, the Ministry of Labour and the Boards of Customs and Excise and of Inland Revenue. The specialized nature of the Department's work was generally adduced as the reason for this deviation. Elsewhere different patterns of Treasury class groupings emerged. Thus some Departments chose a Clerical-Administrative pattern, others a Clerical-Executive pattern. In some the directing class was of the

---

[1] Later, the conditions for men and women were assimilated, and from 1937 the age limits for both sexes were altered to 21 and 24.

technical or professional type; in others all three Treasury classes appeared. The assimilation of members of existing grades to the new classes was a difficult operation with which there is not space to deal here. Guidance on the subject was provided in a later report of the Whitley Reorganization Committee.

## THE TOMLIN COMMISSION, 1929/31

The next comprehensive survey was held too soon and in unpropitious circumstances. Unless a Royal Commission is in a position to study its problem in its long-term aspects it is bound to be at least partially frustrated. This was the situation in which the Tomlin Commission found itself when it was appointed in July 1929 to inquire into, and report upon, the structure and organization of the Civil Service, as well as its conditions of service. The financial crisis was at its height and the new investigations could not avoid being unduly affected by this serious turn in the nation's affairs. Moreover, since the war the situation within the public service had never really returned to normal and in 1929 the Reorganization scheme could hardly be said yet to have been properly tested. The difficult problems created by the special post-war recruitment of ex-Service men were still in course of settlement, while the return to normal recruitment methods, on which the Reorganization scheme was ultimately to have rested, had only recently taken place. In the dire national situation which seemed at the time destined to continue from bad to worse, the call for economy, an admirable enough precept for any investigatory committee if taken in moderation, was too insistent not to colour adversely the whole of the Commission's findings.

The Report, when published in 1931[1], was received with disappointment, especially by the Civil Service itself, which nevertheless in all the circumstances could hardly have expected anything better. In fact much criticism of the Tomlin Report was misdirected and failed apparently to appreciate the measured truth of its diagnosis in light of the existing situation. The chief fault is to be found less in the results than in doubts raised by the investigatory methods adopted by the Commission, which while normal to this type of body pose the question whether in the modern world with its complex structure and procedures the examination of a series of *ex parte* statements, however thorough, is likely to search deeply enough into the fundamentals of the situation. The Tomlin Commission's investigations were certainly thorough, but from an examination of the evidence submitted in the best faith both by

[1] Cmd. 3909.

official and by staff interests, and which indeed formed the bulk of the information before the Commission, it is obvious that the protagonists were concerned primarily with making a case and not in providing an objective analysis of the situation. It would seem that in future to be really successful such a commission will need the assistance of a competent survey team.

As far as the theme of this present chapter goes the Royal Commission had little to suggest. It generally endorsed the grading structure laid down in the Reorganization Report, subject to two suggested readjustments, one of which was eventually adopted and the other rejected. The first was a proposal to extend the range of duties of the Writing Assistants, a class that had attracted a higher educational type than had been originally visualised and whose members were therefore capable of a wider range of simpler clerical work. The new class, rechristened Clerical Assistants, was thus to overlap the Clerical Officer grade at the lower levels. This modification was introduced officially in 1936. The other organisational proposal, largely inspired by complaints of stagnation and lack of promotion prospects in the Clerical Officer grade at the time, was that a new grade should be fitted in between the Clerical Officer and Higher Clerical Officer grades, to which suitable members of the existing junior grade should be promoted. This redivision of the Clerical Class by the insertion of an overlapping grade, as it was called, did not commend itself to the staff nor was it welcomed sufficiently by the official interests to lead to its implementation by administrative action.

With the levelling out of the financial crisis and the change in the political outlook in the 'thirties the situation in the Civil Service gradually changed. Following a period of contraction a mild expansion now began, as the Government, almost against its will, gradually participated more and more in economic control and social amelioration. In the later 'thirties the drive to rearm, again forced upon a government and a nation that had put off the evil day longer than was compatible with public safety, caused this expansion to accelerate. Although the British Civil Service is essentially a non-military body, its professional interest gained considerably from this phase of defence preparation. Between 1929 and 1939 the total of the non-industrial staffs of the central departments rose from 259,000 to 371,000[1].

### AFTER THE SECOND WORLD WAR

On the organisation of the general office, or Treasury, classes the Second World War, which began on September 3rd, 1939, had little

[1] These figures exclude part-time workers (mainly in the Post Office).

effect. The structure stands today very much as it has just been described, although in many ways other conditions have radically changed, as the following chapter will show. During the war, which was much more totalitarian than the previous one, an even more radical expansion of official posts took place and this time, with the cessation of hostilities in 1945, the expected rapid shrinkage back to normal failed to be realised. This was due to a complexity of reasons: firstly, the world itself was in greater chaos and reconstruction meant much more conscious planning: secondly, in this country a new approach to social welfare and nationalization of industry led to the change over from a war economy to a Welfare State, which presupposed little or no diminution in State activity; thirdly, the continued threat of war, due to the division of the victors into two camps, entailed a higher level of defence preparation than had been normal before the recent hostilities; and finally accelerated scientific advances were to affect the administrative situation at every turn. Not only did many of the older Government Departments continue to maintain much larger staffs than hitherto, but new wartime and post-war ministries continued to operate: for example, the Ministries of Supply and of Food, the Ministries of Fuel and Power and of National Insurance[1]. Numerous other new branches were found to be necessary to cope with the new administrative tasks and conditions. The machinery of government, both at the centre and the periphery, was greatly expanded and rendered more complex.

Some structural changes were made which had the effect of narrowing the gap between the three main classes – Administrative, Executive and Clerical – and reducing their separateness. The Clerical Class today consists only of two grades, namely Clerical Officer and Higher Clerical Officer, all of the previous Staff Clerk grades having been assimilated to the equivalent levels of the Executive Class. A plan for a similar tying up of the upper levels of the Executive Class with equivalent levels of the Administrative Class, tentatively proposed in 1945[2], has since been dropped. The structure of the Administrative Class itself has been simplified by the elimination of the Principal Assistant Secretary grade which previously stood between the Assistant Secretary and Under Secretary grades. There were also further moves in the Treasury's campaign to replace the equivalent departmental classes by structures similar to that of the Treasury classes. For example, the National

---

[1] The Ministry of Supply has since gone, the Ministry of Food has been absorbed in the Ministry of Agriculture, Fisheries and Food, while the other two are now known respectively as Ministries of 'Power' and of 'Social Security'.

[2] Cmd. 6680.

Assistance Board, which had its own departmental gradings, went over to the standard pattern and the new Ministry of National Insurance[1] adopted the Treasury gradings, although its work was of the management-specialist type for which departmental gradings would previously have been considered most appropriate. The Ministry of Labour (and National Service), although still maintaining its own gradings approached so close to the general pattern that the main difference is now little more than one of nomenclature. The Inland Revenue and Customs and Excise Departments, on the other hand, while introducing their own modifications to meet changing times, continued to maintain their own patterns of staff organization. The present grading pattern of the main classes is indicated in Diagram I facing page 34.

### THE PRIESTLEY COMMISSION, 1953/55

By the early 'fifties recruitment had become so unsatisfactory and dissatisfaction among civil servants with existing pay standards so great that the Government decided to approach the problem by the time-honoured way of appointing a Royal Commission to go into the whole matter. This was to be the first of the major periodical enquiries since the Tomlin Commission of 1929/31, but with important reservations. Designedly, but unwisely, the Government restricted the new body's terms of reference by excluding the vital question of organization and grading. No doubt they were strongly advised to follow this course by the senior administrators, who are never eager to have outsiders ferreting into their internal arrangements. In any case the new Commission were to find plenty to do in the field of remuneration, but structure and remuneration are so closely inter-related that one cannot be adequately examined without a close acquaintance with the other. It would have been more economical for the Commission to have covered the whole field while they were about it. It is true that there was a widespread belief at the time that the situation was not ripe for a comprehensive enquiry. This may well have been so, but in Britain the time is never ripe to look critically at an old-established institution! We invite change only when we know it is to be inevitable.

On 16th November 1953 a Royal Commission[2] of twelve members, including as chairman Sir Raymond Edward Priestley, was appointed with the following terms of reference:

[1] Now merged in the Ministry of Social Security.

[2] *Report: Royal Commission on the Civil Service, 1953/55* (Cmd. 9613), *Introductory Factual Memoranda on the Civil Service* (H.M. Treasury, 1954) *Minutes of Evidence* 1-28 (1954-5). *Appendix I and Appendix II to the Minutes of Evidence* (1954/55), *Supplement to Introductory Memorandum* (1954).

'......to consider and to make recommendations on certain questions concerning the conditions of service of civil servants within the ambit of the Civil Service National Whitley Council, viz:—

(a) Whether any changes are desirable in the principles which should govern pay; or in the rates of pay at present in force for the main categories—bearing in mind in this connexion the need for a suitable relationship between the pay of those categories:

(b) whether any changes are desirable in the hours of work, arrangements for overtime and remuneration for extra duty, and annual leave allowances;

(c) whether any changes are desirable within the framework of the existing superannuation scheme:[1]

That the Commissioners themselves were disturbed by the narrowness of these terms of reference was placed on record in Chapter III of their Report which they pointedly entitled: 'The Limitations Imposed by our Terms of Reference'.[2] As they rightly pointed out, they had to accept 'as fixed data the existing class and grade structure' which imposed 'considerable limitations on any review of pay rates'. They also made the important point that training arrangements, which were also excluded, were 'relevant to recruitment and retention and so to rates of pay'.

If the Royal Commission's task was a restricted one compared with that of its most famous predecessors, in a rapidly changing situation it was sufficiently complex and difficult to call upon the Commissioners' fullest energies. Apart from the printed materials placed at its disposal it took oral evidence on twenty-eight days, extending from February 1954 to March 1955. The bulk of this evidence was presented by the Treasury and the Departments, the Staff side of the Civil Service National Whitley Council and the several staff associations. Since the Report was concerned entirely with conditions of service its findings will be considered in the following chapter.

### REGIONALIZATION AND DISPERSAL

There are two important developments, however, that call for comment, developments which are bound to have a great influence on future changes in the Civil Service pattern and which already affect in one way or another all the problems that are to be discussed in later chapters. The first is the definite shift of the centre

---

[1] *Report*, p iii.
[2] *Report*, pp 13/14.

of gravity of the Civil Services from Whitehall to the provinces,[1] the second is the emergence of nation-wide Civil Service classes in the professional and scientific spheres.

During the Second World War a pattern of regional government that had already emerged in the previous war and indeed much earlier, was given a definite shape for defence purposes. This specific governmental need never in effect materialized, but a regional administrative structure took shape for war purposes and continued afterwards. Based largely on the administrative pattern already worked out on a divisional basis for the pre-war Ministry of Labour, the new regional scheme, subject to modification for technical reasons in such branches as the Post Office and later in the health service's hospital organization, was well-designed to meet the needs of an administration that required to have offices in close contact with the local communities throughout the country. In these offices the provision of social services brought the civil servant more closely into touch with the public and modified both his outlook and his methods. Indeed, the Employment Exchanges and the National Assistance Board's Offices had already introduced[2] this new element before the Second World War. At the same time the spread of the management function, necessitated by the existence of numerous small offices, which had at one time been largely confined to the Post Office and the Tax Departments, further extended this sector of the Civil Service's responsibilities.

With the slackening of interest in economic planning during the 'fifties the post-war trend towards regionalization of the Central Departments and the development of a co-ordinated regional organization received a setback, but a change of policy towards the end of 1963, when the Presidency of the Board of Trade was associated with a new Secretaryship of State, with extended responsibilities for Industry, Trade and Regional Development, brought regionalization again into the picture. In the following autumn a new Government further strengtehened the planning machinery under a new Department of Economic Affairs, which took over important responsibilities from both the Treasury and the Board of Trade. Under the new system a Regional Economic Planning Council was appointed in each region with a membership drawn from both sides of industry, local authorities and universities, with the task of formulating a regional plan and advising upon its implementation. Each of these Councils is supported by a Regional Economic Planning Board, whose function is to prepare the plan

[1] On July 1st, 1964, of the total staffs, excluding the Post Office, 132,000 were stationed in London and 285,000 elsewhere.

[2] In 1910 and 1934 respectively.

and to co-ordinate the work of the several Departments concerned in its implementation. These Boards are made up of civil servants from the interested Departments, under the chairmanship of a senior official of the Department of Economic Affairs. The new structure is still in course of development but it certainly increases Civil Service participation and departmental co-ordination at regional levels and takes senior administrators more decisively out of Whitehall.

This trend is being reinforced by the governmental policy of dispersal which has been applied with varying seriousness throughout the period. Already before the war the question of reducing the industrial congestion in and about London had been considered for valid defence reasons, but today the new policy, to thin out congestion in the entire South-Eastern area, is being actively pursued for social and economic reasons. London as the site of Parliament emerged naturally as an administrative centre where the staffs of members of the Government were conveniently located to enable them to combine their daily parliamentary and administrative duties most effectively. But as Departments grew larger and acquired more and more purely technical functions it became increasingly difficult and often quite unnecessary for them to be concentrated at one centre. Dispersal of the Civil Service became a sensible national policy both to relieve such congestion and to achieve better employment distribution. As part of the national manpower policy it is desirable to set up public establishments in areas where the labour-supply situation is more favourable than in the Metropolis. The decision, during the war, to locate the Central Office of the new Ministry of National Insurance at Newcastle upon Tyne was an early manifestation of this policy which is now being applied to both new and existing branches of a number of Government Departments with obvious effects upon the structure of the Civil Service.

## THE INFLOW OF SPECIALISTS

The other development, in the extension of the technical sphere, is also very important. Members of the professions have long been employed in the Departments, but usually in small numbers—lawyers, architects, medical officers, engineers. Before the Second World War they had been recruited and organized on a departmental basis. The Carpenter Committee, appointed to investigate the organization of the scientific and technical grades, had in 1930 proposed a general reorganization of these specialist officials on an all-Service basis. The Tomlin Commission endorsed these findings[1],

[1] See their Report (Cmd. 3909), pp. 49–57).

E

but found themselves unable to agree with a proposal from the staff associations concerned that other professional groups should be similarly reorganized. They considered that such posts were too few and their functions too individual to the Departments to render a general service structure practicable. For the time being little was done, even for the scientists.

The greatly extended employment of scientists and other professional technicians during the war and subsequently called for a radical review of the position. While the war was still in progress the position of Scientists was dealt with by the Barlow Committee on Scientific Staff in Government Departments in their Report of 23rd April 1943 which led to proposals for a complete reorganization which was set out in the Government's White Paper on *The Scientific Civil Service* (Cmd. 6679). As a result scientists in the Civil Service are now organized on a Service-wide basis in three broad classes, on a pattern generally similar to that of the three Treasury classes. The present structure is shown in Diagram II facing page 35. At the top is the Scientific Officer Class, recruited mainly from highly qualified graduates capable of undertaking, or of directing others in, fruitful research. Promotion is from the basic grade of Scientific Officer, through Senior, Principal and Senior Principal Officer grades to the highest posts of Deputy Chief and Chief Scientific Officer. The middle sector consists of the Experimental Officer Class whose job is to support the Scientific Officers. They may be graduates, or hold such technical qualifications as Higher National Certificate, or be promoted from the lower Scientific Assistant Class. They too are graded as Assistant Experimental Officer, Experimental Officer, Senior and Chief Experimental Officer, the latter being more or less equivalent to the grade of Principal Scientific Officer. The lowest class, similar in the hierarchy to that of the Clerical Class, is the Scientific Assistant Class, which undertakes the routine work for the senior grades. See Diagram II of Structure and Recruitment of Scientific Civil Service facing page 35.

Other professional groups, like the Works Group which *inter alia* includes architects, surveyors, estate officers and engineers, have also been reorganized on an all-Service basis. Often specialist qualifications are needed by individual Departments. Many specialist groups of a departmental nature, which were already graded long before the war have continued much as before, notably, the Patent Service, H.M. Factory Inspectorate, H.M. Inspector of Schools, and Assistant Keeperships and other senior posts in the various Museums and Galleries. Other professional groups with an all-Service basis are the Medical Officers and the Legal Staffs, while new general classes of senior status, have been introduced of Statisticians, Economists and Psychologists. A somewhat different, but interesting development in the Executive sphere has been the introduction of a specialist Information Officer Class to staff the various Information Divisions of the Central Office of Information and the individual Ministries. The gradings are in parallel with those of the Executive Class from which, apart from general recruitment of experienced outside practitioners, selection may be made, and they too are interchangeable on an all-Service basis.

In the professional sphere a Government Economic Service was set up during 1965, with recruitment at the three levels of Economic Assistant, Economic Adviser and Senior Economic Adviser. An interesting feature has been the introduction of the grade of Cadet Economist, appointees to which need not have included Economics in their first degree course but will be expected to undertake a full-time university course after appointment in order to become Economic Assistants.

## GENERAL PATTERN TODAY

It will already have become apparent that the familiar concept of a three-class Civil Service, based upon a natural development of the Trevelyan-Northcote solution of 1853/54 does not adequately interpret the present structure of the Civil Service, which has had to be extended vigorously into new vocational fields in order to cope with the widening scope of government administration. There are two senses in which the Civil Service is something less than a unified service, deriving from (i) the system of organization in broad classes and (ii) the principle of ministerial responsibility for departmental administration.

(i) Certainly, in an important respect the original principles still stand, namely through the practice of assigning individuals to grades of a class, each of which caters for a range of posts covering a variety of work, designated as falling within the scope of the particular class. Any member of the particular grade is considered available for any post within the grade, although naturally his experience on the work and other factors will be taken into account. Recruitment of suitably qualified persons to a particular class is normally, though not invariably, made to the basic grade of the class, and there are opportunities for grade-to-grade promotion within the class.

The method is applied by first analyzing the work to be performed and then allocating it to the appropriate class and grade. In each Department the number of posts in each grade—known as the complement—is settled on the basis of the volume of work to be performed. Without authority these complements cannot be varied, e.g. to improve the promotion opportunities of a particular class.

This assignment of individuals to broad classes and grades, sometimes known as the 'personal rank' system is a very different principle from that of 'position classification', based upon specific job analyses, which has been preferred and scientifically developed in the United States and depends upon the classification of individual jobs or ranges of similar jobs, to which officials are individually recruited. Of course, there are individual posts in the British system, especially at senior and specialist levels, but here they are the exception and not the rule. The Service generally has a much greater complexity than the three-class pattern suggests. There are a number of distinct personnel groupings which practically form separate corps or careers.

(ii) Apart from these general classifications the Civil Service is further divided by the operation of the principle of ministerial responsibility into separate administrative units and staff entities. The individual civil servant owes direct personal allegiance to the Head of his Department, who is still legally responsible for his appointment, disciplining and dismissal.

At this juncture a broad summary of the several spheres will help to keep in focus at all stages the great diversity of the present Civil Service structure and to avoid the onesideness of so many outside discussions of Civil Service problems. The following headings appear to cover the field, if we ignore a few autonomous or non-Civil Service staffs dealt with in Chapters XI and XII.

(1) *Non-Industrial Civil Service* This is the broad field catered for by the Civil Service National Whitley Council.[1]

(i) *Administrative Class* This senior hierarchy, although an integral part of the Treasury class structure, has characteristics which single it out from the rest of the Civil Service. Its senior members, as joint Permanent Secretaries at the Treasury, with a special grading one step higher than their opposite numbers in the Departments,[2] are leaders of the Home Civil Service. The whole class is in a special sense an all-Service class with obligations to work in any Department. The Class is a restricted elite which forms the leadership element over all the other groupings except (3) below. The several grades, in ascending order, are Assistant Principal (which is a cadet grade and supernumerary),

---

[1] See Chapter VII.

[2] The Secretary to the Cabinet is similarly graded.

Principal, Assistant Secretary, Under Secretary, Deputy Secretary and Permanent Secretary. The equivalent gradings for the two latter in the Treasury are Third and Second Secretary. When it is observed that the entire Administrative Class in 1965 totalled no more than 2,500 out of a grand non-industrial total of 697,600, the selectness of this group is apparent.

The Administrative Class has the dual function of advising Ministers on matters of policy and of organizing and managing the several Departments as executive bodies. It is in this duality that important problems of the class reside.

(ii) *Executive, Clerical and other Office Classes* This group comprises a wide range of classes, from the skilled managerial group of Executives at the top to the Clerical Class, Clerical Assistants, Typists, Machinists, Paper-keepers, Messengers and other minor gradings needed in running the vast administrative machine.

The Executive Class, totalling, in 1965, 77,800 (including both its Treasury and departmental sections) is arranged in grades known as Executive, Higher Executive, Senior Executive, and Chief Executive Officer and, in some Departments, certain higher positions overlapping the Administrative sphere. The class has many specialist duties in different Departments, including statutory inspectoral functions, but the chief innovation since its original introduction has been the great extension of its managerial responsibilities, due to the vast proliferation of Government Departments in offices throughout the localities.

The Clerical Class, numbering with the Clerical Assistants who virtually form a junior grade, as many as 200,500, has only two grades, namely Clerical Officer and Higher Clerical Officer. The latter appears only in some Departments, the normal avenue of promotion being to the junior grade of the Executive Class, so that the Executive-Clerical area now virtually forms one hierarchy. Important changes in the work of these classes are being brought about by the increasing introduction of automation.

(iii) *Professional, Scientific and Technical Classes* (including the specialist Inspectorates). These totalled 82,000. While these groups are also generally subject to the direction of the Administrative Class, senior posts in some Departments – especially those concerned with legal, medical and scientific work – are held by professional men who occupy positions on a par with the Administrative Class. Traditionally professional and non-professional staffs have been organized in distinct units, and the primary responsibility for each Department's work has been placed on the general administrative divisions. Understandably this relationship has given rise to controversy, but the achievement of a satisfactory balance has not been easy, particularly as the situation varies widely as between Departments. Recently a number of mixed teams and integrated posts have been created in some of the more technical Departments, and a solution that is both equitable and efficient is being actively sought.

(iv) *Minor and Ancillary Classes* The Administrative, Executive Professional groups all require the support of a variety of routine workers, manipulatives, laboratory assistants and the rest, varying widely in function and organization as between the different Departments. While there are possibilities of promotion to the senior classes, these groups tend to form more or less specialist self-contained career spheres with their own supervisory positions, although ultimate control is exercised by the senior classes. Possibly the best integrated of these services is the Post Office, in which juniors on the manipulative and engineering sides have good opportunities to rise to the top.

(2) *Industrial Civil Service* Again this group, totalling as many as 235,800 (excluding the Post Office) is not a separate service, though they are invariably considered independently. They include tradesmen and industrial workers who are subject largely to the general industrial and trade union usages operating outside the Service. They are employed in industrial establishments, such as those attached to the Ministries of Defence and of Aviation, Stationery Office, Home Office, Forestry Commission and Ministry of Public Building and Works. They have their own supervisory and directing posts and will be described in more detail in Chapter XI.

(3) *Her Majesty's Diplomatic Service* This is completely separated from the Home Civil Service and has its own Permanent Head, who is equivalent in rank to the Treasury's Joint Permanent Secretaries. The oversea branches were always separately recruited and organized, but it was not until the reorganization of 1943 that the Foreign Service was formally recognised as a separate service of the Crown. Under the present title the Commonwealth Service was combined with the Foreign Service in 1965. Unless specifically mentioned the Diplomatic Service should not be considered part of the Civil Service as discussed in this book, but a more detailed summary will be included in Chapter XII.

CHAPTER III

# CONDITIONS OF SERVICE

The general tone and standards of a public service are ultimately
determined by the official's conditions of service. In those countries
where the official is allowed, and indeed compelled by circumstances beyond his own control, to take bribes low standards of
public service have to be accepted as inevitable. The methods of
recruitment[1] are, of course, of first importance and the offer made
at that stage is embodied in existing conditions of service, usually
embellished by promises of later advancement. It is on the other
hand not possible adequately to assess the offer made without
taking into account the past history and present prestige of the
particular service. A civil service may continue for some time to
live upon past reputation or be dragged back by past inefficiencies,
at any rate to the limits of the working life of the present incum-
bents of public office. The actual conditions offered are the outcome
partly of history and custom, but mainly of public policy put into
operation by the controlling authority. This means in the case of
Britain, by Her Majesty's Treasury.[2] The general social and economic situation of the country is a non-evadable limiting factor and
the degree to which the existing staffs are able to participate in the
revisionary process, through normal or modified trade union channels, is also important.[3] It is proposed in this present chapter to
consider some of the more weighty factors in the civil servant's
conditions of service.

## LIFE CAREER

In an economically unstable world the offer of a secure pensionable
employment has undoubtedly exerted a great influence upon the
recruit to the Service. Parents exert considerable pressure upon their
children to compete for jobs that are sheltered from the normal
economic uncertainties of life, and competitors are willing to accept
less favourable monetary prospects on this account. It is often
alleged that this particular circumstance has attracted to the Civil

[1] See Chapter IV.
[2] See Chapter X.
[3] See Chapter VII.

41

Service profession a larger proportion than usual of persons of unenterprising character. No one would choose public service as a field for adventure: yet there is scope therein today more than ever before for the adventurous spirit and it is no longer just to over-stress this characteristic. Most men seek security, if few find it: there are other valid reasons for the civil servant's lack of enterprise and these originate in the very nature of public administration.

Today the civil servant's security is no doubt less prized than in the past, partly because the Civil Service no longer stands as one of the few careers in which pensionable employment exists, partly because the fear of unemployment has been greatly mitigated by the adoption of a State system of social security and full employ-ment. There is unfortunately the overriding change in the general attitude to life, brought about by the scientific advance in humanity's power to destroy itself, that inevitably colours youth's whole attitude to the future and vitiates appreciably the attractive-ness to them of security of employment. There is also the insidious menace of inflation that constantly threatens any standards that may have been laid up for the future. All pensioners feel the in-justice of the impact of inflation upon their reduced incomes, but the State pensioner is particularly affected by the feeling that the State's life-long pension offer has been eroded by policies for which the State itself has been largely responsible.

The State, when recruiting a permanent official, usually asks for a lifetime's allegiance. Even in the days of patronage official posts were regarded as very much the perquisites of the occupant and there was no question of officials being sacked, as under spoils systems, to make way for the clients of new political leaders. Per-manency is certainly an important characteristic of our Civil Ser-vice pattern and, even if historical reasons partly account for it, the resultant system is not less valid on that account. Quite the contrary in fact: it is important to the efficiency of cabinet govern-ment that it should be able to call upon the resources of a skilled professional administration. Permanency means a gradual accumu-lation of skill and the maximum return from training and experi-ence inside the Service. There is also the important practical point that, other things being equal, permanency maximises loyalty and reduces the dissemination of confidential official information that inevitably follows upon the flow of experienced staff out of the Service.

Security of tenure is therefore offered to the Civil Service recruit as a matter of course. Without doubt those who adopt public ser-vice as a life career are more likely to be faithful servants of the nation that those who regard it as a stepping stone to some other sphere of activity. With increasing service they become more valuable to the State, while on the other hand their abilities become less and less likely to find a market outside the public field. This factor has certainly been modified by the growth of public administration in recent decades and by arrangements that have latterly been introduced to facilitate the interchange of staff between the Civil Service and other public fields.

Until October 1946, when the marriage bar was abolished, security of tenure for women civil servants was assured only so long as they remained single. Subject to a minimum of six years' established service they were entitled to receive as compensation a gratuity based upon length of service, but it was possible, where the interests of the Service were considered to justify it, for married women to continue in employment on an unestablished basis, although this rule was only exceptionally applied. With the removal of the bar, as a matter of government policy in face of the national manpower shortage[1], married women may compete for and continue in Civil Service employment on an equality with men. They retain the right to the marriage gratuity on voluntary retirement and provision has been made for the granting of maternity leave.

This change, which is of course in line with general social developments, was bound to have a considerable effect upon the Civil Service. In the past young girls were administratively acceptable for routine machine and clerical work because of their high rate of outflow, on account of marriage, which rendered it unnecessary to keep them too long on soul-destroying work. In an age when there is a definite shortage of this kind of labour this factor is no longer of great importance, although it still leaves the problem of the routine worker to be solved. On the other hand, despite their subjection to the same conditions of employment as men, married women are obviously less mobile than other workers and naturally more liable to absences through domestic pressures. This is an inefficiency factor that no responsible executive is likely to underrate.

So long as the established civil servant continues to perform his duties with reasonable efficiency and to conduct himself with rectitude he is assured of security of employment. But all civil servants are not established. There is an extensive temporary fringe to which these conditions do not apply.[2]

Recruited temporarily, usually by the Departments and not as

---

[1] A Whitley enquiry had shown the staffs to be divided on the question; see *The Marriage Bar in the Civil Service* (Cmd. 6885), 1946.

[2] On January 1st, 1965, there were approx. 159,000 temporary non-industrial civil servants.

the result of a stringent examination imposed centrally, such officials are needed to deal with emergency conditions which are likely to disappear within a reasonable time. In wartime such temporary recruitments take place on a large scale. At all times some Departments need a fringe of temporary staffs to cope with work of a seasonal and fluctuating nature. Their services will be relinquished as soon as the emergency disappears. That indeed is the theory, and there is an understanding with the staff representatives that temporary officials will be employed only to fill temporary posts, but in fact there is a steady tendency for such posts to become semi-permanent, to exist for long periods and for some temporary officers to be temporary in status only. They continue in State employment without receiving the advantages of permanency. They soon form a pressure group inside the Service whose one object is to obtain permanency of tenure. The permanent officials are concerned at the threat which large bodies of temporaries exert upon their own standards of employment; and the problem has the unfortunate effect of deflecting the activities of the staff associations from more important questions, as well as diminishing the importance of maintaining standards of competence. The mere holding of a temporary post for some time is offered as proving the competence of the holder.

The size of the temporary corps needed by the Administration is not easy to determine. In view of the fluctuating needs of Departments the solution of dispensing with temporary employment altogether, a solution that would have obvious advantages from the public's point of view, would create its own administrative difficulties whenever a contraction or shift of work led to large-scale redundancy.

The grave defect of this form of recruitment is the effect it has upon the efficiency of the Civil Service. It has to be operated locally, varying standards of competence are inevitable and personal nomination is almost unavoidable. When permanency is offered, competency on the job is one of the tests imposed, but it is very difficult to ensure this in public employment and the general efficiency levels of such recruits are usually much below those of the normal competition recruits to the same positions. Persons are thus able to side-step into the Civil Service without being subjected to the sieve of the normal entrance tests. In times of national crisis, such as has occurred almost continuously since 1914, it is impossible to eliminate completely from the most carefully and justly regulated Civil Service the influences of chance and high favour. It has to be admitted that continuing expansion and increasing recruitment difficulties have latterly reduced the relative importance of this factor.

It is not possible to separate the condition of security of tenure from the question of superannuation, but as this is also virtually part of the key-problem of remuneration its discussion will be delayed until this vital question has been considered.

## CAREER PROSPECTS

The entrant to the Civil Service will most certainly be influenced not only by the immediate conditions of employment, but also by the career prospects of the particular branch which he proposes to enter. Advancement has been provided for by the system of grades within the classes which has been gradually evolved to meet this requirement. But the qualifications and qualities required for the different classes may restrict the scope for interflow between classes, and the entrant to the Civil Service cannot normally expect his career to lead outside the class he chooses to enter. This is not strictly true in all cases and does to some extent depend upon competence in the expertise required for the specific class. In the case of the Treasury classes, for example, the promotion avenue of the Clerical Officer entrant now leads into the Executive Class (although before the war there was a separate Clerical hierarchy). Despite official pronouncements equality of opportunity cannot yet be said to exist for all entrants of these several office classes. In their information booklets the Civil Service Commissioners give some indication of the career prospects at the various entry points, suggesting the grade to which a normally successful officer may expect to rise, but in practice this is a matter still dependent very much upon opportunities occurring in the particular Department to which the new entrant is assigned, opportunities inevitably determined by the unforeseeable future developments of the Department's work, and it is quite impossible to give more than a rough and ready forecast at such an early stage. The separateness of the Departments in determining such prospects is not easily appreciated by those who believe the theoretical assumption of the unity of the Service. Having decided to avoid the incalculable element of chance in the field of outside employment the civil servant soon finds himself subjected to a quite different but equally disconcerting chance situation inside the official sphere. As we shall see when considering the promotion arrangements, steps have been taken, constructively but not with complete success, to eliminate some of these faults of the official career system. But we are still a long way from achieving a structure in which the serving official is able to contribute much to his own personal success.

## REMUNERATION

The size of the weekly wage packet, or more appropriately the monthly salary, for many permanent civil servants are paid monthly[1], is the most important of the conditions of service of the civil servant as of all workers. It determines not only the short-term supply of new entrants, but the long-term efficiency of the Service. Poorly paid public services are always inefficient and, although this is not necessarily the only inefficiency factor, little improvement can be hoped for so long as it subsists.

In this, as in all occupations, the complex conditions of supply and demand in the general labour market have a determining influence which is not easy to analyse, but public policy and social context have significant importance in the case of the Civil Service. An expensive civil service may not constitute an undue burden so long as it is small in size. A service with a high prestige and a high sense of public service in an aristocratic community may for long obtain its leading officials for a comparatively modest salary rate. This was undoubtedly the position in Britain up to 1939. At that period the competitions attracted many more suitable candidates than were needed and the examining body could pick and choose. Supply was in the ascendant. Today it is quite otherwise. In the main rather than improve the salary offer the State has preferred to lower the standards called for. But the new situation cannot be wholly attributed to the change in the standards of remuneration or to other conditions of service, for there have been revolutionary changes in the national social and economic context, not least of which may well be the heightened general demand for talents of an administrative type.

Before the First World War the prevailing view was that the Government as employer should set an example, should lead as a good employer in a situation when the bad employer predominated. This principle of the Government as a 'model employer' was accepted by the MacDonnell Commission in 1914[2] and more or less endorsed by a Treasury spokesman in 1922[3]. But the Geddes Axe[4] was already operating over the whole field of government expenditure and with post-war economic stringency a different attitude was bound to grow. The Anderson Committee on the Pay of State

[1] On the basis of one twelfth of the annual salary, paid in arrear.
[2] Cmd. 7338, Chapter IX, para. 87.
[3] Sir Russell Scott, Controller of Establishments, to Select Committee on Estimates, on July 24th, 1922.
[4] The label given to the implementation of the policy recommended by the Economy Committee under Sir Eric Geddes, see Cmd. 1561, 1582 and 1589 (1922).

Servants (1923) set up in accordance with a recommendation of the Geddes Committee, stated categorically, 'In our view there is only one principle in which all the factors of responsibility, cost of living, marriage, children, social position, etc., are included – the employer should pay what is necessary to recruit and to retain an efficient staff.'[1] The Tomlin Commission, which reported in 1931, discarded the model employer doctrine as too variable and contradictory and laid it down that Civil Service remuneration should be based upon broad general comparisons with the remuneration of equivalent outside employments, considered on a long-term basis. This so-called 'Tomlin formula' was adopted as official policy, but there were so many varying factors to be taken into account and so many differences in technical operations between public and private enterprise that strict comparisons were never easy to make.

In the face of hard fact there seems to be little to be argued against the conclusion of the Anderson Committee that the proper level of remuneration for the Civil Service is that needed to recruit and retain an efficient staff. But it all depends upon what is meant by an efficient staff, upon how the long-term trend is interpreted and upon what values are assigned to the other conditions of service that have to be weighed in the balance. The decision is then a matter for a Solomon rather than for a harassed governmental agency impelled by expediency rather than far-sighted statesmanship. At one time H.M. Treasury could be depended upon doing justice to the Service, albeit in its guise of strict parent, without losing sight of its main task as watchdog of the public purse: more recent experience suggests that it has allowed public policy in the direction of economy to obscure the civil service aspect, which is left in the normal trade union manner to the staffs themselves to protect.

Fluctuating living costs and money values have always had a serious disintegrating effect upon salary scales devised for career services. During and after the First World War the situation was met by the application of a bonus to the basic salary, on a sliding scale basis so devised as to give a proportionate increase only to the lowest paid officials and one tapering off steeply at higher salary levels. This system was not liked very much, particularly during the period of deflation when prices were dropping. It is physologically less satisfactory to lose money income when prices are falling than to lose purchasing power when prices are rising, and after the Second World War the staff representatives of the Civil Service, expecting history to repeat itself, were not inclined to press for a cost of living bonus system. They chose consolidation.

[1] See p. 4 of *Reports of Committee on Pay, etc., of State Servants* (1923).

Costs continued to rise and salaries inevitably to drag behind. The staff associations and the Whitley councils had to campaign continuously against the Treasury, whose offers were usually considered unsatisfactory. Consequently the Civil Service Arbitration Tribunal was often given the task of deciding the issue.

In one direction an attempt had been made to change the general salary levels inside the Civil Service, namely for the top grades. Top civil servants during the modern period have never been overpaid. Devotion to public service has been counted upon to attract and retain persons of outstanding capacity for salaries much lower than they could have obtained in outside employment. After the war the worsening of conditions inside the Service was emphasized at the top levels by increased competition from outside: for example, from the newly constituted public corporations. There is also the fact that the Civil Service's need for scientists and members of other professions has made it necessary to offer competitive salaries to them and that the remuneration of the senior administrative officers tended to fall behind. As a result of special enquiry and proposals made by the Chorley Committee in 1949[1] substantial improvement in top-level salaries was introduced.

Except for certain specialist and top-level posts, to which a specific salary is attached, Civil Service remuneration usually involves a system of salary scales whereby regular annual increments are awarded to the individual until the maximum of the scale is reached. In the basic grades the lower steps on the scale are often assigned according to the new entrant's age: this is usually known as the weight-for-age principle. Subsequent advances are made subject to the individual's continuing efficiency on his work, and in light of the natural increase of knowledge and experience that a worker may be expected to accumulate there can be no doubt that the system of increments is a reasonable one. There is, however, an automatic element in the award of such increments and in a large-scale organization there can be no questiton of paying each individual according to his performance. The civil servant is paid not on a precise assessment of his personal merit, but upon the standardized salary conditions of the grade to which he belongs. This is a point that has an important bearing upon the limits of Civil Service efficiency and one that is too frequently overlooked when Civil Service remuneration is discussed.

The campaign for equal pay for women was waged consistently by the staff following the recognition of equality between the sexes

[1] Cmd. 7635.

after the First World War. The Tomlin Commission recommended the principle of 'a fair field and no favour'[1] and this was generally adopted although pay differences were only tidied up by the general acceptance of the rule that women's salaries should approximate to 80 per cent of the male scale, in place of existing widespread variations. The Government continued to accept the general principle, but to delay its implementation on the plea of economy (a recurrent excuse for not making changes in the Civil Service) and of difficulties of implementation. The staff associations pressed strongly for the acceptance of equal pay and there was little vocal opposition from inside the Service. Some women and many men may have had doubts, for rather different reasons, but it was not popular to challenge such an eminently fair principle as equal pay for equal work, although one might cynically ask whether there could be a more difficult principle to apply to the existing Civil Service system. At last the weight of opinion prevailed, supported by competition between the two political parties and an inclination on the part of the Government to use the Civil Service as an example to outside employers. The long-term effect, of course, is to give unmarried women as a class a larger share of the national income, but whether the equating of a married man who has a non-wage-earning wife with a single unit is altogether equitable or socially desirable is another matter. These afterthoughts may be still to come! Unless the principle becomes universal the long run effect on the Civil Service could be to reduce its pay standard to that of the single woman. The agreement of 1955 involved the gradual approach to equal pay over a period of six years. Obviously this particular arrangement was a compromise based upon financial expediency rather than equity, but it was generally welcomed in the Civil Service. The policy is now firmly established.

Formerly salary scales related to the London area and civil servants employed outside the Metropolis were subjected to a system of Provincial Differentiation, involving reduced rates at two levels according to area. As a result of the Priestley Commission's recommendation these arrangements have now been reversed by assigning a National Rate to all areas and granting a special weighting to compensate for additional costs in London area. This addition is subject to periodical revision and is pensionable. The effect of course is the same as before.

As we have already seen[2] the Priestley Commission's main task was to review the whole question of Civil Service pay. They

---

[1] Cmd. 3909, p. 115, para. 398.
[2] See page 32 above.

prefaced their discussion of principles of pay[1] with the following observations:

'. . . Successive Governments have emphasized that in an economy in which full employment is nearly approached significant improvements in pay and conditions of employment (as distinct, we presume, from any which are necessary for the removal of anomalies or the alleviation of patent hardship) should be the consequence only of improved performance; and from the operation of the same principle the Civil Service cannot in our view be exempt.

These considerations are crucial to all our findings because the rates of pay and conditions of service which we recommend are based upon the assumption that the quality and efficiency of the Service has been fully maintained and will continue to stand up to outside comparisons. It is not enough that civil service rates of pay and conditions of service should compare fairly, in the sense we explain . . . with those in other employment. The responsibilities with which the Service is charged and the duties which civil servants have to shoulder are such that they can be properly carried out only if the standards of efficiency and performance in the Service are at least as high as those found elsewhere and if improvements in such standards outside the Service are fully matched within it'.[2]

These are wise words indeed which fairly indicate the quality of the Commission's performance.

The Commission recommended as the first principle of civil service pay 'fair comparison with the current remuneration of outside staffs employed on broadly comparable work, taking account of differences in other conditions of service'. This principle of 'fair comparison', they claimed, took care of the interests of the community in general, of those administering the Civil Service, and of the individual civil servants themselves, all of which should be kept in balance. 'The community must feel that it is getting an efficient service and it is not being asked to pay an excessive price for it. Heads of Departments must have sufficient suitably qualified staff to carry out the tasks demanded of them. The individual civil servant must feel that his remuneration is not unreasonable'.[3] This principle of 'fair comparisons' was to be coupled with a secondary principle of 'internal relativities', which means that existing vertical relativities between grades in a class and horizontal relativities

[1] *Report*, Chapter IV pp. 15 *et seq.*
[2] *Report*, Chapter III p. 14.
[3] *Report*, para. 96, pp. 24–25.

between different classes should be taken into account when pay adjustments are being made.[1]

The Royal Commission agreed that the principle of internal relativities meant that changes in the relative value of different occupations or professions outside the Service should be reflected inside the Service.[2] It was considered that application of the new principle called for much more effective interpretation of the facts than had been possible under past methods of bargaining between the staffs and the Departments or Treasury. They recommended the setting up of an impartial fact-finding body outside the divisions of the Treasury responsible for questions of pay and conditions of service. The Civil Service Pay Research Unit, which was established in 1956 to carry out this function under a Director appointed by the Prime Minister and responsible to the National Whitley Council, will be considered in Chapter VII. It has become established as an interesting and effective part of the Civil Service's machinery of staff consultation.

Following acceptance of the Royal Commission's recommendations pay levels in the Civil Service were substantially raised and further adjustments have followed the investigations of the Pay Research Unit. To this extent the solution has been found acceptable although it can hardly be said that a principle which bases Civil Service remuneration upon changes taking place in other fields, and not upon any fundamental assessment of the institution's worth to the community, can be accepted as an all-time solution. It was an empirical stop-gap answer to an emergency that had long got out of hand. The new methods took time to get established, especially at the outset when the entire field of Civil Service classes had to be covered. Contacts had to be established, information sifted and assessed. There was a good deal of dissatisfaction among the staffs. To get over the inevitable difficulty of the timing of such surveys, especially at a time of steadily rising prices and wages, it soon became the practice to negotiate central pay settlements giving percentage increases to the whole Service on a general assessment of the changing situation, leaving it to subsequent investigations by the Pay Unit to provide the information for adjustments on the basis of fair comparisons. At the end of 1963 such an arrangement was reached between the staffs and the Treasury to cover the three years 1964, 1965 and 1966 amounting to a total increase of ten per cent spread over the three-year period.

The new method received a serious set back in 1961 with a Government pronouncement in the House of Commons on July

[1] *Report,* para. 112, p. 29.
[2] *Report,* para. 120, p. 31.

F

25th of their intention of implementing a national pay pause as one of the means of dealing with the worsening economic situation, but discussion of this must be left to Chapter VII.[1]

## SUPERANNUATION

An important part of remuneration is the superannuation payment which in the case of the Civil Service has been subject to a series of Acts of Parliament extending from 1834 to the present day, and now consolidated in the Superannuation Act, 1965.[2]

It is a peculiarity of these statutes that they do not confer a right to a pension: they lay down the terms on which a pension may be granted by the Crown, a function that is performed by H.M. Treasury. Should a pension be withheld the official would have no legal remedy. It never is in fact withheld where the conditions laid down in the statutes are satisfied. These conditions include the attainment of the normal retirement age of sixty or breakdown of health, and the receipt of the full award depends upon satisfactory service. An allowance may also be granted for retirement on abolition of office, a not very usual occurrence today since there would normally be no difficulty in finding the occupant of such a post equivalent employment in another branch of the Service. Similarly, an officer retired for inefficiency may be granted a proportionate allowance.[3]

Eligibility for pension depends upon appointment to an established post and the tests for this, laid down in Superannuation Act, 1859, are sufficiently interesting to deserve quotation. Section 17 of that Act reads as follows:

'For the purposes of this Act, no person hereafter to be appointed shall be deemed to have served in the permanent Civil Service of the State unless such person holds his appointment directly from the Crown or has been admitted into the Civil Service with a certificate from the Civil Service Commissioners; nor shall any person, already appointed to any office, be held to have served in the permanent Civil Service as aforesaid, unless such person belong to a class which is already entitled to superannuation allowance, or to a class which, if he had been

[1] See page 138 below.

[2] See H.M. Treasury's comprehensive *Digest of Law and Regulations affecting the Superannuating of Members of the Civil Service, Governors of Colonies and the Judiciary* (H.M.S.O., 1965).

[3] These allowances, which are known as compensatory and retiring allowances respectively, must not exceed the amount that would have been granted on retirement for ill-health.

appointed thereto subsequently to the passing of this Act, he would, as holding his appointment directly from the Crown, or as having been admitted into the Civil Service with such certificate as aforesaid, have become entitled to such allowance; and no person shall be entitled to any superannuation allowance under this Act, unless his salary or remuneration has been provided out of the Consolidated Fund of the United Kingdom of Great Britain and Ireland, or out of monies voted by Parliament'.

An important characteristic of Civil Service superannuation is that it is non-contributory. Some earlier superannuation acts did provide for contributions, but the system was finally abolished in 1857.[1] Superficially this may appear as an advantage of Civil Service employment but, coupled with the fact that the pension cannot be claimed as a right, a condition that could not very well exist under a contributory system, it has the effect of making the life contract a reality by rendering withdrawal to another sphere of activity too expensive an expedient for the civil servant to contemplate unless he takes the plunge at an early stage of his career. Nevertheless, pension has usually been considered as deferred pay which should be taken into account when fixing the scales of salary appropriate to the different classes. The Tomlin Commission's recommendations included the introduction of contributory pensions,[2] but the Superannuation Act of 1935, which improved the existing system on certain lines proposed by the Commission, did not include this innovation.

Under the present Superannuation Acts benefit is granted at the rate of 1/80th of a civil servant's emoluments[3] for each completed year of service, with a maximum 40/80ths for forty or more years of service, which thus allows an entrant to the Civil Service whose age is not more than twenty to earn a full pension amounting to half salary by the time he reaches his sixtieth birthday. He also receives at the time of retirement a lump sum based upon 3/80ths of his emoluments for each completed year of service.[4]

[1] Contributory pensions were introduced in an Act of 1822, and repealed two years later. The principle was re-introduced in 1829 and confirmed in the Act of 1834.

[2] See Tomlin Report, Chap. XVII, pp. 201–216.

[3] These emoluments are assessed by averaging remuneration during the last three years of service.

[4] This lump sum allowance was introduced in the Superannuation Act of 1909, which changed the basis for assessment of the pension from 40/60th to 40/80ths. It is also averaged over the salary received during the last three years of service. It is now possible for the pension of officers retained beyond their sixtieth birthday to exceed 40/80ths, but only for completed years beyond that date.

Until 1935 these pensions did not provide for the civil servant's family except in so far as a death grant, based upon 1/30th of his salary for each completed year of service, could be paid to his next of kin if he died while in harness and subject to a minimum period of five years established service. In the Superannuation Act of that year, however, provision was made for the allocation by the retiring officer of a proportion of his pension to a dependant. This arrangement, which is worked out on a strict actuarial basis, involves the definite assignment to a dependant of right to a part of the pension actually awarded and depends on proof of good health on the part of the pensioner.

Since the war a further important advance has been made. Under the Superannuation Act, 1949, pensions on a contributory basis are now provided for the widow and dependants of an established civil servant. In addition, a civil servant resigning after his fiftieth birthday may now retain accrued pension rights, which will become payable on his reaching his sixtieth birthday, although on compassionate grounds the Treasury may grant such a pension immediately. The authorities also have the power to place on pension immediately an officer of over fifty whose services no longer reach a reasonable standard of competence. There is little evidence yet that this option is being very widely used to improve the efficiency of the Service. New regulations also permit the retention of superannuation rights by civil servants transferring to other public services, including teaching, and vice versa.

Until July 5th, 1948, established civil servants were excluded from National Insurance, except as voluntary contributors under the Widows, Orphans and Old Age Pensions scheme. With the introduction of the new comprehensive scheme the Civil Service, together with all other employed persons, became compulsorily insured. This means that existing rights are modified accordingly, National Insurance sickness benefit being deducted from full Civil Service sick pay and pensions of entrants (as from 1st March, 1948) being reduced by the amount of the National Insurance retirement pension. The Graduated Pension Scheme introduced by the National Insurance Act 1959 and operating from April, 1961 permits employees covered by other arrangements to contract out. This the bulk of the Civil Service has done, with certain exceptions such as those on temporary unestablished or casual service.

However, additional contributions under the National Insurance Act, 1966, which have to be paid by civil servants, will affect the sickness benefit and provide a small graduated pension credit at age 65 (or age 60 in case of women).

## HOURS AND LEAVE

The hours of attendance of civil servants have usually been favourable and annual leave arrangements since 1920 have in the main been generous. These were undoubtedly among the factors that made employment in the Civil Service attractive. During the early Victorian period a six-hour day (usually from 10 a.m. to 4 p.m.) was quite common. A minimum day of seven hours for the office staffs was laid down by the Order in Council of 1910, an arrangement which was confirmed at Reorganization, 1920, with provision for a half day's holiday each week. In London the Saturday half-holiday was allowed as a privilege, reducing the 42 hour week to $38\frac{1}{2}$ hours net. In the provinces a week of 44 hours net was applied.[1] Hours in excess of the gross standard week were, except in cases of supervisory and executive grades, paid for as overtime. Longer hours were worked by the manipulative and industrial staffs.

During the wartime emergency these and other conditions of service were suspended by mutual agreement and very long, frequently excessively long, hours were worked by all officials. After the war a standard week of $45\frac{1}{2}$ hours was applied to the office staffs, the excess over 42 hours in London and 44 in the provinces being paid for as overtime. The standard week for the manipulative and industrial staffs remained at 48 hours. To a limited extent the five-day week was granted, namely, in those instances where the office staffs were employed in industrial establishments to which, in accordance with outside practice, a five-day week had been applied since the war. The major part of the non-industrial Civil Service, however, still attended on Saturday mornings.

The annual leave allowance ranged from three weeks for the more junior grades in the clerical sphere up to six weeks for all Administrative and Executive officers. Senior officers of the two major classes were entitled to as much as eight weeks annually, but after the war this privilege was not restored. In addition short periods of special leave, with or without pay according to circumstances, may be granted in cases of domestic urgency and sick absences on full pay may be allowed up to six months, subject to the deduction of National Insurance benefits.

Before the war the Civil Service, especially in London, had been well placed with regard to the length of its working day, but after the war with its longer hours and in the light of improvements in other spheres it is doubtful whether it still held any real attractions on this score, particularly when the general application of the

---

[1] In both cases these totals included a lunch break of 45 minutes.

five-day week or the granting of additional Saturday absences, which had become common outside, were taken into account.

In the matter of annual leave the Civil Service was still in a favoured position. The allowance of six weeks to the senior grades was certainly generous, but there are many factors to be taken into account before coming to a final conclusion on the matter. In the first place many senior officers do not take all their leave (and there is no compensation for not doing so). But this is not necessarily a net advantage to the community. Leave is given for recuperative and refreshment purposes and it can be justly argued that an official who profits fully from his annual leave allowance is likely to be a more efficient worker during the remainder of the year. Some officials, particularly at the top, do not take their full allowance because they are hard pressed. This is a bad thing and relief should be given for efficiency reasons. It may be true that some of these officials do not take all their leave because they find their work so interesting that they do not feel the need for it. This of course depends very much on the nature of the work. There is also the other not uncommon type of official who cannot bear to leave his job to anyone else. By giving up leave he often obtains a reputation for zeal, when the real reason is more likely to stem from lack of confidence in his assistants or an inability to delegate responsibility.

Before condemning the apparently generous leave allowances of civil servants the factor of recuperation needs to be taken very seriously into account. In a sedentary occupation the wise use of leave periods can contribute appreciably to increasing the general efficiency of the Service. Moreover, it must not be forgotten that any time off required by a civil servant (except under those circumstances that justify the granting of special leave) must be taken out of the annual leave allowance and most civil servants take a good number of odd days in this way. Personal privileges that are usual in the private and professional sectors of the economy cannot be granted in a public service.

The Staff and Official Sides were not able to agree on the full restoration of pre-war conditions of hours and leave as was embodied in the wartime promise of the Government to return to pre-war practices after the emergency had passed. The Staff Side naturally pressed strongly for a complete return to the previous conditions, but could make no headway against the adamant attitude of the Treasury, who continued to maintain that the national situation did not permit of such restoration. The truth is that it had long been official policy to reduce the Civil Service's advantages in hours and leave, but earlier attempts by the Official

Side had been unsuccessful. The wartime situation was an opportunity not to be resisted and the official attitude was mean-minded to say the least, a gross failure in good faith which must have played its part in the post-war reduction of the Civil Service's image. In the worsening recruitment situation, to which attention will be given in the following chapter, the policy had little to be said in its favour on any other score.

The whole question was argued at length before the Priestley Commission, which recommended a standardization of hours, varying as before between London and elsewhere; the introduction of the five-day week, with an intermediate stage during which a ten-and-a-half day fortnight should be introduced; and the scaling down on annual leave on the basis of the new weekly attendance but also introducing reduced allowances on the basis of length of service.

As the result of a package deal between the Staff and Official Sides, in which the staff relinquished their claim to certain pre-war privileges, a standardized working week was introduced and the principle of the five-day week, which in fact came into operation more quickly than had been anticipated. Also the less favourable leave allowances were eventually agreed for future entrants and promotees, and this included the giving up of the maximum of eight weeks which had previously been due to senior officials but not operative since 1939. The maximum leave allowance under the five-day week is 30 working days per annum.

The five-day week was introduced in most Departments, subject to safeguarding the interests of the public, which usually entails the attendance of skeleton staffs on Saturday mornings. In fact, despite misgivings regarding probable reactions of the public and a widespread feeling on the part of responsible civil servants that the shorter week was not compatible with their basic responsibilities to the community, the change-over came with little opposition or difficulty. The public on its part had already accepted the principle of the five-day week, except where vital services were concerned, and the skeleton staffing of local offices of such Ministries as Labour, and Pensions and National Insurance and the National Assistance Board has proved quite adequate to deal with enquiries and other business on Saturday mornings. This change went a good way to restoring the balance against the Civil Service as a field of employment.

Further developments in standard hours of attendance have followed an award by the Civil Service Arbitration Tribunal of 2nd July, 1964. The total weekly attendance of office staffs in London is now 41 and elsewhere 42, inclusive of the lunch break. For certain other classes these conditions vary.

## TEMPORARY SERVICE

Apart from being excluded from superannuation, temporary civil servants have often received less favourable rates of pay and other conditions of service than their permanent colleagues. The tendency since the war has been for the gap to be narrowed and on the grounds of justice and equality the staff associations are usually in favour of complete assimilation. However, it does not necessarily follow that there is any injustice in granting more favourable conditions to those who have been subject to more severe entrance tests and have longer experience behind them in a permanent capacity. It perhaps throws a significant light on the decline in general standards that persons recruited outside the normal course can vie sufficiently well with their long-serving colleagues to give an air of reasonableness to a claim to equality of treatment!

However, the practice of maintaining 'temporary' service almost indefinitely without pension rights had long been challenged as unfair and in 1964, by granting the right of establishment to all temporary unestablished non-industrial civil servants who have reached their 60th birthday and completed at least twenty years unestablished service, an important step was taken to ameliorate the position.

## PRESTIGE, CIVIL RIGHTS AND RULES OF CONDUCT

As a condition of service the prestige of an occupation is an imponderable factor, yet none the less important on that account. In the past many, particularly among the highly educated, have been willing to devote themselves to public service as a vocation and to sacrifice the normal opportunities of advancement in economic and social standards that they might have achieved elsewhere. The civil servant's position was held in high esteem and strenuously competed for. Once obtained it was felt to be both a trust and a privilege to be held on to at all costs. This endowed it with an attractiveness that offset a number of manifest disadvantages. One of these is that the civil servant has but one employer, the State: if he is dissatisfied there is usually no alternative market for his wares.[1] He is restricted in his participation in public affairs and

---

[1] This position has been progressively modified by the introduction of reciprocal arrangements for transfer of accrued Civil Service pension rights between the Civil Service and a wide range of other public employments, while it is also possible in other cases where the arrangement is specially approved.

subject to special rules of personal conduct, which to some extent involve a sacrifice of some of his citizenship rights. These important matters, which are discussed in Chapter VIII, must be taken fully into account when assessing the conditions of civil service employment. By some they may be considered to more than offset the accepted advantages of the Service. The completely efficient civil service calls for a high degree of self-sacrifice and dedication from its members.

WELFARE

Another post-war development has been the increased attention given to staff welfare. Formerly this was recognised as a function of individual heads and supervisors: the general situation outside and the quality of the staffs inside the Civil Service meant that this responsibility was well within the capacity of all supervisory officials, supported as a matter of course by the Whitley councils and wise departmental regulation. Now care for the personal difficulties of individual officials has been given to specially selected Welfare Officers.

As was to be expected there were a number of reasons for this development: the generally poor quality of accommodation in government premises, albeit for long the concern of the staff representatives and at least subjected to certain minimal standards; the inflow after the war of many persons without a Civil Service background including many temporaries of rather lower health gradings than had previously been normal; but, more than these, the great change in attitudes to such matters as staff welfare and premises standards throughout the community, and their embodiment as an important factor in official health and employment policy. The Government felt bound to apply to its own servants at least the minimum standards it was advocating for industry at large, and once again it was impelled to use the Civil Service as an example in this field!

Great improvements have been made in public office accommodation on behalf of both the public and the staffs, with an eye on overall efficiency. But building shortages and demands in many directions for the resources needed for constructional work has meant that, while many new modern-type premises have been provided, some older offices still remain very much behind the times and too expensive to bring up to even modest standards. There is also the fluid technological factor that buildings devised for today's uses soon get out of date in face of the developing requirements of the new administration and of new constructional materials and methods.

The Welfare Officers are carefully selected from and continue as specialist members of existing grades. Members of the staff have direct access to them for the consideration of personal matters and strict confidentiality is the rule. In other words the Welfare Officer is not in the chain of command. Supervisors may seek his advice where they have a particularly stubborn staff problem to solve. It has to be remembered that care for the welfare of his staff is an essential aspect of the supervisor's job. He knows quite well that the efficiency of his unit often depends upon good personal relationships and that non-official happenings to individual members can have an adverse effect upon their performance. Merely to ignore the possible existence of personal complications when no official cause can be diagnosed and to hope for the best is too negative an approach for safety.

The new Welfare system in the Civil Service, upon which a senior Welfare Adviser at the Treasury exercises a general oversight, seems to work very well. The danger is that the handing over of this task to experts may create the impression that the supervisor needs no longer to concern himself with such matters, but, in fact, apart from his unavoidable involvement, he is still the nearest responsible person to the source of the trouble who is in a position to prevent in many cases the need for expert advice ever arising.

## HONOURS

It is a fact that proportionately more civil servants than other citizens figure in the Honours Lists. Traditionally, the sovereign rewards his servants for services rendered. Awards to the Civil Service are made on a strictly graded system, which appears to work out as follows: K.C.B. for Permanent Secretary, K.B.E. for Deputy Secretary, C.B. for Under Secretary, C.B.E. for Assistant Secretary, O.B.E. for Principal or Chief Executive Officer, and M.B.E. for all lower grades.[1] One consequence of this is that, while a civil servant's official grading may not be known, or if known may convey little, to the outsider, an honour will definitely signify that he has not risen above a certain level! It is doubtful whether civil servants bother very much about this sort of award, unless perhaps it carries a knighthood, which has a prestige and can have a cash advantage. The possibility of receiving an honour is often put forward as forming part of a civil servant's remuneration, although it is doubtful whether, under the present system of fair

[1] See P. G. Richards, *Patronage in British Government* (Allen & Unwin, 1963).

relativities, any such makeweight would be appropriate in any case. In the lower honour gradings there has of late been such an inflationary trend that it is doubtful whether many who receive such honours any longer feel that there is much reason for personal congratulation.

The official performance of senior civil servants can be pretty clearly assessed by the authorities, so that higher awards could be made strictly according to special merit, if that were the real objective, which is doubtful. Further down the line, where comparatively large numbers are involved, a pattern of precedence by grade and seniority and geographical distribution has to be worked out, and the designation of a specific recipient will depend upon the luck of the draw, i.e. upon his being at the right moment at the actual point towards which the award is more or less directed. As things are it can be hazarded that only a few civil servants would feel aggrieved if the present honours system were superseded. Obviously it has little impact upon the Civil Service's drawing power from the career point of view. Of course there could be no objection to a system of honours based upon outstanding performance or exceptional contribution, and bestowal irrespective of rank, like the Victoria Cross. Such awards do honour to the Crown, to the recipient and to the community on whose behalf they are made.

# CHAPTER IV

# RECRUITMENT

The efficiency and morale of the Civil Service depend ultimately upon the standards prescribed and the methods adopted at the recruitment stage. It is an immemorial characteristic of public employment that it should be regarded as a bounty to be conferred upon the adherents of the governing power, a return for services rendered rather than a creative opportunity to promote the public weal. Throughout history administrative offices have been in the gift of the ruler; sometimes by mere whim to retainers about the court; sometimes in accordance with hereditary precedence; sometimes even by sale to the highest bidder, a practice not rare in English experience and habitual in France under the *ancien régime* that fell with the Revolution. The degree to which the competence of the candidate was taken into account would depend upon the selector's assessment of current necessities. Too frequently the meeting of an irksome obligation or a chance to replenish the coffers of the State would overshadow any thought for day-to-day administrative efficiency, and the loss as time went on would be cumulative. Sometimes, of course, the right man was chosen for the job. Self-interest could be counted upon to ensure that none but the most incompetent of rulers should completely ignore the immediate needs of the situation. Where specific qualifications were laid down special arrangements might be made; as in Rome where the magistracies were subject to a scale of precedences, in Greece where election rather than lot might be preferred for filling technical posts, and in medieval England where churchmen for long monopolized the Royal Household positions in virtue of being practically the only competent clerks in the community. Even where the power of appointment was delegated to lesser authorities some form of patronage was almost bound to operate. It is natural that the responsible minister should fill vacancies from among those with whom he is acquainted or on whose behalf the pressures of relations and friends have been exerted.

## THE CIVIL SERVICE COMMISSION AND ITS TASK

With the advent of the modern state the need for more efficient methods of selection became apparent. Even the patronage wielders sometimes found entrance examinations desirable, but they were usually loath to give up privileges which seemed to be an essential perquisite of their office. We have already seen how, at the birth of the modern Civil Service in the middle of the nineteenth century, the storming of the citadel of patronage was the reformers' first and most difficult task. In seeking an objective method of selection to substitute for the subjective ways of patronage, open competition was chosen as the most satisfactory solution. But before any such objective tests could be imposed an independent recruiting agency had to be established. Thus, in 1855, the Civil Service Commission was first set up.

The Commissioners[1] are appointed by the Crown and hold office during the sovereign's good pleasure. They are responsible only for recruitment. The general conditions of candidature for the various posts and rules for the examinations are settled by the Treasury and Heads of Departments, and the latter continue to make the actual appointments after the requirements of the Commissioners have been satisfied. The Civil Service Commissioners' sphere of responsibility is therefore a restricted one, but within that sphere they act quasi-judicially and are not subject to outside interference, even from the Treasury or the Prime Minister. Assisted by a normal Civil Service staff they are indeed one of the smaller Departments. They also arrange examinations for certain other public authorities on an agency basis.

The Commissioners now hold their authority under the Civil Services Order in Council of 3rd August 1956,[2] which lays down the following rule:

'The qualifications of all persons proposed for permanent appointment shall before they are appointed, be approved by the Commissioners, and no person shall be so appointed until a certificate of his qualification has been issued by the Commissioners:

Provided that the provisions of this Article shall not apply to appointments to situations

(a) to which the holder is appointed directly by the Crown;
(b) filled by the appointment or transfer of classes of persons by or in pursuance of any Act of Parliament which exempts such persons from the requirement that a certificate of qualification shall be issued before appointment.'[3]

---

[1] Originally there were three; today there are five.
[2] This recent Order in Council supersedes all previous Orders in Council on the subject. It is reproduced (together with General Regulations of 31st August, 1956, issued under the Order) in the *Report of Her Majesty's Civil Commissioners* for the period 1st April, 1956, to 31st March, 1957.
[3] Order in Council, 1956, para. 2.

These exceptions merely represent the existing constitutional powers of the Crown, under the prerogative, and of Parliament, through legislation, to make special provision when necessary. They are sparingly used. Of course the Civil Service Commissioners themselves hold Crown appointments!

Under the General Regulations the Commissioners have to satisfy themselves as to the following conditions:

*Age* That the candidate is within the limits of age prescribed for the particular post.

*Health and Regularity of Attendance* That the candidate's health is such as to qualify him for the situation he seeks and that he is likely to give regular and effective service up to the normal minimum age of retirement.

*Character* That the candidate's character is such as to qualify him for the situation which he seeks.

*Knowledge and Ability* That the candidate is qualified in respect of knowledge and ability to discharge the duties of the situation which he seeks.

*Nationality* Subject to certain additions and qualifications, a candidate must be a British subject, a British protected person or a citizen of the Irish Republic.

From the first the Commissioners have built up a high reputation for the effectiveness and impartiality of the tests which they impose. Various types of test have been adopted, but for open competitions to the 'Treasury' classes the written literary type of examination, based upon a general educational pattern, was for long favoured to the exclusion of other methods. It is only since 1919 that the variety of tests has been extended. By basing the syllabus of the examinations for the Administrative Class on the curricula of the universities, particularly of Oxford and Cambridge, it was possible to ensure not only that these universities should supply the majority of the cadets to the leadership group, but also that the Commission's examinations and the standards and methods of the educational establishments should keep in step. Similar principles were applied at lower levels, although before the First World War some steps were taken to include appropriate clerkship subjects in the examinations for certain of the subordinate grades.[1] Examinations for certain departmental classes, e.g. the Customs and Excise Officerships, included subjects that were considered helpful in the performance of the Department's work, but even in these cases the examinations remained predominantly of the general literary type.

[1] E.g. such subjects as précis writing, copying manuscripts, book-keeping and shorthand in the Second Division examinations.

One point should be specially emphasized: for the purest type of open competition a specific educational experience or qualification was not laid down. Anyone satisfying the general regulations as regards age, health, character, etc., could compete, but in practice success came over-whelmingly to those who had undergone the type of education to which the examination syllabus was so closely related. Occasionally, it is true, a brilliant privately tutored candidate passed the examinations, but the advantages of having had the right type of schooling were so great that even the new universities made a poor showing beside Oxford and Cambridge. In practice this pure form of open competition has never been appropriate except for a limited range of office posts. After 1919 a *viva voce* test was introduced for the Administrative Class with the object of assessing personality and the use of this method has since been extended in accordance with modern thought on the subject.

Technical and professional posts need vocational qualifications, which are laid down as the minimum requirement for candidature: formal selection is then usually settled by means of competitive interview. For many subordinate posts, and also for the allocation of a proportion of vacancies to a particular type of candidate, limited competitions have also been widely adopted. For example, a special limited competition has for long been available to members of the manipulative classes in the Post Office who aspire to transfer to the Clerical Class.

The examination system, built up during the later decades of the nineteenth century, probably had its heyday in the period immediately preceding the First World War. Relatively to the rest of the community the Civil Service from top to bottom was a highly educated vocation built in a strictly hierarchic form. Already, however, the expansion of the Post Office into the telecommunications sphere and the recent extension of government participation in the social service spheres of employment and health had led to the absorption into the Civil Service of older persons with special outside experience. Following the war recruitment from among school-leaving candidates was delayed by the need to absorb large numbers of ex-Servicemen. This again radically altered the normal age grouping of the Civil Service and was not effected without gravely lowering the entrance standards hitherto considered as the minimum essential to efficiency. A similar situation arose after the Second World War, but in this case, profiting by previous experience, a carefully devised Reconstruction scheme of recruitment[1]

[1] See *Recruitment to Established Posts in the Civil Service During the Reconstruction Period* (Statement of Government Policy and Civil Service National Whitley Council Report, 1944), Cmd. 6567.

ensured that tests which were both fair and effective should be applied in the recruitment of the ex-Service men and women. These tests did involve the suspension for the time being of the general principle of open competition and the prescription of a specific educational experience as one of the conditions determining eligibility to compete. In the main, however, it is changes of a more general and radical nature that have created special recruitment difficulties, but it is proposed to leave the consideration of these matters until the present system of recruitment has been briefly examined.

### THE CHANGING SITUATION

Following the Second World War new situations arose to delay reinstatement and to affect development of Civil Service recruitment. Before the end of the war arrangements had been agreed on the National Whitley Council for the recruitment during the Reconstruction period of persons whose service with the armed and auxiliary Forces of the Crown had deprived them of the normal opportunities to compete for posts in the Civil Service. Every effort was made to avoid the somewhat haphazard approach of the previous 'Reconstruction' period.

The new 'Reconstruction' examinations usually consisted of a written part which was of a general nature, suitable for persons who had got out of the habit of formal study, followed by an interview. In the case of the highest posts the so called 'house-party' system was adopted, as previously mentioned. Age limits were extended to allow for the candidate's period with the Forces and a prerequisite for entering the competitions was an educational experience suitable to the level of the normal competitions for the particular class. Thus for the Clerical Class the requirement was full-time education to the age of 16 or the holding of a School Certificate. This was a new principle for examinations for this type of post and the competitions were therefore limited and not open even within the restricted field of recruitment. Generally speaking these competitions presented a fair compromise in a difficult situation and seem to have worked effectively.

The maintenance of the size of the Civil Service in order to cope with the new post-war policy of increased economic planning and social reform prevented any serious redundancy problem from arising. Numbers of temporary civil servants left of their own accord, but for a time the outflow was restricted by the Control of

Employment Order (Civil Servants) which operated from 1945 to early 1947. Some permanent posts were given to suitable temporaries, who were selected by interview boards. But the temporary element continued to be large and inevitably pressure began to be exerted through the staff associations for establishment to be offered to suitable temporary officers in the lower grades, e.g. Clerical and Sub-clerical. Naturally the general shortage of normal recruits at this level disposed the authorities to look at these proposals more favourably than they might otherwise have done and schemes were agreed from time to time for limited competitions to be held. Despite the modest educational levels of these competitions it was never easy to fill the quotas agreed with the Staff Side, without lowering standards below any reasonable level. In any case it is obvious that the majority of recruits through these channels were not up to the minimum standards normally required by the Civil Service.

The unanticipated continuance of certain wartime Departments meant the assimilation of numbers of older entrants with a limited Civil Service background, but an even more important development of this type followed the passing of the National Insurance Act of 1944, which authorized the establishment of the Ministry of National Insurance[1] to administer a comprehensive social security scheme. In the staffing of this new Central Department, whose main function was to be the implementation of the Beveridge proposals, not only were the Civil Service staffs of the several Departments already concerned with this work brought together under one control, but large blocks of non-Civil Service workers were assimilated from the Approved Societies, the Public Assistance Departments of the Local Authorities and certain private insurance offices concerned with Workmen's Compensation. These groups included many experts whose experience and skills were invaluable to the new Ministry, but there were many others, particularly at lower levels who inevitably fell below the normal standards of the Civil Service. Their new grading was settled in terms of their previous status which was bound to have varied between one outside organization and another. They included many middle-aged workers who were too old to be completely assimilated to the Civil Service outlook and traditions. The cynic may suggest that that might have been a good thing. In some ways perhaps, but it must be remembered that civil servants are still expected to have certain virtues that outside organizations are less insistent upon. One interesting deviation from existing Civil Service practice was the provision that certain of these outside entrants should retain the right to work on

---

[1] Subsequently the Ministry of Social Security.

till the age of sixty-five, instead of the normal Civil Service sixty. The object of this was to preserve the value of their previous super-annuation rights.

It may be thought that developments peculiar to the post-war period having once been dealt with, the Civil Service, repeating the experience of the previous post-war era, would gradually return to normality, but apart from the general factors in the market situation briefly touched upon in Chapter III there were other extra-Civil Service developments that were bound to have a long run effect upon recruitment. These were specifically the encouragement of employment of married women and of extending the active working age, both advocated nationally as essential ingredients of the full employment policy, as well as the conceding of equal pay to women civil servants, largely to meet the pressure of staff groups inside the Service. The lifting of the marriage bar in October 1946, although decided upon as a matter of national policy and despite divided opinion inside the Civil Service,[1] can be adjudged a logical outcome of the failure of the Service to recruit sufficient numbers of young girls for routine work. The field of clerical recruitment was subsequently extended by opening the competitions to adults, first, in 1955, to the 40–60 age group and later to the entire adult period up to age 59. The conceding of equal pay also made the Civil Service a relatively more attractive field of employment to members of the fair sex and this has certainly had the effect of increasing the proportion of female recruits, although whether this may have been offset by rendering the Civil Service less attractive to the male is a matter for conjecture. Yet, taken in their aggregate these expedients have done no more than slow up the tide that has been running steadily against the Civil Service's attractiveness as a career.

### DECLINE IN OPEN COMPETITION

All these changes, and others still to be mentioned, have been necessitated by the dwindling attractiveness of the Civil Service as a field of employment and the difficulty of attracting sufficient school leavers to the competitions. The overall effect has been to restrict the operation of open competition as understood for the best part of a hundred years following its formulation by Trevelyan and Northcote in 1853.

Immediately following the First World War, the introduction of the straight-forward interview as an ingredient of the written examinations had already sown the seeds for a drift away from the complete objectivity of the examinations as originally projected.

[1] See *The Marriage Bar in the Civil Service*, Cmd. 6885 (1946).

This is not to suggest that the selecting authorities did not continue to approach their responsible task with the strictest impartiality, but as the late Sir Stanley Leathes, an expert on the interview procedure as then applied by the Civil Service Commission, stated in 1926,[1] 'If jobbery is suspected, it is almost as bad as if jobbery exists'. When personality meets personality across even the friendliest table it is possible for all sorts of class and social prejudices to influence the proceedings without the participants themselves being aware of what is happening, and even when they are aware the very effort called forth to ensure strict impartiality almost inevitably leads to over-emphasis in the opposite direction.

It is argued, with truth, that the written examination fails to eliminate candidates who are obviously unsuitable on the score of personality. This is a more valid objection where personality is an important factor in the actual job to be performed, but usually there is such a wide range and variety of tasks open to an entrant to a general grade in the Civil Service that there should be little difficulty in finding an effective niche for any generally suitable candidate. Even in an age when social contacts by civil servants in course of public business have grown so much more important than in the days before the Welfare State, efficiency in the back-room positions is still vital. One of the difficulties of attempting to pick and choose on the basis of personality is the lack of any generally accepted measure by which administrative ability—using the term in its broader sense—can be assessed, particularly for younger people in whom such ability can be little more than potential.

In the restricted labour supply situation after the war there was a decisive swing against undergoing the strains of a competitive written examination for entry to the middle and lower grades of the Civil Service, when equally attractive posts were widely available without any such effort. To meet this trend the Civil Service Commissioners, in default of any serious governmental effort to make the Civil Service more attractive, tentatively decided in 1953 to accept the General Certificate of Education (or its equivalent) with certain passes in lieu of the normal written examination. Actual selection was to be by interview. At first the new method was applied in a limited way to the London area, where recruitment had become exceptionally difficult owing to the high demand for school leavers in all directions, and it was made available concurrently with the ordinary examinations. This was to prove the thin end of the wedge. Its immediate effect was to improve the recruitment position. But as poor weight money drives the good coin out of circulation so was it inevitable from the outset that the

[1] See *Public Administration*, Vol. I, p. 356.

less burdensome test of educational competence would drive out the more testing written examination. By 1966 the GCE method had spread so widely as to cover the greater part of the Clerical-Executive field, and to extend elsewhere.[1] Even in the Administrative Class recruitment the written examinations are steadily losing ground before the alternative Method II tests which, while they do apply a searching probe into the candidate's character and capabilities, cannot avoid imposing standards that have a degree of subjectivity which is more likely to be emphasized than diminished at the interview stage where the final decision is reached. In this field at least the State's offer of a highly privileged position virtually for this one-time effort, is sufficient to maintain open competition even if the universities do fail to produce enough candidates to fit the specification that, for good or ill, has been laid down.

Even if it is agreed that the Commissioners have had little alternative in face of the dwindling competitiveness of the Civil Service in so many areas, no one who prizes the high reputation built up by the Service over its first hundred years can regard without apprehension the thought that so many entrants today, to what should still be a great profession, do not consider it worth any real preparatory effort to attain. For let us be clear about this general school qualifications, from GCE to high degree or diploma, are properly a preparation for life but cannot constitute a promise of eternal reward in any truly democratic society.

The only selective element now left in the new-style recruitment process is the interview and even that has been waived in some cases and may be expected to become much of a routine with the general dispersal of the GCE selection of Clerical Assistants and Clerical Officers. It has become a national habit to place the straight across-the-table interview on a pedestal as essential in numberless selection situations and it is to be wondered whether its widespread use in this way does not mark a general unwillingness to do some real hard thinking about its demerits as well as its merits. Committees, however well-intentioned, perhaps even because they are well-intentioned, can be hopelessly irresponsible. Could it be possible that an interviewing computer, programmed with all the leading questions, would give results that were equally reliable but less open to challenge on grounds of inconsequential human bias?

Before briefly surveying the more important current competitions in order to see how the various changes and innovations have been woven into a new pattern some further details of the so-called 'house-party' method will be of interest.

---

[1] For example to recruitment of certain Engineering and Postal Telegraph Officers in the Post Office.

### 'HOUSE PARTY' METHOD

Officially known now as Method II (particularly in connection with the Administrative Class examinations), this is essentially a modern approach, aimed to place special emphasis on personality and quickwittedness as opposed to sheer intellectual ability. It stems back to the house-party scheme adopted for the selection of Army officers during the war and subsequently by the Civil Service Commission for recruitment to the Administrative Class in the Reconstruction examinations. These examinations were devised for candidates whose career had been dislocated by war service and for whom the old type of examination was certainly not suitable. Under the original scheme candidates attended the Civil Service Selection Board (at that time known as CISSB) located at Stoke D'Abernon, Cobham, Surrey, organized on a residential basis for two or three days. For reasons of economy the Board now sits in London and candidates attend daily, apparently without any distinguishable falling off in efficiency.[1] The procedures adopted allow for a friendly but searching review of the candidate's personal qualities and intelligence to be undertaken by the Board. The following explanatory extracts from the Civil Service Commission's Report on CISSB, published in 1951, summarizes the several factors in the process:

'The procedure by which it was hoped that the CISSB assessors would be able to form reliable judgments was to obtain evidence of a candidate's suitability from four sources. The first was the external evidence, that is to say, the documents in the case, comprising the candidate's record, his referees' reports and the results of his Qualifying Examination; the second was the psychological tests; the third, oral and written exercises based on problems broadly analogous to the work of the Civil Service; and the fourth, interviews by the Observer, Psychologist and Chairman attached to the candidate's group.

'Although the procedure can be considered under these four headings, it would convey a wrong impression of the CISSB method if it were thought that a poor showing by a candidate under any one of them was regarded as decisive. The aim was to arrive at an estimate of the candidate's suitability by means of all the evidence available and to attach to each part its right degree of importance in relation to the whole.[2]

[1] See *Ninth Report from the Select Committee on Estimates (Session 1947–8) on the Civil Service Commission* (H.M.S.O., 1948) and *Memorandum by the Civil Service Commission on the use of the Civil Service Selection Board in the Reconstruction Examination* (H.M.S.O., 1951.)

[2] *Op Cit.*, p. 10, paras. 37 and 38.

The Report then goes on interestingly to describe some of the practical methods and exercises adopted by the CISSB. Originally there was a good deal of excited publicity on the so-called psychological aspects of an approach which is really designed to increase the candidate's participation in the selection process and to give him a chance to face up to live situations by such means as taking the chair of his group, organizing the strategic approach to a specific administration problem, or reporting back upon the group's solution. Each candidate's reactions are objectively assessed by the observers attached to the groups.

It is to be emphasized that the Civil Service Selection Board, which continues today on the lines described, does not come to a final decision. Its findings are passed to the Final Interview Board whose task it is to determine the final placings. This new method has become firmly established and its specific applications will be mentioned in the following section.

### THE ENTRANCE TESTS TODAY

Compared with the simpler system of written tests which predominated the Civil Service Commission's Reports up to 1938 the present pattern of tests looks excessively complicated. As the foregoing section will have amply demonstrated, the system of Civil Service recruitment is in a state of flux from which any sort of stability appears unlikely to emerge in the near future. The object of this section is to provide a general picture of the examinations available in 1966 for some of the main classes.[1]

*Administrative Class* The ordinary competitions are now open to candidates between the ages of 20 and 28 (with some extension for those serving in the regular Forces or in H.M. Overseas Civil Service). As we have already seen there are two forms of examination, known as Method I and Method II.

Method I is the traditional type of academic examination, which is now divided into two parts. The first part consists of a qualifying examination made up of an essay, an English paper, and a general paper. Only those candidates who attain the requisite standard in this part are allowed to proceed to the more competitive second part, which consists of an interview and of written papers in a

---

[1] Up to date information should be sought from the Civil Service Commission at 23 Savile Row, London, W.1, or in the case of purely departmental posts the headquarters of the particular Ministry. It is a matter of interest that the Commission left its historic headquarters at 6 Burlington Gardens during 1963 and dispersal out of London is contemplated.

wide range of studies covering most university honours subjects. The order of merit is determined by the total of marks awarded at interview and for the optional subjects. In this case no one is barred from entry through lack of educational qualifications but, as the Commissioners assert 'candidates who are not of at least second class honours standard have little chance of success.'[1] This of course had always been the position in the past although occasionally a candidate of outstanding intellect had managed to get through, largely on the basis of private study!

Method II has already been briefly discussed. To be eligible in this case the candidate must hold (or obtain during the year of the competition) a first or second class honours degree or diploma in technology. The examination is in three stages: (i) a preliminary qualifying written test as in Method I; (ii) subject to satisfactory performance in (i) attendance at the Civil Service Selection Board for tests and interviews; and (iii) appearance before the Final Interview Board which reviews all the information now available, including its own judgment at the interview, and arranges those whom they declare successful in order of merit.

Originally a third only of the vacancies were assigned to Method II, but with its increasing acceptance and popularity over 50% are now filled by this method. Very high standards are applied by the Commission and these examinations are still highly competitive, as the figures for 1964 clearly show, when, for the 88 advertised Assistant Principal vacancies in the ordinary competitions, there were 835 applicants of whom 699 were examined, and out of the 90 declared successful 71 took up appointments.

Latterly, in accordance with a statement in Parliament on 9th June, 1964 limited competitions by Method II have been held to recruit to higher positions older experienced persons from outside the Civil Service. The first competitions covered the recruitment of six Principals, between the ages of 30 and 35, from among persons holding responsible positions in other employment, and three Assistant Secretaries, between the ages of 40 and 45, who could bring specialized experience into the Civil Service. The Civil Service Commissioners comment upon the first of these competitions for Principals, which was held during 1964:

'Candidates were required to have held a senior post in industry or commerce or at a university or in some professional field. There were some 380 applications from a wide range of occupations, and 56 candidates were invited to tests and interviews at the Civil Service Selection Board and to interview by the Final

[1] *Civil Service Posts for Graduates* (C.S. Commission, 1965), p. 93.

Board. In keeping with the purpose of the competition, the standard for acceptance was high. Three of the successful candidates were from the business and commercial world, one, with experience of computer projects, was from local government but had formerly served in industry, one came from university administration and one was a Grammar School Headmaster. One of the successful candidates had a science degree and another a degree in economics combined with a Higher National Certificate in Mechanical Engineering. Two had obtained accountancy qualifications in the course of their careers.'[1]

In this field and also for the Executive and Clerical Classes mentioned below there are special competitions for members of the armed Forces and H.M. Overseas Civil Service.

There are also special limited competitions for serving civil servants but these have something of the nature of promotion examinations and will be dealt with, together with similar examinations for other classes, in Chapter VI.

*Executive Class* Open written school-leaving competitions for this important group have now been superseded by the G.C.E. form of entry already described. The failure to attract a sufficient number of suitable candidates to fill an increasing number of vacancies has rendered the holding of highly competitive examinations futile. Candidates must be aged at least $17\frac{1}{2}$ and under 28,[2] and hold G.C.E. with passes in five acceptable subjects, including English language, two of which must be at Advanced Level. Selection is by interview. For 1,704 advertised vacancies in 1964, 2,496 candidates were interviewed, of whom 1,650 were declared successful and 1,369 actually took up appointments.

*Clerical Class* Under new arrangements introduced in 1966, the competitions are divided broadly between the London area and elsewhere. The general qualification is G.C.E. with five passes at Ordinary level, including English language. The Civil Service Commission still organize a number of competitions to fill vacancies in the London area, and other shortage areas, where recruitment has been increasingly difficult for some time. These include open written competitions for school leavers between ages 15 and 20, and for older entrants between 20 and 40, and from 40 to 59. There are also separate G.C.E. competitions for under 20's, and over 20's.

Elsewhere authority has been given to the Departments to fill their own vacancies locally, i.e. in the Regions, on the basis of the G.C.E. qualification. Suitable candidates will be nominated by the Department to the Civil Service Commission, who will have the

---

[1] C.S. Commissioners 98th Report for 1964 (1965) p. 2.
[2] Increased from 24 to 28 in 1966.

final word in granting establishment, subject to the evidence of age, health, character and nationality, as laid down in the regulations, which has been collected by the Departments. The age limits now range from 15 to 59, but Departments are urged to continue to place emphasis on the recruitment of school leavers! They are also recommended to act collectively wherever circumstances dictate. It is difficult to see on what grounds the Departments will be justified in rejecting any eligible candidate with the necessary qualifications, and if they do some element of arbitrariness seems bound to enter into the process. Thus has the much vaunted open competition principle been finally discarded over important areas of the Civil Service.

Apart from the ordinary competitions some vacancies are filled by the offer of appointments to unsuccessful Executive Class candidates, while limited competitions are organized from time to time for serving members of both non-industrial and industrial grades, aged 20 to 59, who lack the prescribed educational qualifications.

In 1964, out of 19,173 applicants in the open competitions for 9,103 vacancies, 8,003 were declared successful, of whom 7,884 were actually appointed.

*Clerical Assistants* After numerous experiments in choosing Clerical Assistants, including short-answer tests, recruitment of this grade, which is now open to both sexes, is conducted on similar lines to the Clerical Class competitions, except that qualifying levels are more modest, namely G.C.E. with two passes at Ordinary level, including English language.

*Typing Grades* These are widely employed throughout the Departments, both in personal secretary posts to senior officials and in pools more generally available to responsible members of the staff throughout the branch. The minimum age of entry is 15. Typists in the lowest grade must be able to type at least thirty words a minute. Shorthand typists must also be able to write a minimum of eighty words a minute in shorthand. There are also supervisory posts. To cover more senior secretarial posts calling for higher qualifications and previously graded as Clerical Officer (Secretary), in January 1966 a new grade of Personal Secretary was introduced, with a higher grade of Senior Personal Secretary.

In this field in particular the Civil Service is placed at a disadvantage both by the heavy demand for typists or various grades in industry and commerce, and also by the high salaries that these fields can offer younger recruits, especially if they are presentable! Consequently typists and shorthand typists are in short supply and there are vacancies for almost any qualified applicant. They usually begin in an unestablished capacity, but the normal rules for establishment apply. Recruitment is undertaken by the individual Departments and the necessary speed tests are applied locally. Limited competitions for establishment are organized by the Civil Service Commission for existing unestablished typists and shorthand typists under the age of 60 who otherwise lack the prescribed educational qualification.

*Special Departmental Classes* Three distinct classes are concerned here, differing radically in function: namely, H.M. Inspector of Taxes in the Inland Revenue Department, the Cadet Grade of the Ministry of Labour, and Assistant Postal Controllers (Class II) in the Post Office. Annual vacancies have amounted to about 60, 10 and 15 respectively. The requirements of this group fall somewhere between Administrative and Executive, but they are generally classified under the latter heading.

The entrance requirements are the only common basis to these three senior groups. Candidates must conform to the same age limits and conditions as for the Administrative Class competitions, but for the Method I examination there are fewer optional papers, while for Method II the degree or diploma in technology does not require first or second class honours. However, for those who can offer such qualifications or are chartered accountants, there is also continuous recruitment to the grade of Inspector of Taxes only. Selection for these posts is by Method II, but with a preliminary interview substituted for the written examination.

*Scientific and Professional Classes* Holders of suitable qualifications are recruitable by interview at any time to the grades of Scientific Officer or Senior Scientific Officer. For the former the upper age limit is 29, while candidates for the latter must have at least three years post-graduate or other approved experience and the age limits are 26 to 32. Similarly there is recruitment to the Assistant Experimental Officer and Experimental Officer grades, requiring more modest qualifications and with age limits between 18 and 28 and 26 and 31 respectively.

The Civil Service Commission organize competitions for many other professional and technical classes, and these are summarized in their annual Reports. For example, in 1964 the number of advertised vacancies in this field ranged between single or a few posts and over 500 for the same type of appointment, and in few instances were all the vacancies filled. For such appointments there are usually prescribed minimum professional qualifications, often coupled with evidence of specific experience. The competitions are usually continuous and carried out by interview boards.

This method of continuous competition was introduced to counter the widely held view that the Civil Service loses suitable recruits because of the normally long drawn-out nature of the official selection process, which has to run strictly according to the rules with the result that many, naturally impatient, candidates accept other offers in the meantime. Such strictures apply particularly in the sphere of professional recruitment where there is a widespread demand for qualified candidates. The long-established system of selection by competitive interview, which is appropriate in fields where the written test would be out of place for candidates already fully attested by academic qualifications, has latterly been speeded up by making it practically continuous, enabling the interview board to reach an immediate decision on the candidate's suitability and to make an offer of appointment on the spot, or soon after. This method can only operate where there are more vacancies than suitable candidates.

*Other Recruitment* There is also a wide range of temporary and unestablished positions of various types which are filled by the several Departments, who adopt similar rules and methods. Holders of such posts may subsequently qualify for establishment, which is effected through nomination by the Department to the Civil Service Commission for certification. During 1964 the Commissioners certified for appointment after such nomination a total of 16,892 men and 7,122 women, throughout the non-industrial Civil Service.

### SOME GENERAL CONCLUSIONS

The quality of Civil Service recruitment must be inevitably affected by the extended demand throughout the community for administrative talents. From a period when the Civil Service had access to a surplus of talents of the type required, we have moved rapidly into a situation when such talents are being spread more widely to meet the increased demands of many large-scale services in both the government and the non-government spheres. The expanding education field constitutes an important rival to the Civil Service in its higher ranges. Despite the rapid advances in general education it is doubtful whether the national pool of clerical abilities is keeping pace with the vast new demands that have been created. Thus a restoration of the relative attractiveness of the Civil Service as a career, as discussed in Chapter III, would not be likely to bring back the favourable situation that existed before 1939. In this complex modern world the community has need of all its human capacities.

Although patronage, as a system presenting opportunities for personal advantage in the allocation of official posts, can be eliminated by a wise recruitment policy and was indeed so eliminated in principle in Britain in 1870, political policy may still have the effect of granting privileges to particular groups in the recruitment of the Civil Service. Pressures may be exerted through Parliament to this end. Thus, after the First World War numerous ex-Servicemen were absorbed into the Civil Service, against the better advice of both the Treasury and the Civil Service Commission, as the result of political decisions. True, limited competitions were set, but as no minimum educational standards had been imposed at the original recruitment of these temporary officers their general educational standard was bound to be substantially below that of the ordinary open competitive recruits. Despite more carefully planned Reconstruction recruitment after the Second World War similar pressures operated, mainly through the staff associations, who had recruited the new temporaries to their membership and were therefore in honour bound to advocate the absorption of all who could be considered fit. But here again the competitive tests imposed were not such as to ensure the educational standards that are normally required for this type of work. The abolition of the marriage bar and the policy of recruiting older persons to the Clerical and Sub-clerical grades—both adopted by the Government in pursuance of the full employment policy—were further instances of policy affecting the recruitment of the Civil Service and substituting political for administrative tests of effectiveness. The established policy of the State to use the Civil Service as an example to the rest of the community has already been touched upon. It is not necessarily to be inferred that this sort of thing is avoidable or even undesirable, but it is an important factor that must be taken into account when considering the position of the Civil Service in the modern State.

It is difficult to compare the quality of one age with another. Older people, among whom writers are mainly to be found, almost invariably suffer under the delusion that things spiritual and intellectual have declined since the days of their youth. Mr. H. E. Dale in his authorative work on *The Higher Civil Service of Great Britain* (1941) suggested that even then the Administrative Class was not quite what it had been. There are today certainly good reasons for concluding that the Civil Service, man for man, is not up to the standards of its predecessors, but much of this is due to special historical circumstances and make-shift expedients in recruitment that could have had no other effect. Whether a sustained period of normal recruitment will gradually restore the position remains to be seen. The difficulty today, in a situation that is so extremely volatile, is to decide just what is meant by 'normal recruitment'.

On one subject there certainly was general agreement after the war, namely a widespread decline in the general literary ability of school leavers at all levels, a situation that was reflected in the widely recognized inadequacy of performance in this sphere of entrants to the universities. The ability to write lucid reports is an essential prerequisite to academic study. It is an even more essential prerequisite to all administrative work. The poor general standards of official correspondence was widely remarked upon and the two official publications of Sir Ernest Gowers (1880/1966), referred to in the next chapter, were commissioned with a view to rectifying this failing. Even in a mechanized age ability to use the pen is a basic skill of every office worker and we should not be far wrong in hazarding a guess that there are more civil servants today whose competence in this direction is mediocre than at any time since the modern Civil Service was shaped by the reformers.

In the meantime there is one factor that is adding steadily and to some extent unconsciously to the recruitment problem, namely the growing complexity of the administrative process. The men of the old Civil Service had much simpler tasks to perform. With the growth in scale of organization and the extension of the functions of the State over an expanding community the art of public administration has become more and more involved. The law to be administered is inevitably more complicated; new techniques have to be acquired and constantly modified; the processes of co-ordination require more forethought and conscious planning; supervision and management are expanding activities in the public field. This changing situation presents a challenge to the new officials beyond anything that the older civil servants had to contend with. The truth is that the old standards are no longer good enough and all the problems of yesterday have to be thought out afresh. Paradoxically there are fewer talents available to cope with greatly increased administrative complexity and extending responsibility.

## ESTIMATES COMMITTEE'S REVIEW, 1965

Recognition of the increasing seriousness of the problem of Civil Service recruitment led the House of Common's Select Committee on Estimates, which had long been extending its scope to probe into the working and methods of the Central Administration, to turn its attention to this field.[1] The task of looking into 'the Civil

[1] *Sixth Report from the Estimates Committee, Session* 1964/65, *Recruitment to the Civil Service.*

Estimates, Class I, Vote 9, Civil Service Commission, and other Votes in so far as they relate to recruitment to the Civil Service' was given to Sub-Committee E, which heard oral evidence on fourteen occasions both from witnesses representing Government Departments and from witnesses outside the Civil Service. The breadth of this enquiry is further indicated by the number of written statements received in evidence and the fact that visits were made by the Sub-Committee to the Civil Service Commission, including attendance at sessions of the Civil Service Selection Board and of the Final Interview Board.[1]

The Committee were much concerned with the continuing failure to fill all Administrative Class vacancies and the increasing failure to do so in the Executive, Scientific, Technical and Professional fields. In the examination of witnesses many important points were brought up which it was certainly useful to have discussed but which were obviously beyond the Committee's range. Thus evidence indicated the very high standards and the particular image applied to candidates for the Administrative Class, not only from the universities but also from within the Civil Service itself, by way of transfer or promotion. This affected the career prospects of the Executive Class and raised the question whether in the modern situation there was any longer any real distinction between the administrative and the executive function as defined and applied in the Civil Service. The Committee were so concerned about the discontent evidenced in the Executive Class that they recommended that the authorities should undertake a follow-up survey of Executive Officers 'to determine the efficacy of selection methods and to isolate particular reasons for wastage in the early years of service'.[2] Relationships between the Administrative Class and the several major professional groups were also considered. Obviously the position had been improved by steps already taken inside the Departments to raise the standing of the specialist but there still remained a good deal of discontent with the administrator's superior status, though one would hardly have thought that surprising in what is still a predominantly administrative field. These and many other general topics, which so obviously impinge upon recruitment in one way or another, receive attention in the Estimates Committee's Report, and will be touched at appropriate points in following chapters.

The Estimates Committee was, however, particularly concerned with the impact of Civil Service recruitment and the need for

[1] *Op cit*. para. 1, p. v.
[2] *Op cit*. para. 44, p. xvii.

improved publicity. This was a matter to which the Civil Service Commission had already given a good deal of attention, but the position was still not considered satisfactory. The Committee felt that 'the Commission's procedures still concentrated on keeping people out rather than attracting them.'[1] The public's image of the Civil Service was incomplete and inadequate.

The Commission maintains close liaison with the schools and universities through their Information Section and they work through Regional Representatives appointed from working civil servants in offices up and down the country. There always had been a close relationship between the schools and the Civil Service. Formerly it came very actively from the side of the Education authorities and, as the evidence of the MacDonnell Commission of 1912/1915 clearly shows, in those formative days the schools consti- tuted something of a pressure group which regarded the Civil Ser- vice as a special preserve for its more promising scholars. In the post-war full employment situation the position became just the opposite and the Civil Service has to compete with other occupations for staff and to go out actively to get them. The Commission's staff make periodical visits to the universities and there is also a system of liaison officers who are as far as possible civil servants who were formerly members of the particular university, with inside information and acquaintanceship with its staff, though this is difficult in the case of those 'redbrick' Universities from which re- cruitment to the Administrative Class has been thin. It was also alleged that Administrative Officers so appointed were 'up to their eyes in work in the departments and available to visit their univer- sity or college only for odd days in the year.'[2] To use a colloquialism, anyone who has any inside experience of Civil Service working, will regard such an assertion as all my eye and Betty Martin. It all depends upon the degree of importance assigned to the particular responsibility. If the man at the top rates it lowly it will come well down in the list of the official's responsibilities. This is not to deny that efforts to sell the Civil Service to any of the people are in- evitably confronted by special difficulties which will need to be referred to later.[3]

The problem of delays, inseparable from the recruitment methods operated by a public service commission, reducing the effectiveness of the Commission's performance was also discussed. But the Commission had already gone a good way in speeding up the mass recruitment process, especially by the introduction of the continuous

[1] *Op cit*, para. 22, p. xi.
[2] *Op cit*, para. 63, p. xxi.
[3] See p. 177 below.

competition which had considerably changed the position in the professional field where recruitment had previously been most affected by such delays. In broader fields the substitution of the GCE type of qualification in place of the written examination had also considerably speeded up the process. But the question now to be asked is whether such attempts in speeding up have not passed the point at which the loss in selective effectiveness is not greater than the gain from such procedural improvement. After all, this again returns us to the problem of the Civil Service's image with candidates and impels us to ask whether there is not something wrong with an occupation which fails to attract sufficient recruits even though, unlike many of the professions with which it has to compete, it does not stipulate any specialized pre-entry studies. Below the topmost levels candidates to the Civil Service seem today to receive their jobs on a plate. They lack the requisite enthusiasm from the outset and the new recruitment methods are at the root of the trouble. Yet it would be futile to seek solutions by retracing steps. The answer will no doubt be found in other and forward directions.

The Estimates Committee did not presume to propound solutions. They did excellent work by providing a stimulating preliminary survey of the problem and recommended a wider survey of the structure, recruitment and management of the Civil Service on much more intensive lines.[1]

Having thus discovered that the recruitment situation in the Civil Service is much more fluid and problematical than ever before it is now time to examine, in the next Chapter, what sort of training and other arrangements are required to fit the new entrant to his job.

[1] *Op cit,* para. 113, p. xxxv.

# CHAPTER V

# FITTING THE OFFICIAL TO THE JOB

When the civil servant has been accepted by one of the Central Departments the problem of his assimilation immediately faces the establishment branch of the Department. He has to be made aware as soon as possible of the general rules of the Service as well as of the special needs of the work of the particular Department, and a suitable job has to be found for him. This problem of assimilating a new member to a team, which is of course common to all recruitment systems, is complicated in the British Civil Service by two important factors: namely (i) the general educational nature of the entrance tests and (ii) the general grading of posts, which means that a wide range of different jobs is included within the scope of each class. The functions of the Clerical, Executive and Administrative Classes are broadly defined, as we have seen, but their actual work varies considerably, not only as between the Departments, but also as between the branches and sections of the same Department. This does not apply to the comparatively few specific posts and it is less true where definite manipulative, technical or professional skills are prescribed. On the other hand, although the Treasury classes are largely in mind in this discussion, many of the problems of assimilation inevitably arise in connection with appointments to more specialized posts.

The staffs of the Departments are strictly limited to needs, and appointments are made to fill existing vacancies. Newcomers will normally be assigned to those branches in which vacancies exist and at this stage the question of geography is important, especially today when it is not easy to move officials about freely in order to create vacancies in the positions most suitable for new entrants. The object therefore of choosing posts that are both suitable for the new entrant's training and likely to be particularly suited to his temperament and potential qualities is not easily achieved. All that can be said is that the establishment branches do their best, but that the accidental incidence of vacancies is bound to have a good deal to do with the new entrant's initial allocation.

H

## PROBATION

The rules of the Service impose a period of probation usually lasting a year or two, during which confirmation of the recruit's appointment is withheld pending satisfactory reports on his progress. All the investigatory committees on the Civil Service have emphasized the importance of the probationary period. Indeed it is particularly important in a system depending upon selection by a general educational test, which if effective in assessing the potential suitability of a sample group for Civil Service work does not presume to certify that a particular individual will not only be suitable, but will take to his new occupation and derive full satisfaction from it.

It is one thing, however, to recognize the importance of probation, quite another to ensure its effective accomplishment, as each succeeding investigation has had to admit. The tendency inside the Civil Service is to give the newcomer the benefit of the doubt, if there is any. After all, he has much to learn and should improve. Only the obvious misfits are rejected at this stage, and once the appointment has been confirmed on the evidence of a favourable report the time for reassessment has passed, unless the new officer's incompetence is too blatant to be ignored.

It is a weakness of State employment that no one is likely to suffer personally if an unsuitable official is recruited. The individual chief will be content to attribute the main responsibility for selection to the examining authority; the individual supervisor will see no good reason to be hard on a newcomer who may well improve: especially when an adverse report may bring his own judgment under immediate scrutiny. It is much easier to take the line of least resistance.

Since the war new regulations have been issued by H.M. Treasury with the object of improving the operation of probationary reviews. Heads of Departments are enjoined to ensure that suitable tests are imposed to assess the conduct and capacity of the recruit, with the general aim of making probation a more positive stage. In view of the importance of the Administrative Class a Central Probation Board has been established under the control of the Civil Service Commission to consider the personal representations of new Assistant Principals upon whom an adverse probation report has been made. The Establishment Officer of the probationer's Department is a member of the Board. It is of course of particular importance to the Civil Service that an unsuitable person should not be confirmed in the top class.

The importance of probation is generally recognized and the

existence of a real problem is not challenged. One point in favour of a more rigorous attitude is often overlooked: namely, that it is not a kindness to allow a young person to become rooted in a life employment for which he is not fitted and in which he is never likely to find real satisfaction. It is important that a right decision should be reached while suitable alternative employment is readily accessible.

### TRAINING BEFORE THE WAR

A civil servant has to be trained for his work. Under some systems this training may commence before he enters the Service, particularly where special skills and qualifications are called for as a prerequisite to entry. Thus the shorthand typist may be expected already to have acquired a minimum skill in the appropriate techniques and recruits to the technical and professional classes are required to hold suitable qualifications, which presuppose university study or professional experience, or both. For the general Treasury classes, however, the policy of recruiting from among juniors with the widest possible range of academic experience has hitherto been justified in practice and the presupposition of special studies at this stage would have narrowed inadvisably the scope of the competitions.

All new entrants, however highly qualified, have to learn the ways and attitudes of their new occupation, and various means are adopted to speed up their initiation. It was for long assumed, rightly in the circumstances, that for the general office work of the Civil Service no other initial instruction was required. The successful candidate's educational abilities – his proved capacity to write and to cypher – were all that were needed to enable him to get on with the job. The open competitions not only precluded the need for professional pre-entry training, but the nature of the work to be performed also reduced the need for initial training to little more than a formality. Not only was it sufficient to learn the job by doing it, as dogs learn to swim, but it was unnecessary to encourage the recruit to do anything more to broaden his professional knowledge.[1]

With the steady development of administrative techniques and the extension of the work of the Central Departments into new fields the pattern of work assigned to the general classes became

---

[1] Some special exceptions to this are mentioned below. Furthermore the system encouraged entrants at lower levels to compete in the open competitions for more senior classes. Such efforts normally absorb any surplus energies of officials in their early years of service.

more and more varied and complicated, until today the simple assumptions of the older Civil Service no longer apply. Open competition is still effective in selecting the right sort of human raw material for the Civil Service, but the competent official can no longer be said to spring fully fledged from the schools. He has to learn his profession's techniques and his task is by no means a light one. Unlike almost every other profession the public official has to accept practical responsibilities while fitting himself to his work. This difficulty is to some extent met in the important Administrative Class by making the lowest grade, namely the Assistant Principals, mainly a cadet or training grade. It was originally the intention of the Reorganization Committee of 1919/20 that the basic grade of the Executive Class should also be a training grade, but that idea was never implemented.

Between the two wars the Central Departments were feeling their way towards new methods of training. Although there was little formal training more thought was given to desk training, for example, by way of preliminary explanations and planned tours of the office and allied branches. Some Departments recognized the importance of planning a young officer's tour of duties, so that he was given, by means of periodical transfers from one branch to another, an opportunity to learn different aspects of the Department's work. This scheme might extend over a number of years during the young officer's early service. Some attention too was given to the dissemination of information, which had often been carried out, if at all, in a somewhat haphazard way. For example, the Post Office in the 'thirties issued a valuable series of *Green Papers* explaining the Department's work and also introduced a house journal, *The Post Office Magazine,* superseded in October, 1966 by *Courier,* the GPO Staff Newspaper.

Formal training at special schools was not generally considered necessary, although here the Post Office, largely on account of its special problems and needs, had led the way in setting up separate schools for teaching Counter, Telephone, and Engineering work. These schools are so equipped as to reproduce the actual work situations and thus to enable students to exercise manipulative skills, to face up to practical problems and to gain confidence before actually entering upon their new duties.

Little encouragement was given to officers to undertake sparetime studies either in subjects having a close bearing upon their work or in others having a general relationship to the Civil Service's broader activities. As advancement within the Service did not depend upon such professional studies there was little urge within the Service to improve its quality in this way. To this situation there were a few interesting exceptions. In the Inland Revenue Department, for example, Tax Officers were required to study for an internal examination in income tax law and procedure as a minimum qualification for promotion, which did not, however, follow automatically upon success in the examination. Instructional courses were organized by the officers' association, the Inland Revenue Staff Federation.[1]

## THE WAR AND THE ASSHETON REPORT

With the onset of the Second World War the objectives of training were immediately switched to the briefing of officials in new work and the inducting, as quickly as possible, of temporary officials to the ways of the Civil Service. Under the exceptional impact of war conditions existing training schemes closed down and the resources, so far as they were tangible, were switched to more urgent work. Whether this strictly empirical approach was wise is another matter. One would have thought that the special wartime conditions would have called for a special and prolonged training effort. Be that as it may, the practical, and therefore essentially English, tendency to regard all training and education as something of a luxury invariably attracts the economy axe to this sphere of activity as soon as emergency conditions begin to appear.

Yet the war itself was quickly to teach the lesson, applicable in many fields, that the old haphazard rule of thumb methods would no longer do. The easy thinking of active, and oftimes blundering, practical men was clearly not enough for the complex administering of the sort of war effort that the nation was being called upon, albeit reluctantly, to undertake. In 1942 the Select Committee on National Expenditure issued, as its Sixteenth Report for the Session 1941/42, a paper dealing with the *Organization and Control of the Civil Service*. This important document contained recommendations which led to the present notable development of Organization and Methods work in the Central Departments and the setting up of a committee, under the Chairmanship of the Financial Secretary to the Treasury,[2]

'To examine the general question of the training of civil servants, including the question whether a Staff College should be

[1] For further details see E. N. Gladden *Civil Service Staff Relationships* (1943), pp. 128–32. This excellent scheme has since been absorbed into a comprehensive official staff training programme.

[2] The Rt. Hon. Ralph Assheton, M.P., who was assisted by three senior civil servants, three administrators from outside the Civil Service and two representatives of the Staff Side of the Civil Service National Whitley Council.

established, and if so, the particular form and character which that College should take.'

The Assheton Report,[1] which appeared in 1944, does not deal with the Foreign and Colonial Services or the various manipulative grades, or dwell in detail upon the professional and technical classes, each of which has its own training needs and problems. Its proposals are primarily concerned with the clerical-administrative sphere, which was, after all, the sphere in which training had been most neglected.

After touching briefly upon the defects for which the Civil Service is criticized the Committee go on to state, 'But whatever shortcomings there may have been in the past, our aim has been to consider in what ways, at their different levels, the servants of the State can be assisted to attain and maintain the wider outlook, greater adaptability and the technical knowledge which the State service will call for in the years that lie ahead.'[2] The objects of training, they suggest, are twofold. 'In any large-scale organization, efficiency depends on two elements: the technical efficiency of the individual to do the particular work allotted to him, and the less tangible efficiency of the organization as a corporate body derived from the collective spirit and outlook of the individuals of which the body is composed. Training must have regard to both elements.'[3]

The Committee laid down five main aims of training, which may be summarized as follows:[4]

(i) Attainment of precision and clarity in the transaction of business.

(ii) Continuing adjustment of the official's outlook and methods to the new needs of new times.

(iii) Inculcation of broad views to counteract the tendency towards robot-like efficiency and mechanization by the machine.

(iv) Vocational training, not merely to fit the individual to his present work, but also to develop his capacity for higher work and greater responsibilities.

(v) The payment of special regard to staff morale, in order to offset the adverse effects of routine work.

For the achievement of these aims a new organization was proposed. H.M. Treasury were to exercise general control of training

---

[1] *Report of the Committee on the Training of Civil Servants* (Cmd. 6525) 1944.

[2] *Op cit.*, para. 14.

[3] *Op cit.*, para. 15.

[4] *Op cit.*, para. 16.

in the Civil Service and for this purpose a Director of Training and Education was to be appointed. The importance of each Department having a systematized training scheme was emphasized and this was to be controlled by a Departmental Training Officer directly responsible to the Department's Principal Establishment Officer. Special care was to be taken in selecting the instruction staff, and the use of up-to-date equipment and accommodation was considered vital. The close participation of the Staff Sides of the Whitley Councils was also recommended.[1]

In their classification of the types of training to be provided the Committee were perhaps a little confused. They defined the four main types of training as (i) vocational training, (ii) background training, (iii) further education and (iv) centralized training.[2] But four further divisions were also used in the Report, specifically to indicate the ends in view, namely, (*a*) initial training, (*b*) training for mobility, (*c*) training for supervision, and (*d*) training for higher administration. The latter headings speak for themselves and it is to be assumed that any or all of the preceding types of training may be employed as appropriate to achieve each or all of these specific objectives. The Report suggests how the different types of training may be adopted for each of the main classes, i.e. Clerical, Typing, Executive and Administrative, with some reference also to the Professional and Technical Classes.

A summary of the Committee's proposals for the four main types of training will be of interest:

(i) *Vocational training.* Each Department was to organize a scheme of training for its own recruits, who were to be put on their actual duties straight away. At this stage they should be given a booklet, containing a brief history and outline of the functions of the Department and a guide to office procedure. The technique of the model public office should be adopted wherever suitable. This initial stage would then be followed by a period on the actual work under the supervision of an experienced officer. During his early years the young officer would be moved from branch to branch at reasonable intervals in order to broaden his experience. Later on the problem of acquiring the faculties for supervision would be tackled. The interchange of staff in the higher ranges with the business world was not recommended, but it was thought that the secondment of officers to local government might sometimes prove useful.

(ii) *Background training.* The Departments should aim at giving their staffs, by such methods as conferences and the circulation of an office bulletin, as much information as possible about their

[1] *Op cit.,* paras. 19–23, pp. 11-12.
[2] *Op cit.,* para. 10, pp. 6–7, and later.

work. Each large Department should have a house journal and a good library available to the staff. The exploration of the use of films was recommended. Visits to other branches were advocated as a means of broadening horizons.

(iii) *Further education.* Departments should encourage their staffs to acquire outside vocational qualifications by the provision, in approved cases, of time off and the payment of fees. Non-vocational further education should also be encouraged in co-operation with the authorities in every way short of paying the fees. All civil servants should be expected to pursue their education up to the age of 18 on a part-time basis.

(iv) *Centralized training.* Institutional training was not recommended for the Clerical grades and only to a limited extent for the Executive and the Professional grades, but for Administrative cadets the Civil Service should have its own central organization for training. It was not considered desirable that the Government should associate itself with the establishment of the proposed Natitonal Administrative Staff College, although if such were established some civil servants might attend experimentally.[1]

The Assheton Committee also gave special attention to the problems of training in higher administration. They were favourable to the idea of granting sabbatical leave, to promising officers in their early thirties to pursue an approved course or undertake a specific task of research. Short-term transfers might be arranged to Services outside the United Kingdom. These proposals were clearly intended mainly for the Administrative Class, but the Committee disowned the notion that they should be confined to that class and stated 'On the contrary we attach considerable importance to the application of some of them to selected members of other grades, especially the Executive and Professional or Technical.'[2]

As a summing up of the Assheton Committee's aims a quotation from the closing paragraphs of their Report will not be out of place. They stated:

'While our scheme is experimental in the sense of being the first attempt to devise a system of training for all civil servants, aiming both to increase the competence of the individual and to give the whole profession a higher conception of the contribution it can make to the welfare, happiness and good government of the community, some of the features are already in successful operation in the Service or elsewhere, and we do not doubt that the rest will also be productive of good and early results. But

[1] The Administrative Staff College, established long since, receives such students.
[2] Report, para. 117, p. 32.

alone they will not suffice to attain our objective of a Civil Service keyed up to meet the demands of its generation not only successfully but acceptably to the community. For this the Service must be pervaded with a sense of its obligations to the citizen as well as to the Crown. The faults we have recited earlier can be pointed out and to some extent prevented in the lecture-room, but if there is to be an ever-present consciousness of the importance of clarity of thought, directness of action, simplicity of expression, speed, initiative, considerateness and the other virtues in which civil servants are said to be deficient, these must be the keynotes of daily practice in all ranks from the highest downwards. It is our hope that if training—the idea that, besides being told what their jobs are, people need to be guided into the right way to do them—is given due prominence as a cardinal feature of good staff management, and if our scheme is worked with enthusiasm and vision, the whole Service will in due course be brought to an appreciation of the higher standards attainable and will be inspired by the force of example to attain them.'[1]

## THE POST-ASSHETON ERA

The Report was well received though, as usual, the extremists wanting the moon failed to realize just how much the Assheton proposals did contain. These proposals were certainly not revolutionary, but the great thing was to ensure that they were carried out as quickly as possible. Then would come the time to look further in the light of experience.

Staff training was now placed positively upon the Civil Service map. With little delay a special Training and Education Division was set up at the Treasury, under a Director appointed from the university field,[2] and steps were taken to implement the main proposals. In 1945 a central school was set up at the Treasury to provide training in special cases: for example, initial training of new entrants to the Administrative Class and certain technical training where the whole Service was a suitable field for selection, such as the instruction of training officers in the techniques of their new job. In the main, however, training was delegated to the Departments, who appointed their own training officers and usually equipped their own training centres. The larger Departments in their turn devolved training to their regions, retaining at headquarters only such training as could be most efficiently and economically

---

[1] *Op cit.*, para. 119, p. 33.
[2] Strictly speaking the first Director was already serving as a wartime temporary member of the Administrative Class.

provided centrally; for example, introductory courses for new entrants, courses for officers returning from the Forces and technical courses for which there would be insufficient demand in any one region.

Thus, it will be seen that staff training in the Civil Service is now conducted generally at three levels—Treasury, Department-headquarters, and Region—and, while there is a constant flow of information and advice between these levels, the general practice is to allow in each sphere a reasonable latitude and scope for experiment. This training is conducted on modern lines. Instructional methods appropriate to the adult are adopted and in particular the normal class-room atmosphere is avoided as much as possible. Discussion methods are favoured and practical demonstrations, by means of case study, role playing and the like, are widely used. Instructional visits to other offices and to outside organizations are included in the training scheme wherever suitable. Visual aids in the form of charts, films and film strips, are much in favour. Staff training handbooks have been prepared on such subjects as interviewing, letter-writing and statistics. H.M. Treasury issues to all new recruits a brightly written brochure, with the title *A Handbook for the New Civil Servant*, which briefly surveys the Civil Service as a career and the civil servant's rights and duties. In order to improve the conduct of official correspondence, the standard of which had fallen to a deplorably low level (partly owing no doubt to the influx of poorly educated types into the Service), Sir Ernest Gowers was commissioned to write *Plain Words* (1948) and *An A.B.C. of Plain Words* (1951). Issued through the Stationery Office, these books achieved unexpected success and became best sellers.[1]

While the Civil Service makes use of outside lecturers and experts of all kinds at the training centres, instruction in internal techniques, which is the main task of staff training, is provided by experienced members of the staff, selected as having both suitable technical knowledge and a capacity to impart it. In contrast to the normal practice of moving officials from one post to another purely to meet administrative needs—although of course the official's personal needs are taken into account—staff trainers are allocated on a voluntary basis, since the individual's personal attitude to the job is of primary importance. Such appointees are provided with a special course in training techniques at the Treasury centre. It is generally agreed that their tour of duty should not be so short as

---

[1] Now combined in *The Complete Plain Words*, also obtainable as a Pelican Book.

to fail to make the most of their training and accumulating teaching skill and not so long as to put them out of touch with the practicalities of the actual work, which today is usually far from static. Five years seems to be about the right period, although the more senior staff training officers may stay longer. It is a good thing for staff training to have a constant inflow of officials with new ideas and again for the Departments to have an accumulating band of officials who at some time have had direct experience as staff training instructors.

The system seems to work efficiently and there is no dearth of the right sort of talent, even in those Departments where the volume of training is quite considerable. It has been suggested that a more permanent corps of instructors should be built up, but this is not to be recommended in the training field. School teachers without experience of adult education are sometimes unaware of the adverse effect upon the student group of teachers who are obviously out of touch with the living reality of the students' day-to-day work and problems. In any case the instructor with the practical approach will have a more effective impact even when his teaching technique leaves something to be desired, although in fact the Civil Service staff training organizations have had no difficulty in finding skilled teachers.

The courses provided at the training centres are usually short, varying from a day or two, up to a week or more, and only exceptionally over a fortnight. But officials should return time and again to the centres at various stages in their careers, for training in new work and new techniques, refresher training, development of supervisory and management skills and so on. No longer can training be considered as a once-for-all process, if ever this was the correct approach! In a changing administrative world the process goes on to the moment of retirement.

For a few years the new training policy was pressed forward with enthusiasm and efficiency. Although it was extremely difficult to assess the immediate results of such training there can be little doubt that the post-war Civil Service has greatly benefited from this wave of instructional activity. For the time being the doubters, of whom there are always many among the practical men, were forced to lie low.

By the autumn of 1951, however, this wave of enthusiasm had passed its peak, although the full objectives of the Assheton proposals were still far from achievement. The rod of economy entered the official classrooms where its normal scholastic counterpart had no place. In response to a Government demand that less money should be devoted to staff training—an obvious but expensive 'economy' if ever there was one—H.M. Treasury issued an edict that in future, except where technical training was in question, Civil Service staff training should become the task of the first line supervisor, as it had of course always been in the pre-Assheton era. For the attainment of this end more emphasis was to be placed upon the training of supervisors. A definite gain from this change was the giving of more attention to training in supervision and management, subjects that had always been neglected but were becoming the most urgent concern of staff trainers everywhere.

But the loss following this change of policy was far-reaching. The status of training officers was often reduced, particularly at Treasury level; the training staffs were cut and activities at the centres reduced or even abolished entirely. In many Departments training quickly became a matter of minor importance. The enthusiasm with which this retrogressive movement was undertaken will surprise only those who do not understand the traditional outlook upon training of many civil servants.

In 1956 the present writer, from inside the Civil Service, offered the following judgment:

'There is a large body of opinion in all grades that holds formal training to be so much waste of time: jobs can best be learned by doing them, as was ever the case in the happy past. Staff trainers are starry-eyed theorists not entirely unconcerned with the creation of cushy specialist jobs. Staff training in fact is considered an example, if a minor one, of empire building! These two schools of thought—the enthusiasts and the denigrators—are struggling all the time for supremacy. During the Assheton period the starry-eyed enthusiasts carried all before them: now the pendulum has swung in favour of the practical men. In the Civil Service as in the nation at large we suffer incalculably from the specious common sense of the rule of thumb. For, alas, the simple truth, in a world growing every day more complex, is that the empiric way will no longer do. The scientific approach is necessary in public administration as elsewhere and a return to nature—unfortunately, many will feel—is out of the question. A half-trained Civil Service is a luxury the nation cannot afford.'[1]

### RENEWED INTEREST IN STAFF TRAINING

A similar pulsation between active interest and a sort of quiescence in staff training has continued right up to date, with the Treasury, in its financial non-training aspect, acting its traditional

[1] E. N. Gladden *Civil Service or Bureaucracy?* (Staples Press, 1956) p. 93.

economy role, though less insistently than in the past, for the exigenciees of the situation have been convincing more and more people in key-positions that the Civil Service's responsibilities cannot be properly fulfilled unless its members are better trained and, for that matter, re-trained to cope with the Administration's developing role. Gladstone's negative influence is at last passing into the shadows!

That the need for better training is not concentrated only upon the administrative hewers of wood and drawers of water was pinpointed in the Plowden Report on *Control of Public Expenditure*, published in 1961.[1] Among other vital matters this Report dilates upon the growing importance of management in the Central Administration, on the need to develop adequate management services, and on the training and selection of men and women for posts at each level of responsibility.[2]

An outcome of this Report was the establishment by the Treasury, in the neighbourhood of Regents Park, the Centre of Administrative Studies with the task of developing such services. It took over responsibility for the training of the Administrative Class and one of its innovations in this field is a special course of from 14 to 21 weeks duration for Assistant Principals following the completion of their probation. The course covers such subjects as economics and the general principles of public administration. The existing Training and Education Division, together with the new Centre, have since been placed under a Director of Training and Education of Under Secretary rank.

The intensification of the Government's administrative activities with the increasing interest, from 1962 onwards, in economic planning, and the creation, towards the end of 1964, of a number of new major Departments, has also had its effect in emphasizing the Civil Service's need for new techniques and thus in the value of staff training in this field.

With the tide thus running strongly the time was surely ripe for a follow-up on the Assheton Report to discover how far its proposals had been adopted and what further developments were now desirable. To this end the Civil Service National Whitley Council set up a working party, confined to representatives of the two sides, to look into the question. Its report appeared towards

[1] Cmd. 1432. This Report arose out of an enquiry by a group appointed as a result of a recommendation by the Select Committee on Estimates in their *Sixth Report* (*Session 1957/58* on *'Treasury Control of Expenditure'*).
[2] *Op cit.,* para. 44, p. 16.

the end of 1964 in the Staff Side's *Whitley Bulletin,*[1] an arrangement that somewhat restricted its circulation.

The Working Party commented strongly upon the serious effect on staff efficiency of retrenchment in 1952/53, in particular by nourishing the idea that training was a suitable field for quick economies and encouraging in some quarters the notion that training could be regarded 'as an optional extra, not carrying the same weight in management as, for instance O & M', rather than 'one of the most useful tools of management'.[2] It was generally agreed that in many Departments considerable progress had been made on Assheton lines. No doubt this was mainly in those Departments which had long recognized the need for effective training. In other areas much less had been done and this was excused by pressure of work and shortage of staff. Improved co-ordination between Departments was recommended, particularly to assist the smaller Departments, which often found it difficult to assemble the resources needed for a full-scale training programme. The perennial proposal to establish a Civil Service Staff College, which the Assheton Committee had found unacceptable, was again examined but no definite decision was reached, although the Working Party did support the establishment of a Central Institute of Higher Training, which they considered should not be confined to civil servants and might eventually develop out of the recently introduced Centre of Administrative Studies.

Important changes in this field have been going on all the time, notably through the use of improved techniques, often following the advice of the Training and Education Division, one of whose important functions is to keep in close touch with such matters and to try out new ideas, which can be passed on to the departmental training branches. Not that the latter are completely dependent upon the Treasury for ideas. Much depends upon the vigour and foresight of the Departments' senior training officers at both headquarters and regional levels. One advantage of a high degree of delegation in this field is that it facilitates the undertaking of training experiments at the several levels, in close touch with the needs of the situation which, in a large widespreading Service, are bound to vary infinitely. Conferences of training officers across the Departments, whether organized at the centre or out in the field are of great value in this connexion.

Even before the Plowden Report made its important pronouncement on the need for more and improved management training much had been done in this field by the Departments

[1] *Whitley Bulletin,* Vol. XLIV, pp. 155–171.
[2] *Op cit.,* para. 27, p. 157.

with numerous local offices, mainly at middle management, or, as it is called in the Civil Service, executive levels. More use had been made of available facilities for arranging management seminars on a residential basis which, by extending the opportunity for informal contact and exchange of ideas, greatly increases the effectiveness of such courses. Important recent developments include the setting up of a Training Centre for Small Departments, also in the Regents Park area, and the appointment of four Senior Executive Officers by the Treasury to act as Liaison Officers and advise groups of Departments, respectively over the four fields: (i) Economic and Revenue, (ii) Social Services, (iii) Defence and Scientific, and (iv) Small Departments.

### FURTHER EDUCATION FOR THE OFFICIAL

Official training activities at best deal with only part of the problem of fitting the official to his work and keeping his mind alive to the world that public administration is devised to serve. There are also further education in the general sense and professional education in its theoretical and philosophical aspects. For some time civil servants have run an active further education movement to organize on their behalf a wide range of spare-time educational activities. After the war the Civil Service Council for Further Education was reconstituted on a tripartite basis, consisting of representatives of staff and official interests as well as co-opted members from the world of education. This is a body of the Whitley type associated with H.M. Treasury, which provides it with a Civil Service staff. There are also committees for Scotland, Wales and the English Regions,[1] appointed by the Treasury from local representatives of the Official and Staff Sides. The function of the Council and the Committees is to encourage spare-time activities of an artistic, intellectual or skilled nature. The Council also organizes arts and crafts exhibitions, publishes a quarterly journal but does not itself provide courses of study. Its main task is to encourage civil servants to use their spare time creatively, to bring to their notice existing facilities and to persuade the educational authorities to meet the  needs of civil servants where such facilities do not already exist. The Council does not set out to encourage vocational studies in preference to other types of study. However, it has executive responsibility for the organization of continuation schooling for juveniles in the Civil Service, which is compulsory, on the basis of one day a week, up to the age of 16 and voluntary thereafter

---

[1] As well as a committee for Northern Ireland, which represents both the United Kingdom and the Northern Ireland Civil Services.

until the age of 18. All such officers are officially encouraged to continue their studies in subjects of their own choosing,[1] and executives, who may sometimes be inclined to place the day-to-day needs of their work above the long-term needs of the individual officer, are expected to release them.

The civil servant has not been active in the furtherance of his strictly professional education. Indeed, study of public administration in the broad sense is still not very advanced in this country. There are various reasons for this, apart from the general apathy of the majority of civil servants; for example, (i) the traditional academic supremacy of the Administrative Class (now being somewhat tempered by the inflow into the Service of large numbers of qualified members of the professions); (ii) the departmentalization of the Civil Service, which leads each Department to consider the acquirement of its own techniques as of overriding importance and more general administrative studies as largely a waste of time; (iii) the predominantly empirical outlook of most civil servants, whose intensive concern for the trees often leave them little time to worry about the wood, and (iv) the essentially academic outlook of the universities, who seem as little concerned as the Civil Service to construct a bridge between the bread and butter activities of official staff training and the rarefied intellectualism of the high seats of learning.

Except where specific instruction generally available outside was needed by an official in the performance of his normal duties, the approach of the Departments to further education had generally been lukewarm. It is true that the more go-ahead Post Office had long made it a practice to invite members of the staff to advise their chiefs of any academic success however modest and to list this performance annually in the *Official Circular* which was distributed to the staff, but general regulations did not give much scope for more concrete encouragement. It was not in fact until as recently as 1956 that the Treasury decreed that:

'Departments should be enabled to give greater encouragement to non-industrial staff who wish to follow in their own time, worth-while external courses in subjects of general background value to the work of the Civil Service as a whole, such as public administration, economics, law and other social sciences. For this purpose the distinction is to be drawn less sharply than hitherto between background training of specific vocational value and the more general type of course . . .'[2]

[1] Not specifically for examination purposes, but to broaden their outlook and prepare them for a fuller life.
[2] Quoted from Treasury Establishments Circular No 61/56.

Such aid could take the form of a contribution towards costs and re-arrangement of leaving times to facilitate attendance at evening classes. It was still somewhat minimal and, in accordance with normal practice, it left the decision to the Departments whose attitudes and interpretations were to vary widely. Nevertheless this step from a definitely negative to a relatively positive approach was a vital one, creating a situation from which further constructive advances could be made. The Whitley Working Party referred to above[1] discovered that eight years after this change of policy Departments were still prone to 'regard external courses as being valuable for specific jobs and gave little encouragement to their staffs to undertake general background studies, such as those for the Diploma in Government Administration'. A more liberal interpretation of the regulations was therefore recommended.

## DIPLOMA IN GOVERNMENT ADMINISTRATION

An even more important step forward was made the following year when the National Whitley Council, the Treasury, the Royal Institute of Public Administration[2] and certain Civil Service staff associations combined to sponsor the introduction of a Diploma in Government Administration to help civil servants, through spare-time study, to improve their general professional knowledge. Existing studies in the field of public administration were few and far between and those at the universities generally out of reach of the working official. Excellent degree courses in various branches of administation were available at Manchester University but elsewhere students usually had to be satisfied with a Diploma and the demand was not usually so great as to encourage developments in this field. The most popular university qualification had been the Diploma in Public Administration awarded by the University of London. Although it was misnamed, in the manner of the times, since it dealt with the broad field of government and politics rather than the more specialist sphere of public administration, it could be obtained by external students and was fairly popular among civil servants. After the war the University decided to restrict the Diploma to graduates and certain professional categories, consequently barring junior civil srevants who needed such a course of studies. The new professional Diploma in Government Administration (D.G.A.) came therefore to fill an undoubted gap.

The sponsoring of this innovation by the Civil Service is of special interest, in the light of the previous attitudes of both official

[1] See page 95 above.
[2] See page 103 below.

J

and staff interests, which had been overwhelmingly against the introduction of any such professional qualification. The rank and file of most staff associations were antagonistic to academic acquirements, as any staff representative favourably disposed to such developments very quickly discovered. What was the reason therefore for the sudden *volte face* ? Certainly there had for long existed a modest movement in favour of improved studies in public administration but no sudden break-through had been foreseeable.[1] Changes in the external situation had obviously had a greater impact upon both official and staff leaders than had been outwardly apparent. It could very well have been that the new approach to salary assessment through the medium of the Civil Service Pay Research Unit[2], which was discovering the weight given to the holding of professional qualifications in certain comparable outside occupations in contrast with the relative weakness of the Civil Service in this respect. Obviously such differences affected the comparability of similar posts!

In launching the new Diploma advantage was taken of the existence of the Local Government Examinations Board, which had been set up after the war to introduce suitable promotion qualifications for general clerical and administrative workers in Local Government. The new Civil Service qualification was patterned on the existing Diploma in Municipal Administration (D.M.A.), sharing such papers as are suitable to both fields. The Local Government Examinations Board devises and manages the examinations through an Examinations Committee but for the D.G.A. the Board is advised by a special Civil Service Examinations Committee which includes representatives of the several Civil Service interests.

The D.G.A. examination is in two stages[3]: Intermediate and Final, the latter being divided into Parts I and II which may be taken separately. Normally study is spread over two to three years and the standard of the Final is of university ordinary degree level. The subjects of the Final are: for Part I, three compulsory papers, two of which cover Principles and Problems of Public Administration in their General and Central Government aspects separately, and a third paper on either the Social Services or Nationalized Industries Administration; and, for Part II, two optional subjects

---

[1] The present writer, a long-standing advocate of more intensive studies in public administration by civil servants, was as surprised as anyone by the rapid change of front!

[2] See page 51 above.

[3] Under new regulations to operate in 1967 the Intermediate, for the D.M.A. and probably for the D.G.A. is also to be divided into Parts I and II.

chosen from: (i) Social and Political Theory, (ii) Political Institutions, (iii) Social Statistics, (iv) Economics and Public Finance; (v) Administrative Law, and (vi) the alternative not offered as the third paper in Part I. A new optional paper on 'Management in the Public Services' is being added to Part II of the Final of the Diploma in Municipal Administration in 1967, and it is to be expected that a similar addition will be made to the D.G.A. Tuition for these examinations is available through evening classes and correspondence courses.

It cannot be said that this attempt to interest civil servants in professional studies has been an outstanding success. During the first seven years of the examination a total of 220 D.G.As were awarded. The Diploma is not restricted to any particular class or grade. The D.G.A.s awarded over the four years 1962/65,[1] totalling 130, were distributed as follows: 6 to Senior Executive Officers, 24 to Higher Executive Officers, 56 to Executive Officers, 14 to Clerical Officers, and 30 to other grades, which included a few members of the Administrative Class. Thus the range of interest was quite wide although, appropriately, the qualification commended itself mainly to the Executive Class and naturally a high proportion of these belonged to the junior grade. But if we compare the total over the four years of 86 successful Executive Class officials with the total of the Class (42,200 in 1964) the response is seen to be ridiculously small. It is of some interest that members of the senior grades considered the effort worthwhile, and this makes the age spread of the successful candidates of particular interest. Over the five years 1961/65, taking all five-year groups up to age 50, least interest was shown by the lowest age group 20–24, the next three groups showed high and more or less equal interest, while the highest participators were the 40–44 age group. There was then a steep falling off, although there were some successes among the over-50s! This is not what one would have expected and at least throws some doubt on the oft repeated assertion that examinability falls off consistently with increasing age. Normally the D.G.A. should have commended itself more to new entrants to the class and the figures suggest that there was a widespread lack of faith among the younger members that such studies would prove of any real value in their career. In fact, unlike the Local Government service, where the D.M.A. was actually designed as a promotion qualifying examination, the Civil Service bends over backwards to assure holders and everyone else that it will not be considered as qualifying

[1] The basis of the figures as quoted in the annual reports of the Local Government Examinations Board has been modified and do not provide a complete picture over the entire period of the examinations.

for promotion. Of course it would be taken into account, as are so many other factors, but this could mean anything or nothing. Certainly one would have thought that, to Clerical Officers and other grades junior to Executive, it could very well constitute a guarantee of promotion, since it is a much weightier and more appropriate test than the accepted G.C.E. qualification for new entrants. This negative aspect of official policy is undoubtedly widely reinforced by the lack of encouragement given by senior officers to juniors undertaking such studies, and a real stimulation of interest in this worthy innovation will come only through a change of heart on the part of all responsible officials concerned with the deployment of staff. More enthusiasm for such studies must certainly be generated at the top, and this applies to senior Executives at least as much as to senior Administratives. A gradual improvement in this direction should come about, almost as a matter of course with the normal retirement from the active Civil Service scene of those senior officials, particularly at middle management levels, who love to boast that what was good enough for them in the simpler situation of their youth, should still be good enough in our complex administrative society.

Evidently the effort of introducing the D.G.A. was sufficient to exhaust the Civil Service reformers, at least for the time being, and the examination has tended to stagnate, rather than to accumulate interest and support. This is a pity, since the mere introduction of a qualification cannot constitute an end in itself. What is wanted is a vigorous extension of this comparatively new field of study. The syllabus of the Diploma needs to be extended to include more specialized technical subjects as options, and the holders of the Diploma should be drawn on to undertake research and, at least for the younger ones, there should be increasing opportunities for them to obtain secondment to other fields, especially overseas, to expand their administrative experience. There is nothing like this in sight at present, and on the number of successes to date this was hardly to be expected.

For those officials who, while personally desirous of extending their professional knowledge, cannot spare the time required to undertake such an extended programme of studies as that of the D.G.A., admirable as it is, courses in Public Administration are not easily come by. There is a need for suitable programmes on a single subject basis, and one such has certainly been made available by the Royal Society of Arts since the war. This began with the introduction at their advanced level (Grade III) of a Certificate in Public Administration, followed subsequently by a supporting paper at intermediate level (Stage II) in Central and Local

Government, and finally going down further, to stimulate interest in the schools, of an Elementary (Stage I) qualification in Civics. The Stage II and Stage III papers, in this order, provide an admirable two year course in Public Administration (although each paper is offered independently) which is particularly suitable for public officials, but this has not received official encouragement of any sort and courses on this basis are few and far between.[1]

## ROYAL INSTITUTE OF PUBLIC ADMINISTRATION

There is, of course, the Royal Institute of Public Adiministration, established in 1922 by a band of enthusiasts to promote the study and improve the practice of public administration in all its branches. Membership is open to officials in all branches of public administration, as well as teachers in the subject, and obviously the Institute is concerned only partially with the interests of the Civil Service. It arranges lectures by well-known administrators, organizes conferences, provides library facilities, undertakes research, and publishes *Public Administration,* a journal with a worldwide reputation in this field. It also provides special services for its corporate members. The Institute is not an examining body and does not provide qualifications of any sort. Since the war the Institute, in line with so many other bodies of this type, has changed from a voluntary and somewhat amateurish organization to a partially professionalized and subsidized institution. The Institute's new responsibilities towards its corporate members (public authorities and departments of all types) tend to endow it with a near-official outlook and this further restricts its capacity to meet the needs of individual officials or to do much to rescue them from the deadening influences of the large-scale organizations by which most of them are employed. As is the way of institutions its new air of impersonal efficiency is no substitute for the inspiration and enthusiasm of individuals. Certainly the personal element has been admirably maintained in the Royal Institute's Regional Groups, which do not, however, cover the whole country and, except in the London area, often do not have a sufficiently large membership to facilitate the organization of meetings and other activities. Significantly the Institute's individual membership is now substantially greater overseas than it is at home, especially in Australia where the Groups are much more active.

[1] Further information may be obtained from the Principal, Royal Society of Arts (Examinations Department), 18 Adam Street, Adelphi, London, W.C.2.

The introduction of corporate membership has most certainly strengthened its finances, but probably at the expense of its individual membership, which is very small for an organization of its scope. However, the lack of support from the Civil Service is due as much to the apathy of the latter as to the failings of the Institute, which after all must find its support where it can. It is doing essential and invaluable work. If it had more enthusiastic Civil Service support it could certainly do much more than it does for civil servants as a body. The activities of the Royal Institute of Public Administration and the provision of certain funds have since the war encouraged the development of research in public administration.

In accordance with the policy laid down in the Assheton Report a few higher civil servants have been give sabbatical leave both for research purposes and on an exchange basis for service in Commonwealth and foreign administrations. Latterly arrangements have been made to second civil servants to industry. The results should be mutually advantageous and of wide interest.

### CONCLUSION ON TRAINING

In the Civil Service staff training has generally flourished in those sectors where the immediate advantage, indeed necessity, of such training has been recognized, particularly where supervisors realize that they cannot get their work done without trained staff and that such training is a responsibility they cannot shirk. Where specific techniques have to be acquired the aid of organized training facilities has to be invoked. Early cases of such training, going back at least as far as the early 'twenties are the Post Office and Inland Revenue schemes briefly mentioned in the text.

Close staffing of posts, under the general budgetary process applied to the Civil Service, has often left little apparent margin for training purposes. Even where a definite staffing scheme made such provision the time allocated for this purpose could easily be absorbed by other more immediate tasks, and supervisors were usually not enthusiastic either in themselves making the training effort or in releasing staff to attend courses elsewhere. This position is being considerably improved by the more purposive allocation of staff time for training, and in the case of new entrants in particular by assigning specific initial periods of service solely to training. Apart from the special arrangements for the Assistant Principals of the Administrative Class which has been mentioned, new entrants to the other Treasury classes are allowed such initial training periods, while new entrants to certain technical grades often begin with a period at a training school; for example, sorters, counter clerks and postmen in the Post Office.

Except in the cases mentioned where special skills have to be acquired before the work can be undertaken, or when the introduction of new work obviously calls for some special briefing to enable the staff to cope with an unusual operational situation, staff training is definitely a long-term process. Immediate results are difficult to assess. The problem of estimating the effect of training upon the staff is often discussed by staff trainers themselves and many ingenious methods have been devised to follow up the effect of training on individuals who have attended courses, but there are so many imponderables to be taken into account that it is practically impossible to assign any specific improvement or failure to staff training. As with education one must have faith in training as an ameliorating process, and it is futile to attempt to assign statistical symbols to results. Managers and supervisors, in the public services as elsewhere, must be moved by the conviction that a highly trained and continuously re-trained staff, will produce better results than one left to its own devices. In practice this is self-evident and only the incompetent supervisor could believe otherwise. The training responsibility is an essential factor of supervision, and the supervisor who fritters away his present training margin at the expense of the future is self-condemned as incompetent.

Latterly interest in staff training and education in public administration has been rising steeply under the impact of demand for aid in this field from the many new, and usually comparatively underdeveloped, countries which have come upon the international stage. In their case the urgency of the need for improved and expanded education and training has been too obvious to be denied. The slow process of apprenticing officials in administration could not be left to the admirable but time-consuming process of learning on the job. Definite instruction in theory and practice was urgently needed. Practical administrators, especially in Britain, had to revise their prejudices against theoretical studies in such a practical subject. The Americans, largely as a consequence of the considerable attention that had been given to just this sort of approach in the numerous universities and other centres of higher education in a Federation and fifty States which has a multiplicity of separate public administrations in which to experiment, were able to make an early and quite considerable contribution in areas where the Colonial powers had long priority in practical administration. All this is having a powerful influence upon the Civil Service, which is closely involved in the consequences. A more dynamic outlook on the professional training of civil servants is implicit both in the internal administrative situation and in the complex of outside influences bearing upon and remoulding the wider administrative structure.

CHAPTER VI

PROMOTION: SENIORITY, MERIT OR CHANCE?

Promotion is an important process in the Civil Service, as indeed it is in all graded services. It covers both advancement between grades within the same class and between different classes, although the latter process sometimes has something of the characteristics of recruitment. A civil servant has career prospects within the class to which he is recruited, but transfer to other classes is usually considered exceptional. This situation is certainly modified within the scheme of Treasury classes: for example, since the war the Clerical Officer's normal promotion outlet has led direct to the Executive Officer grade. While this present chapter is mainly concerned with the promotion process it should not be overlooked that this process is part of the greater problem of placement within the Service, the problem of so allocating the available personnel that the most efficient result is obtained through the maximum use of existing abilities. Such a result would also have the inestimable advantage of affording the highest satisfaction to the individual officials involved and thus would considerably enhance the general morale.

The promotion system in the British Civil Service is considerably influenced by the personal rank scheme of organization which assigns to the several ranks or levels of the hierarchy a wide range of duties of equal responsibility but varying techniques, and the promotion requirements of such a system are bound to be much more complicated and less easily assessed than under the alternative position classification scheme under which posts are determined by detailed job analyses, competence for which can be more specifically prescribed as a minimum requirement for appointment or promotion.[1] Under the classified scheme vacancies can be more readily thrown open to all who can prove competence, and promotion will not be very different from recruitment. The individual tends to specialize and may have a wide range of similar posts in many quarters open to him, but has diminished prospects of advancement in his own branch. The organization gains from the inflow of new blood but loses through the loss of invaluable experience.

There are of course advantages and disadvantages in both

[1] See page 38 above.

107

approaches but the general adoption of the one should not completely exclude the use of the other. Organization in personal ranks enhances the integrated-service element, while organization in classified posts places the emphasis on unit autonomy. Thus the classified post type is widely used in the highly deconcentrated Local Government Service in Britain, and can be useful for promotion between Departments, or in such organizations as the Post Office where Head Postmasterships are filled partly in this way from specified Post Office grades, whose members regard this as one of their accepted avenues of promotion.

### FITTING THE SQUARE PEG INTO THE SQUARE HOLE

Establishment branches are constantly concerned with filling vacancies arising here, there and everywhere from various causes. Officers have to be transferred within the Department. Where no geographical change is involved this may not be difficult, although persons with the requisite experience may not always be available, or if available may not be releasable from other positions. In theory all the members of the same grade are available for any jobs allocated to that grade: in practice the range of work covered by one of the Treasury grades is so varied as to render some degree of specialization highly desirable. This is particularly so in the Executive Class. For example, an Executive Officer supervising a block of work in a Post Office department would require a completely different corpus of knowledge to supervise a block of work in a local office of the Ministry of Social Security, and vice versa. Within each Department there is also a wide variety of work and it is generally considered desirable for officers to obtain experience in a number of branches. As was pointed out in a previous chapter this may also be a factor in the training process. In small offices where staff absences might otherwise bring current operations to a standstill a high degree of interchangeability has to be aimed at by the manager. It is therefore a characteristic of the Civil Service that members of the general Treasury classes are expected to be versatile. They may eventually become specialists, but they are not recruited on that assumption.

Where the nature of the work varies—for example, as between case work and supervision, desk work and public relations, considerative work and inspection—it is clear that establishment branches must take into account an officer's particular flair, if the best results are to be achieved. Moreover, an officer allotted to a type of work for which he is not particularly fitted will be discontented and liable to spread his discontent to others. It is no easy task to match official with job and the blind application of the theory that all the members of a grade are interchangeable may lead to a good deal of unease and inefficiency. In practice this situation is bound sometimes to occur in a large-scale organization.

Inefficient personnel management may not be the only reason for unsatisfactory results in this sphere. It cannot be assumed that the staff is completely mobile. Where a Department is decentralized the effective allocation of some members of the staff may involve a geographical movement which is unduly expensive or actually prevented by social and economic circumstances. Civil servants are expected under their terms of service to be mobile, but it is not usually expedient to transfer persons against their will, particularly in the present housing situation. Expenses of removal and subsistence allowances are paid in cases where transfer is made for the benefit of the Service, but such upheavals are often so unattractive that officers may even refuse a promotion that involves uprooting their homes. Wives, of course, have a considerable influence upon such decisions. All this means a high degree of immobility unless the Department is concentrated geographically. Particularly for those serving in areas they do not like there is usually a Whitley agreement on the order of precedence to be followed when transfers are made. Marital status, personal disabilities, hardship grounds and such matters are usually taken into account.

Although there are similarities between the work of the same grade in different Departments there are also vital differences that substantially alter the relative attractiveness of the work to different individuals. Transfers between Departments can be arranged, but this is not easy unless a Department, usually because of some exceptional expansion, offers transfers to fill up gaps for which it is unable to find experienced officers. Transfers on a personal exchange basis are possible between officials in different Departments. These are not easily arranged and while they no longer suffer from loss of certain privileges the transferee usually finds he has much to learn before he is fully at home in his new Department. The British Civil Service has no machinery for rationalizing transfers between Departments. Despite certain arrangements to the contrary, which will be mentioned later, the broad assumption is that an officer is the servant of the Department to which he is assigned and has no rights elsewhere in virtue of his membership of an all-service class. Constitutionally, departmental loyalties still override general service loyalties. To some extent an inherent parochialism in the system defeats the desirable policy of fitting the square pegs into square holes.

These are only a few of the difficulties that confront the establishment sections, and indeed all senior officers and managers with responsibility for staff allocations, in their endeavours to make the most of the human resources at their disposal. Moreover, this is not only a problem of making use of the positive capacities of the efficient, but also of getting the best out of the inefficient despite their negative qualities. With these preliminary observations in mind it is time to examine the more dynamic problem of selection for promotion.

### PRINCIPLES OF PROMOTION

Historically, in all graded services the practice of arbitrary selection is at an early stage tempered by the emergence of an order of precedence—based upon privilege, heredity, prestige of office, and possibly relative power—in accordance with which certain rights, including consideration for other official positions, are decided. Seniority has always been accepted as an important attribute, as indeed it is if merely as a measure of the experience of the individual official, and promotion in accordance with the seniority list of a grade has for long been a common practice in the Civil Service as elsewhere. Where selection by this method was rigid it led inevitably to the placing of incompetents in high positions and at a time when officials could retain their posts indefinitely this was a serious drag upon the Civil Service's general efficiency. It was not surprising, therefore, that under such conditions patronage had a certain virtue in allowing the alternative of direct appointment from outside in place of routine advancement within. The Trevelyan-Northcote Report, 1853/4, condemned this system and in its place advocated selection by merit. Each subsequent enquiry supported this view and a dictum of the Playfair Commission, 1875, is well worth quoting. They wrote: 'A man should be promoted, not because those above him are unfit, but because he is the best man for the place. If this course be pursued no man is branded as unfit, and it would not at all follow that the senior man, passed over for one promotion, might not be the fittest man for the next.'[1] To some extent the principle was tempered for the more junior grades; in which case it was widely agreed that seniority should be given more weight. The general practice was to follow the seniority list, but not slavishly, so that an officer adjudged not suitable for the higher post could be 'passed over'. In the main the seniority principle was supported by the staff who felt that it was the one method not open to favouritism and other underhand influences.

[1] Quoted in Report of Royal Commission on the Civil Service, 1929–31 (Tomlin), p. 79, para. 293(1).

The trouble is that the words 'seniority' and 'merit' have merely to be uttered in conjunction to prejudge the issue. Seniority seems to conjure up automatically the idea of bureaucracy, of working to rule, of selecting the elderly merely because of their age and, therefore, lack of enterprise: merit on the other hand suggests both justice to the chosen and vigour to the system. Thus, to defend seniority is to mark oneself down as a stick in the mud.

The truth is that we are not called upon to make this particular choice. Seniority and merit are complementary factors: a system that denies either is almost inevitably bad, for if the first on its own means stagnation and lack of enterprise, the second is almost as likely to be challenged because the standards adopted are not generally acceptable by those to whom they are being applied. The real difficulty indeed is to define merit in this particular context and to evolve a method whereby the merit choice can be made in a way acceptable to the majority. Ultimately, in many merit systems the choice is made by individuals who are rightly making a personal judgment in the light of standards that are not easy to lay down. In fact, merit selection has been advocated by practical investigators, and applauded by publicists and scholars, but the problems involved in applying it are left, not merely unsolved, but often unrecognised. An effective promotion system has to achieve at least three important goals, namely (i) to select the best man for the higher position, (ii) to satisfy those to whom it is applied that it is fair and just, and (iii) to have a creative influence on the whole staff structure. Merit selection is aimed primarily at (i); seniority selection is effective generally in achieving (ii); an ineffective merit system or an excessive seniority system are likely to fail under (iii) by their adverse effect upon individual initiative and the general morale of the Service.

## THE PROMOTION MACHINERY

Promotion in the Civil Service is primarily a Departmental and not a general service matter. Responsibility for the selection of his staff rests with the Head of the Department, traditionally the Minister of the Crown, by administrative delegation in practice the Permanent Secretary. At the highest levels this principle is modified by the constitutional practice of consultation between the Joint Permanent Secretary of the Treasury, acting in his capacity as Head of the Civil Service, and the Prime Minister in filling the departmental posts of Permanent Secretary, Deputy Secretary, Principal Finance Officer and Principal Establishment Officer. The principle is also tempered by the fact that the Administrative Class is, as an all-Service class, freely transferable between Departments, and by the fairly recent growth of promotion pools. There is also more inter-departmental promotion in the specialist, professional and technical classes employed in more than one Department.

In the earlier period of the modern Civil Service, when the majority of Departments were still sufficiently compact for the senior officers to know personally all the staff of the Department, it was not difficult for the head to exercise this prerogative. With the general guidance of the seniority list, as the key to experience, and the personal reports of senior officers under whom members of a specific grade were working, it was not difficult for such a head to reach an honest and effective decision. It was a grave responsibility, but one not beyond his capacity to fulfil. With the growth in size of the Departments the task passed beyond the range of practical fulfilment and unavoidable mistakes of judgment caused a widespread dissatisfaction among the staff, who were not easy to convince that *bona fide* mistakes, however regrettable, were not due to favouritism or worse.

It was for this reason that the newly appointed Civil Service National Whitley Council decided at an early stage to tackle the problem of promotion. The present promotion machinery stems back to their first report, issued in 1921. The new system provided for (i) the constitution in each Department of a properly organized promotion board, and (ii) the introduction of a standardized report for officers within the range of promotion.

Departmental promotion boards are now appointed by the Head of the Department, to whom they act in an advisory capacity. The final decision still rests with him, although in a large Ministry he will usually find it expedient to accept the recommendations of the board as they stand. He can, where he considers it necessary— e.g. for filling a post requiring special experience or qualifications— waive the normal procedures but, as such a decision is bound to create difficulties with the staff representatives, it is resorted to only where circumstances are exceptional. The promotion board will include the Principal Establishment Officer and other senior officers. It may reach its decision informally after consideration of all the available evidence, or it may first interview recommended candidates. For the latter purpose interviewing panels may be set up, consisting of officers senior in grade to those being interviewed. It is desirable also to include on such panels officers who have a reasonably intimate knowledge of the work of the branches in which the candidates are serving.

Staff representation on these promotion boards is not usually considered expedient. In the first place it would be difficult to find staff representatives who were not themselves involved in the specific promotional process, unless the staff themselves selected fairly senior people who are almost as likely as the official element to be out of touch with the outlook of the rank and file: in the second place the staff interests might find that participating in the responsibility for choosing would create invidious difficulties with their own constituents unless they religiously selected the most senior aspirant. In any case they would find their important function of criticizing the official decisions largely abrogated by their direct participation.[1] However, they may be given an opportunity to make recommendations and such a system is applied in the Post Office to the selection of certain first-line supervisors.

One of a promotion board's biggest problems is to ensure that they have all the facts needed to make a proper comparison between all the officers eligible to fill the particular vacancies, which are almost invariably restricted to the members of the grade next below the one in which the vacancy exists, a field which may be further restricted by the imposition of a minimum period of service in the lower grade. These boards have before them the normal personal records of the officers concerned as well as any special reports that have been made during that officer's career; they have also specific recommendations of senior officers and some of them will have personal knowledge of at least some of the officers involved. The real problem is to reduce so much information to a common denominator and to fill the gaps where scrappy personal knowledge is in question. To assist in this a system of standardized periodical reports was introduced.

### ASSESSMENT OF THE INDIVIDUAL

A scheme of systematized reports has three main aims, all closely interwoven, namely:

(i) the achievement of an objective assessment of the capacities of the individual officer in the performance of his duties;

(ii) a just forecast of his capacity for different and more responsible work; and

(iii) the gearing of such assessments to a common standard throughout the promotional area, which may be a large Department with branches throughout the country.

The third and culminating objective is very difficult to attain,

[1] See E. N. Gladden, *Civil Service Staff Relationships*, p. 134, for details of an interesting promotion scheme in the Admiralty in which the staff co-operated.

since the basic assessments must necessarily be made by different supervisory officers in a number of different branches, possibly dealing with different types of work and probably distributed over a wide geographical area. This is one of the main reasons for the introduction of interviewing boards to assist, or act for, the promotion board.

The main object of the annual report form introduced for the Civil Service as a result of the proposals of 1921 was to rationalize the process of making such assessments and to provide the materials upon which sound conclusions on the reportee's achievement and capacities could be drawn. While such reports are an essential element in the promotion system they also provide an invaluable aid to Establishment Officers in selecting suitable officials when transfers and other postings have to be made. The Model Report Form proposed by the National Whitley Council and later amended in the light of experience[1] is reproduced on pages 116 and 117.

Such a report is made periodically, usually each year, on officers within the range of promotion in all grades up to a certain level. It will be seen that the Model Report prescribes two distinct operations, namely (i) assessment of the officer's performance on his present work, under the twelve quality headings shown, by means of a marking on the following scale:[2] A—Outstanding, B—Very Good, C—Satisfactory, D—Indifferent, and E—Poor; and (ii) assessment of his suitability for promotion under one of four headings, namely, 'Exceptionally well qualified', 'Highly qualified', 'Qualified', and 'Not yet qualified'. The report is normally made by an officer at least two grades above the reportee and countersigned by a more senior officer. The former should insert, under 'general remarks', a note on any special qualifications or weaknesses not covered in the schedule, and the latter may add his remarks on the report in general. The report is treated as confidential and not communicated to the reportee except in the case of an E marking, details of which have to be given him unless broadly it is due to inexperience or, owing to health reasons, its communication is likely to have an adverse effect upon the official. In fact this information is merely passed on to the official to give him an opportunity to put right his failings, a matter that should have already received attention in the ordinary course of supervision.

Each Department is left to adopt its own type of report. Some Departments have adopted the Model Form, some have adapted it

[1] Revised in 1938.

[2] But A or B markings are not appropriate under heading No. 11—Official conduct.

to their specific needs, others—notably the Inland Revenue Department—have devised report forms of their own.

The Model Form has been criticized, mainly on the grounds that it does not give a complete picture, and amendments to the schedule of character factors have been suggested. It has been pointed out that these character factors are in some cases ambiguous: e.g. 'initiative' may refer either to intellectual initiative or to the initiative of the energetic and adventurous temperament. In some Departments, therefore, the reporting officers have been supplied with a set of definitions, or 'pointers', as they are called. The introduction of further headings, such as 'mental powers', 'speed of working', 'adaptability'—three notable omissions—has been suggested. There is also the difficulty of integrating the various character factors into a comprehensive judgment on the individual, complicated by the fact that different levels in the hierarchy call for different types of general capacity. The main difficulty, however, is to obtain equivalent standards of marking, particularly in a widely distributed staff organization. It is almost necessary to devise a 'coefficient of marking ability' for each reporting officer in order to bring each report to a common denominator, a fantastic idea perhaps, but one that at least suggests the almost insurmountable difficulty of devising a just scheme of comparison for a promotion system in a large-scale organization.

Various alternative solutions have been sought, particularly in America where much thought and experiment have been devoted to the problem. Ultimately all reporting systems depend upon an act of judgment, or more usually a series of such acts. Broadly two kinds of process have been applied in an effort to improve upon the report under character factors in a restricted range of markings as in the Civil Service Model Report. In the first an attempt has been made to add a numerical element to the process by which the different character factors are individually scaled and mutually weighted. The most popular is the rating scale method under which each element is assessed on a scale rising to 100, a total numerical assessment being reached by adding up the individual assessments, suitably weighted, in accordance with the relative importance of each quality required for the efficient performance of the work under review. The numerical result by which the candidates are eventually graded has an appearance of precision which is misleading, to say the least, and masks the fact that the whole scheme is based upon a series of personal judgments. Scientific precision in this sphere is unattainable and it is dangerous not to recognize the fact.

The rating scale appears to be much less popular in America than

K

it was. It has never found favour in this country. An alternative
method has been sought in the direction of simplifying the marking
process by breaking it down into a number of simple stages. The
Probst system, which is based upon a number of short answers, is
perhaps the best known.[1] Under this method the reporting officer is
asked to mark a series of short statements about the reportee: on
the following lines: Lazy; Slow moving; Quick and Active; Too
old for the work; Minor physical defects; Indifferent and not
interested; Talks too much; Good team worker; etc. Only those
headings that definitely apply to the individual concerned are

*MODEL REPORT FORM*

CONFIDENTIAL                                    E 53.   ESTAPORT (Code 5.53.0)

**ANNUAL REPORT ON MEMBERS OF THE STAFF**

*1st January* 19....

*Name*................................................................ *Rank*.................. *Branch*.................

*Date of Birth*.................................... *Date of entry into (a) Public Service*.................

*(b) Department (if different from (a)*.................... *(c) Present Grade*.................
(For notes on compiling the report, see overleaf)

SECTION 1.   PERFORMANCE OF DUTIES IN PRESENT GRADE

| | *Marking* (see note (1)) | *Remarks* |
|---|---|---|
| 1. Knowledge (a) of Branch . . . | | |
| (b) of Department . . . | | |
| 2. Personality and force of character | | |
| 3. Judgment . . . . . | | |
| 4. Power of taking responsibility . | | |
| 5. Initiative . . . . . | | |
| 6. Accuracy . . . . . | | |
| 7. Address and tact . . . | | |
| 8. Power of supervising staff . . | | |
| 9. Zeal . . . . . . | | |
| 10. Ability to express himself herself clearly . (a) in writing . . . | | |
| (b) orally . . . . | | |
| 11. Official conduct (see note (2)) . | | |

*General Remarks* (including note of any special qualifications not included above):

[1] This was experimented with by the Inland Revenue Department in 1931.
See E. N. Gladden's *Civil Service Staff Relationships,* p. 140.

SECTION II.  DEGREE OF FITNESS FOR PROMOTION

Indicate by placing a cross against the appropriate degree of fitness:

Exceptionally well qualified   |...............|     Qualified
Highly qualified                       Not yet qualified   |...............|

*Remarks*

(May be continued overleaf)

I HEREBY CERTIFY that in my opinion the conduct, standard of efficiency, and degree of fitness for promotion of the officer named hereon are as stated.

nature............................................................................ Rank.......................................................................
       (Certifying Officer)

*marks by
untersigning Officer.*

                             Signature.......................................................................
                                             (Head of Sub-Department)

(For professional and technical qualifications as supplied by the officer see form annexed)

NOTES

CTION I

NOTE (1). Insert in this column A, B, C, D, or E, against each item according to the following appraisement:

     A. Outstanding.   B. Very Good.   C. Satisfactory.
     D. Indifferent.   E. Poor.

NOTE (2). An A or B marking is inappropriate for this item.

NOTE (3). This report is to be regarded as confidential: but an E marking against any item must be communicated in duplicate by the head of the sub-department to the officer concerned except in the following circumstances:

     (i) Where in the opinion of the head of the sub-department communication is considered likely to affect adversely the officer's health.

     (ii) Where the marking is due to inexperience owing to less than one year's service on the grade (except in cases of unsatisfactory conduct, laziness, etc.).

     (iii) Where the weakness has already been notified and it is clear that no useful purpose can be served by repeated notification. In such cases the officer should be advised of the proposal to discontinue further notifications to the same effect as those he has previously received. Any change, for better or worse, should be notified to the officer.

     The officer should be required to sign and return to the Establishment Officer, one copy of intimations of E markings as evidence that he has been notified: he may, if he so desires, add observations.

CTION II

NOTE (4) The estimate of fitness for promotion should be related to the officer's capacity for the performance of the duties of the grade above. If he is marked "Exceptionally well qualified" or "Not yet qualified" the reasons for the markings should be stated; and in general reporting officers should make the fullest use of the "Remarks" space.

ENERAL

NOTE (5). Every effort should be made to arrive at a just estimate of the qualities of the officer at the time the report is made. Reporting Officers should rely on their own judgment and experience and should in no circumstances have access to previous reports on the same officer by other reporting officers.

*marks (continued from overleaf):*

marked and the resulting assessment is worked out by means of a special scoring device. A different set of virtues and failings is selected for each type of appointment. Whatever can be said in favour of such a pseudo-automatic system it appears to be inevitably restricted to the assessment of work of a routine nature.

In Britain the line of development most thoroughly explored has led in the direction of rendering the individual character factors more precise by attempting to define more carefully the meanings of the different headings, either by means of definitions or by inserting pointers to indicate the particular aspects of the main quality to which the judgment should be orientated. This is done by means of questions, e.g. 'Energy'. (Is he thorough in his application to work? Does he put his heart into it?)[1] It seems that this type of report is the most suitable for Civil Service use and that improvement of the present system should be sought in this direction.

Attempts were made to introduce an improved standardized report form on these lines but in default of general agreement, in 1954 a set of new Model Forms was made available for the Departments to adopt if they so decided. From the form suitable for the Clerical-Executive field, section B covering 'Qualities and Performance of Duties' is reproduced on pages 124/5. It looks less straightforward than the previous form, but, while it calls for a more concentrated effort on the part of the reporting officer, the pointers should assist him to reach more rational judgments under the several character headings. Other sections of the form have been brought into line, but they follow generally the pattern of the Model Form which we have been discussing.

Yet when all is said and done, and assuming that the real difficulties of obtaining a series of comparable reports have been overcome, the resultant report can present little more than an emasculated version of the real personality of the reportee or fail to do more than suggest how effectively he may be expected to grapple with an actual job of work. The real problem of the selectors is so to equate these reports, and all the other information available to them, as to choose the best man for the job, and there are so many imponderables in any system which is too large for the selectors to have intimate personal knowledge of all the candidates that it is not surprising that they sometimes fail in this. It seems possible that in any organization beyond a certain size, the job of selection is too big to place entirely upon the shoulders of a group of senior officers, and that some active element of individual competitive participation needs to be introduced. The tests and exercises adopted by the Civil Service Commission in their Method II recruitment deserve consideration for this purpose.

### WORKING THE SYSTEM

Application of the general principles of promotion through the machinery of the promotion boards and periodical reports varies

---

[1] Quoted from the Inland Revenue Form (E1).

throughout the Civil Service. This is due partly to the varying size of the Departments and the degree of geographical dispersion of their staffs and partly to the different attitudes adopted by the Departmental Whitley Councils in applying the general scheme. The system is most adequate to the needs of the smaller Departments where the personal knowledge of the heads is sufficient to bring an element of reality into the selecting process. In the larger Departments the defects of the system are more manifest, although here special factors may create unusual difficulties: for example, frequent changes in the selection policy adopted at the top, inconvenient age groupings in the staff that render periods of stagnancy inevitable, and factors affecting the expansion or contraction of the Department's activities at different periods.

It is important that the promotion system should be accepted as just by the staff themselves and, of course, Whitley co-operation in devising the system has gone a good way to ensure this. In some instances an even closer participation of the staff in the process of selection has been attempted. One important aspect is the question of appeal. How far should an official within the range of promotion who has not been selected be given the right to appeal and to what authority? The practice varies. Again the smaller Departments have an advantage, for there it is not too burdensome a task for the head himself to see any aggrieved officer if he so desires. It is important to the health of the system for an officer who feels that he has a grievance to be able to get it off his chest, as it were. In the larger Departments there may be an avenue of appeal, but unless an oral hearing is possible—and frequently such appeals can only be made on paper, usually within very restricted terms of reference—that is not very satisfying to the aggrieved individual, who unless he succeeds will feel that no real review has taken place. In any case the appeal is to the official who is ultimately responsible for the promotion; namely, the Permanent Head of the Department. There is no provision for appeal to a higher authority and thus no true appeals system exists. Since the civil servant, as the employee of a Minister, is considered a servant of the Crown, there could be no fundamental objection to the provision, by the Joint Permanent Secretary to the Treasury as Head of the Home Civil Service, of a final Promotion Appeal Body for civil servants who had exhausted all other appeal channels open to them. Under the British system of government the civil servant is barred on pain of dismissal from writing to his Member of Parliament about it and is not provided, as he would be under a system of *droit administratif*, with recourse to an administrative court. In this sense he is a second-class citizen!

The experience of other countries, notably Australia, where a system of central appeals has been in operation for some time, suggests that the solution of this problem is not easy. For in removing grounds for one sense of injustice the appeals system can easily introduce others and in effect merely shift the problem from one point to another. But the difficulty of finding such a solution must not be allowed to blind us to the fact that there is a problem. Securing that justice is done both to the individual civil servant and to the Service as a whole, is of extreme importance and a matter to which much more consideration needs to be given.

One way of introducing an objective element into the promotion process would be to use competitive examinations. This is of course practicable through the entrance examinations during the officer's early years of service, when he is given facilities to enter the ordinary competitions for posts in a higher class or may even be afforded an opportunity to sit a limited competition reserved for his grade alone. Since the war such competitions have been widely introduced into the Civil Service, so that an entrant to a class lower than his capacities justify now has good opportunities to obtain advancement in this way during his early years of service. There is even a so-called promotion examination for Clerical Officers between the ages of 21 and 25,[1] during which period no officer of this grade can obtain advancement to the Executive Officer grade by normal position. But this is really a special type of entrance examination, particularly as the successful candidate is available for posts in any Department.

The difficulty with the promotional examination is that it cannot easily take into account the qualities of mind and character that are so important as soon as the official begins to rise in the hierarchy. On the other hand it cannot be said that the application of the examinatiton process to promotion has been widely tested in this country, for the idea receives little support inside the Service. Nor does much consideration appear to have been given to the application to promotion selection of methods adopted in the Method II system of recruitment. Yet one would have thought that to test candidates for more senior positions by confronting them with case studies or special exercises with a managerial slant might have at least been more revealing than subjecting those on the final short list to a desultory general conversation of no more than twenty to thirty minutes duration, which is the method at present often adopted by promotion interview panels.

There is in fact a notable example of a promotion examination

---

[1] Until 1965 the limits were 21–28.

in the British Civil Service, namely in the Customs and Excise Department, where the important post of Surveyor is filled by examination from among Officers of the next lower grade who have usually about fifteen years service to their credit. The examination appears to have been introduced because it was felt to be the fairest way of selecting, from a large number of experienced Officers widely distributed over the country, the comparatively small number of people required to fill the higher posts. The examination comprises written papers, based entirely upon the work of the Department, and an interview to which real importance is given.[1] This interesting example of a promotion examination shows how in its varied nature the Civil Service can break away from general practice and thus render difficult the making of dogmatic pronouncements on its methods.

From what has been written it will be clearly seen that the promotion system in the Civil Service is based firmly in the Departments. It is not to any great extent a service system and in this respect at least the Service is not one but many. Opportunities vary not only as between the grades but also as between members of the same grade in different Departments. Some steps, however, have now been taken to mitigate this situation.

At one time it was difficult, below the top levels, to make promotions between the Departments and any suggestion that vacancies should be pooled was anathema to officials in Departments where the number of prospective vacancies was above the average. Limited pooling schemes had been introduced before the Second World War to ameliorate the differences in opportunity for promotion from the Clerical to the Executive Class which had arisen inside the Post Office[2] at that time. After the war, however, when the separateness of the Departments had been somewhat broken down under the exigencies of the great emergency, the principle of pooling a margin of vacancies was generally accepted and, with the approval of the Staff Sides, pooling schemes were introduced by the Treasury. The general method is for Departments where the proportion of recent promotions is below average to be assigned a certain number of appointments from the pool, which is made up of posts contributed by Departments with better than average promotion. Officers recommended by the below-average Departments as fully suitable for promotion are seen by a specially constituted

---

[1] Since this examination was first introduced this problem has become much more general by the spreading out of the Departments, but the particular solution has not been copied.

[2] This large Department is, exceptionally, divided into a number of promotion fields.

Treasury Pool Board, who compare the candidates and choose the most suitably qualified to fill vacancies in the pool. The selected officer will have to move out of his Department: Departments have to accept officers brought up elsewhere, but, although they no doubt prefer members of their own staffs to be promoted, in practice they do not lose by an inflow of 'new blood', or should one rather say 'different blood', since the newcomers are likely to be rather older than their own potential promotees. This scheme has been applied to promotions from the next grade below to the Executive Officer, Higher Executive Officer and Senior Executive Officer grades respectively. It has been of great value in levelling out the great discrepancies between promotion opportunities that were prevalent in the Civil Service between the wars. It is a simple and logical procedure, but its earlier development was obstructed by the prejudices and vested interests that exist in the Civil Service as in all professions.

It is clear that in large Service classes like the Treasury classes, the operation of a general scheme of promotion is fraught with almost insuperable difficulties. The same problems do not arise so acutely in the Departmental classes whose field of opportunities is strictly defined and many of these classes have specialized duties that would in any case confine their members to their own Departments. For example, there are in the Post Office large Manipulative groups for which there would be little employment elsewhere. On the other hand the professional classes, many of which worked in small Departmentally recruited pockets before the war, have been reorganized on a Service basis and it is possible, the numbers not being too large, for promotion to be made between the Departments. It is probably easier fairly to compare the capacities of officers in different Departments who are master of a specialist technique than to compare those with varying experience in the vastly miscellaneous field of general administration.

Promotion for the acquirement of recognized qualifications is not admitted in the Civil Service, although members of the professional classes who improve their qualifications are likely to stand well when higher vacancies arise. The position of the new professional Diploma in Government Administration for civil servants, which is not accepted as a promotional qualification, has been mentioned in the preceding chapter.[1] Clearly there is room for the development of more positive official attitudes on this subject, particularly in view of the increasing complexity and intensification of the large-scale element in public administration, which render the

[1] See page 101 above.

highly subjective content of present promotional procedures both less acceptable and less efficient.

In this chapter we have briefly summarized the principles and methods of promotion applied inside the Civil Service. It would be wrong to deny that much thought and goodwill have been devoted to the solution of the many difficult problems arising, but optimistic to suggest that satisfactory solutitons have invariably been achieved. During the course of this and previous discussion numerous references have been made to the co-operation between the staff and official elements, upon which the success of the system so much depends, and it is now time to consider this very important factor as a whole.

APPENDIX TO CHAPTER VI

*Extract from Revised Report Form* (**1955**)

# B   Report on Qualities and Performance of Duties

**CHARACTER AND PERSONALITY** *Tick appropriate boxes*          REMARK

### 1. Responsibility
Seeks and accepts responsibility at all times  .  .  1  ☐
Very willing to accept responsibility  .  .  .  .  2  .  ☐
Accepts responsibility as it comes  .  .  .  .  .  3  .  .  ☐
Inclined to refer up matters he could himself decide  4  .  .  .  ☐
Avoids taking responsibility  .  .  .  .  .  .  5  .  .  .  .  ☐

### 2. Relations with Colleagues
Wins and retains the highest regard of all  .  .  1  ☐
Is generally liked and respected  .  .  .  .  .  2  .  ☐
Gets on well with everyone  .  .  .  .  .  .  3  .  .  ☐
Not very easy in his relationships  .  .  .  .  4  .  .  .  ☐
A difficult colleague  .  .  .  .  .  .  .  .  5  .  .  .  .  ☐

### *3. Contacts with Public
Outstandingly effective in dealing with them  .  .  1  ☐
Considerate and firm as required  .  .  .  .  .  2  .  ☐
Handles them quite well  .  .  .  .  .  .  3  .  .  ☐
His manner tends to be unfortunate  .  .  .  4  .  .  .  ☐
Poor at dealing with them  .  .  .  .  .  .  5  .  .  .  .  ☐

## CAPACITY

### 4. Penetration
Gets at once to the root of any problem  .  .  .  1  ☐
Shows a ready appreciation of any problem  .  .  2  .  ☐
Usually grasps a point correctly  .  .  .  .  3  .  .  ☐
Not very quick in the uptake  .  .  .  .  .  4  .  .  .  ☐
Often misses the point  .  .  .  .  .  .  .  5  .  .  .  .  ☐

### 5. Constructive Power
Always produces a comprehensive solution  .  .  1  ☐
Generally makes a valuable contribution  .  .  .  2  .  ☐
His solutions are normally adequate  .  .  .  3  .  .  ☐
Seldom takes any constructive action  .  .  .  4  .  .  .  ☐
Fails to respond to a new situation  .  .  .  .  5  .  .  .  .  ☐

### 6. Judgment
Judgments consistently sound and well thought out  1  ☐
His view of a matter is nearly always a sensible one  2  .  ☐
Takes a reasonable view on most matters  .  .  .  3  .  .  ☐
His judgment tends to be erratic  .  .  .  .  .  4  .  .  .  ☐
His judgment cannot be relied on  .  .  .  .  .  5  .  .  .  .  ☐

## PERFORMANCE OF DUTIES

### 7. Output
Outstanding in the amount of work he does  .  .  1  ☐
Gets through a great deal of work  .  .  .  .  2  .  ☐
Output satisfactory  .  .  .  .  .  .  .  .  3  .  .  ☐
Does rather less than expected  .  .  .  .  .  4  .  .  .  ☐
Output regularly insufficient  .  .  .  .  .  .  5  .  .  .  .  ☐

* To be completed only for officers with relevant experience.

## Report on Qualities and Performance of Duties—*continued*

**ERFORMANCE OF DUTIES**—*continued*    *Tick appropriate boxes*    REMARKS

**Quality**

Distinguished for accurate and thorough work . 1 ☐
Maintains a high standard . . . . . 2 . ☐
His work is generally of good quality . . 3 . . ☐
His performance is uneven . . . . . 4 . . . ☐
Inaccurate and slovenly in his work . . . 5 . . . . ☐

**Expression on Paper**

Brilliant on paper . . . . . . . 1 ☐
Written work always clear, cogent and well set out 2 . ☐
Generally expresses himself clearly and concisely 3 . . ☐
Written work just good enough to get by . . 4 . . . ☐
Cannot express himself clearly on paper . . 5 . . . . ☐

**Oral Expression**

Extremely effective . . . . . . . 1 ☐
Puts his points across convincingly . . . 2 . ☐
Expresses himself adequately . . . . . 3 . . ☐
Barely competent . . . . . . . 4 . . . ☐
Ineffective . . . . . . . . . 5 . . . . ☐

**1. Figurework**

Exceptionally good at all kinds of figurework . 1 ☐
Handles and interprets figures very well . . 2 . ☐
Competent at figurework . . . . . . 3 . . ☐
Handling of figures leaves something to be desired 4 . . . ☐
Poor at figures . . . . . . . . 5 . . . . ☐

**2. Management of Subordinates**

Always inspires them to give of their best . . 1 ☐
Manages them distinctly well . . . . . 2 . ☐
They work quite well for him . . . . . 3 . . ☐
Does not control them very skilfully . . . 4 . . . ☐
Handles them badly . . . . . . . 5 . . . . ☐

**3. Organization of Work**

An exceptionally effective organizer . . . . 1 ☐
Shows considerable organizing skill . . . 2 . ☐
Plans and controls work satisfactorily . . 3 . . ☐
An indifferent organizer . . . . . . 4 . . . ☐
Cannot organize . . . . . . . . 5 . . . . ☐

. . . . . . . . . . . . . 1 ☐
. . . . . . . . . . . . . 2 . ☐
. . . . . . . . . . . . . 3 . . ☐
. . . . . . . . . . . . . 4 . . . . ☐
. . . . . . . . . . . . . 5 . . . . ☐

To be completed only for officers with relevant experience.

# CHAPTER VII

## TRADE UNIONISM AND JOINT CONSULTATION

Inside the Civil Service trade unionism, where it exists, is bound to be modified considerably by the special nature of State employment and the peculiar loyalties of the public official. Although the history of mutual combination by civil servants to protect and further their own interests can be traced back to earlier, less conventional days, there has always been an air of respectability about this movement and a disinclination to accept the assumptions of a full-blooded trade unionism. Combinations of officials are referred to as 'staff associations' and the label 'trade union' is usually avoided.[1] An important factor is that in the British Civil Service, where the political administrator remains aloof from establishment activities, the normal master-servant relationship does not exist. The employer or 'Official' element is supplied by the senior civil servants in charge and thus both sides are really members of one and the same interest group. The mythologies of the class war are not there to confuse the issue, although one has to admit that confusion may arise in other ways.

### BRIEF HISTORY

Leadership in the Victorian Civil Service was essentially authoritarian, tempered with a good measure of paternal benevolence. The upper stratum expected their intellectual inferiors to know their place and providing they did, were usually willing to give sympathetic consideration to their modest aspirations: as far, that is to say, as regulations might permit. It could safely be left to the fiscal strictness of Her Majesty's Treasury, as guardians of the Nation's financial resources, to refuse anything that transcended the barest justice. There is therefore no reason to be surprised that the legal recognition of trade unionism by the Trade Union Act of 1871 was not accepted, even by any large number of subordinate officials, as granting a similar privilege to the servant of the State. Certainly the administrative-clerical classes as a whole, typifying the black-coated worker, continued right up to the First World War to

[1] This is not the case with the Industrial Civil Service or with such an organization as the Union of Post Office Workers which has always advocated a more activist approach.

consider mutual aid in seeking better conditions of service as a sign of ill-breeding, not calculated to enhance their status as civil servants.

Nor is it surprising that recognition when it did come in 1906 was granted by the Postmaster General[1] to the rather more menial sections of the Civil Service. For a quarter of a century at least the chronically underpaid manipulative workers of the Post Office had been struggling for better conditions and one of the strongest weapons in the official armoury was the refusal to listen to representations by staff unions except in accordance with procedures that made it difficult for representatives to act without prejudicing their own official prospects.

There were indeed earlier examples of incipient trade unionism in the Civil Service, even before 1879 when the letter carriers of the Post Office began to consider united action in their own defence. In reply to Tom Paine's statement on behalf of his former colleagues in the Excise Service,[2] Pitt stated in the House of Commons in 1788 that the only proper mode of applying to Parliament was through the Commissioners of Excise and that he would never countenance an application to the Legislature by petition from the Excise Officers themselves. This statement, which could have been made as authoritatively a century later without appearing the least old-fashioned, indicates that even in the eighteenth century the house union might be tolerated provided it made its represenation through 'normal official channels'. Associations were formed for special purposes, as in 1846 when one was established to pursue reform of the pensions system. This was dissolved as soon as a select committee had been set up to investigate the problem.[3] In the 'sixties of the nineteenth century, and probably earlier, revenue officers were again in the picture. Through a Central Committee representing certain grades statements were made both to the Commissioners of Inland Revenue and to Parliament not only suing for pay increases but also proposing an extensive re-classification of the Excise Branch.[4] The Royal Commission, as a method of investigation into Civil Service conditions, also had its influence on the shaping of such associational activities. Both the Playfair (1874–5) and the Ridley (1886–90) Commissions received information from civil servants and from groups of civil servants on behalf of their colleagues.[5]

[1] On February 13th, 1906, by Mr. Sydney Buxton.
[2] In *The Case of the Excise Officers* (1772).
[3] Select Committee on Superannuation Allowances, reported 1857.
[4] See E. N. Gladden *Civil Service Staff Relationships* (1943), pp. 13–16.
[5] See *Introductory Memoranda relating to the Civil Service*, H.M. Treasury (1930), p. 71, which also mentions in this connection the Tweedmouth Committee on Post Office Establishments, 1895–7.

128     *Civil Services of the United Kingdom*

Already in these early manifestations of staff collaboration in the Civil Service, manifestations that were no doubt much more widespread than the surviving records disclose, there clearly appears—in addition to the natural objective of such groups to advance and protect the interests of the membership—their supplemental but hardly less important function as collectors and disseminators of information.

The success of Post Office unionism in 1906 was followed by a steady advance in staff co-operation throughout the Civil Service, so that by 1914 even the black-coated civil servants were building up their own associations. Collective bargaining as a principle was by that date more or less generally accepted, though progress was very slow in many Departments, where the old method of solicitation for the removal of grievances by memorial was still favoured. Traditionally couched in language that mixed pomposity with servility, the memorial had the dual advantage to the administrators of allowing their staffs the psychological relief of bringing their grievances out into the open and at the same time permitting those grievances to be quickly incarcerated in the official pigeonhole from which they would only emerge, if ever, after a good deal of procrastination. The Treasury suggested[1] that any reluctance to recognize associations arose not from any fundamental antagonism but because of the difficulty of reconciling the doctrine of ministerial responsibility with direct recognition by the Treasury of an association representing a grade common to the whole Service. That is as may be, but there can be little doubt that in 1914 the *élite* of the Civil Service still regarded staff activities as generally obnoxious and their instigators as vulgar and distinctly disloyal, while the rank and file themselves, rightly or wrongly, entertained a strong suspicion that those who were intrepid enough to stand up for the rights of their colleagues were foolishly, if nobly, jeopardizing such opportunities for advancement as might in the future arise.

ENTER WHITLEYISM

The First World War offset to some extent its tragic destruction of many promising civil servants, among those who rushed into the armed forces before the system of voluntary recruitment was superseded, by ensuring that those who returned from the battlefields of Flanders and the Somme to the humdrum offices of Whitehall should no longer feel the same subservience as in the past. The juniors of the post-war Civil Service were not prepared to go cap-in-hand to their superiors or to be content with fair words that masked

[1] *Introductory Memoranda*, p. 74.

specious excuses. If in other spheres the Civil Service was destined, for some years at least, to follow the even tenor of its ways, in the sphere of staff relations a revolution was certainly at hand.

While the international struggle was still at its height a significant movement had been taking shape inside the nation's factories. The workers were demanding a greater share in the management of the industries in which they worked. A Committee, under the chairmanship of the Deputy-Speaker of the House of Commons, the Rt. Hon. J. H. Whitley,[1] which had been appointed by the Minister of Reconstruction, reported[2] during 1917 and 1918 in favour of the introduction into industry of a system of joint councils on which representatives of the workers should share with the management the decision of questions particularly concerning the workers' interests. After substantial initial successes this system of Whitley Councils, as they came to be called, was not destined to make universal headway. The times were not yet ripe. In the Civil Service the new system was accepted for the industrial establishments, where the Government felt they had to set an example, but originally there was no intention that it should be adopted for the administrative sectors. Indeed the Reconstruction Committee had not had any such application of their scheme in mind.

The new plan, however, commended itself very favourably to the rank and file of the Civil Service. The staff associations, growing in strength by the inflow of new members, put pressure upon the Government to apply the Whitley scheme throughout the Departments and persisted in their representations with such good effect that the understandable reluctance of the Government was overcome. The Departments and associations discussed jointly the application of the scheme to the Civil Service and produced, in May 1919, an agreed report.[3] This was a consummation that in itself demonstrated at the very outset the potentialities of the Service as a field for operating the Whitley method of joint consultation. The report recommended the establishment at an early date, for the non-industrial classes of the Civil Service, of a National Whitley Council and appropriate Departmental Whitley Councils.

It is laid down in the constitution adopted for the new system that 'the objects of the National Council shall be to secure the greatest measure of co-operation between the State in its capacity

[1] He was to be Speaker from 1921 to 1928.

[2] *Interim report on Joint Standing Industrial Councils* (Cmd. 8606); *Supplementary Report on Works Committees* (Cmd. 9001); *Second Report on Joint Standing Industrial Councils* (Cmd. 9002); *Report on Conciliation and Arbitration* (Cmd. 9099); *Committee on Relations between Employers and Employed, Final Report* (Cmd. 9153).

[3] Cmd. 198.

as employer and the general body of civil servants in matters affecting the Civil Service, with a view to increasing efficiency in the public service combined with the well being of those employed; to provide machinery for dealing with grievances, and generally to bring together the experience and different points of view of representatives of the administrative, clerical and manipulative Civil Service.'[1]

The main functions of the National Council, modified to meet the needs of the Civil Service from the more detailed definitions suggested in the Whitley Reports for industrial joint councils, are covered by the following six headings:

(i) 'Provision of the best means for utilizing the ideas and experience of the staff.'

(ii) 'Means for securing to the staff a greater share in and responsibility for the determination and observance of the conditions under which their duties are carried out.'

(iii) 'Determination of the general principles governing the conditions of service, e.g. recruitment, hours, promotion, discipline, tenure, remuneration and superannuation.'

(iv) The encouragement of the further education of Civil Servants and their training in higher administration and organization.'

(v) 'Improvement of office machinery and organization and the provision of opportunities for the full consideration of suggestions by the staff on this subject.'

(vi) 'Proposed legislation so far as it has a bearing upon the position of civil servants in relation to their employment.'

The scope of these functions is very wide, covering not only many of the normal objectives of trade unionism, but also those of a professional body. There was no intention, however, that the councils should displace the staff associations, and to avoid any possibility of this happening staff representatives on these councils were to be selected by the associations. There is no provision for individual membership. Employee organization in the Civil Service is therefore divided into three distinct but closely inter-related sectors; namely the National Whitley Council, the Departmental Whitley Councils, and the staff associations. Broadly their respective fields of responsibility may be defined as follows: the National Council deals with matters of interest to grades in more than one Department, Deparmental Council deals with the affairs common

[1] The terms of the constitution of the National Whitley Council are reproduced as an appendix to *Staff Relations in the Civil Service,* H.M. Treasury (H.M.S.O. 1965).

to the various grades within its own Department, while an association pursues the interests of the grade or grades, which it has been
formed to represent, whether its members serve in one or a number
of Departments.

Under its constitution the Civil Service National Whitley Council has a membership of fifty-four, one half of whom, appointed by
the Government, is known as the 'Official Side', and the other half,
appointed by associations or groups of associations, is known as
the 'Staff Side'. However, the constitution has been flexibly interpreted and the membership total and equal division have not been
strictly adhered to. The Official Side, appointed by the Chancellor
of the Exchequer, consists of the Joint Permanent Secretary to the
Treasury designated Head of the Civil Service, as chairman, together with the other Joint Permanent Secretary, the Permanent
Secretaries of the major Departments and the senior Treasury officials responsible for establishment matters. The Staff Side consists
of representatives of the staff associations, who may be either civil
servants or permanent association officials, and also *ex officio* the
Chairman, Secretary-General, Secretary and Assistant Secretary of
the Staff Side. The Secretary-General, as the Staff Side's chief negotiating officer, has been appointed Vice-Chairman of the National
Whitley Council: In the Chairman's absence, however, another
member of the Official Side takes his place.[1]

Originally the Council met regularly, but even then much of its
business was transacted through joint committees. Today full meetings are rare and practically all business is handled by committees
or by spokesmen for the two sides. No doubt much of the Official
Side's own co-ordination is carried out through the normal informal
meetings of senior departmental officials at the Treasury, while
the Staff Side set up several committees for this purpose.

From the outset the Staff Side had to establish an office and
staff of its own, at first under the direction of joint Secretaries
seconded from the Civil Service for a number of years, but with
the growth of Whitley business after the war this organization,
which for a time had come under the control of one man, had to
be strengthened and extended, first by making the Chairmanship
a full-time appointment and then, in 1956, by the appointment of
a permanent Secretary-General to take over the Chairman's executive duties, while the Chairmanship again became elective for terms
of two years. This post is invariably filled by a prominent association leader. The Staff Side publishes a monthly *Whitley Bulletin*
which, not only reports current Whitley and association news, but
gives publicity to official decisions and pronouncements relating to

[1] A similar rule applies to the joint committees.

staff matters and thus provides a valuable publication of near-official status.

At first sight this joint council on which civil servants or their representatives sit on both sides of the table would seem to have a somewhat artificial character, differing fundamentally from the typical industrial council on which the 'we' and the 'they' are more clearly differentiated. In fact this arrangement is entirely in line with the conventional distribution of the Department's political and administrative functions between Minister and Permanent Secretary. That the position was not clearly seen at the outset is suggested by the original inclusion in the Official Side of Members of Parliament from the Government party. Understandably they were unable to contribute very much in this capacity and found themselves to be veritable fish out of water. It is hardly surprising that the arrangement was dropped, following the recommendations of the Tomlin Commission (1929–31).

While the Official Side have welcomed and encouraged the co-operation of the staffs in the spirit of the new system they have never been free in granting concessions that would impose an undue burden on the State. Indeed, as representatives of the Government it is certain that the Official Side will never come to a decision that is likely to be contrary to the wishes of the Government of the day. As decisions on the National Council are operative, subject always to the constitutional overriding powers of the Cabinet and Parliament, as soon as they have been reached, it is common sense to assume that the Official Side will always have made the position absolutely clear to their political chiefs before an agreement is concluded.

There are special arrangements for reviewing the remuneration of the Higher Civil Service. In accordance with recommendations of the Priestley Commission[1] general oversight of the pay of the Higher Civil Service (which is defined as 'staffs whose salary maximum or whose fixed rate exceeds the maximum of the Principal') is assigned to a Standing Advisory Committee, appointed by the Prime Minister, after informally consulting staff interests, from among persons chosen to reflect a cross-section of informed opinion in the country at large. Its present membership is made up of a chairman and five members, all prominent people from outside the Civil Service. The Committee's function is to advise the Government from time to time on changes they consider desirable in the remuneration of the Higher Civil Service. Such advice is offered when the Government so requests, or upon the Committee's own initiative, or on the occasion of general pay settlements, or when a claim from a staff

[1] See *Report*, para. 377 *et seq.*, pp. 88–91.

association touching any of the grades in the Committee's sphere has not been satisfactorily solved.

The jurisdiction of the National Whitley Council does not extend to matters of purely departmental interest. Consequently there are in most Departments a Departmental Whitley Council independently appointed, with Official and Staff sides very much on the plan of the National Council. There is also provision for district or regional committees to deal with the Whitley problems of staffs distributed in offices throughout the country. It must be emphasized that this departmental system constitutes a distinct layer without hierarchic connnection with the National Council, which does not constitute a court of appeal from the Departmental Councils. Membership of the two systems is independently determined but, so far as the staffs are concerned, coherence between the activities of the two layers is ensured by the fact that membership rests upon the associations, which operate at both levels. A more precise inter-relationship would hardly have been compatible with the principle of ministerial responsibility.

Two specialist Whitley organizations have developed since its inception, namely the Civil Service Council for Further Education[1] and the Civil Service Pay Research Unit,[2] which have already been mentioned, but the latter is so interesting that further consideration is called for.

### CIVIL SERVICE PAY RESEARCH UNIT

In order to operate the Priestley Commission's[3] recommendations on the application of the principle of 'fair comparisons' to the pay of civil servants the Civil Service National Whitley Council in 1956 established the Unit, together with a Steering Committee of six members from each Side to supervise it. To give the new body appropriate prestige and to emphasize its impartiality its Director appointed by the Prime Minister. The post has hitherto been filled from the higher ranks of the Civil Service, while the staff has been drawn from appropriate grades, seconded from their Departments for limited periods. The Director has charge of administration, but is responsible to the Committee.

The Unit's function is to provide the Committee, the Departments and recognized Civil Service staff organizations with objective facts to assist in the process of pay negotiations. The Royal

[1] See page 97 above.
[2] See page 51 above.
[3] *Report*, pp. 23 *et seq.*

Commission laid down that pay settlement involved two distinct processes. They said:[1]

'The key to a solution seems to lie in the division of the process of pay settlement into two distinct sets of operations: on the one hand the operations of assembling and analysing the factual material upon which comparisons are to be made, and on the other hand the application of the results of these operations to the subsequent negotiation of rates of pay. Failure to make this distinction must tend to bring the principle of fair comparison into disrepute and to place an unnecessary and undesirable strain upon the negotiating machinery . . .'

The Unit is confined to the first set of operations and to this end is directed to limit itself 'to the description and definition of the similarity or difference in the duties of the grades with which comparison is being made' and 'not attempt to evaluate those differences.'

The Unit has to investigate the pay and conditions of the employees of outside firms presenting suitable fields for comparison. Such outside approaches have depended upon the goodwill and co-operativeness of both employer and employee in the concerns approached and this has generally been readily forthcoming, on a strict understanding that all such information is treated as strictly confidential. Consequently the Unit's reports upon their investigations cannot be communicated except to the authorized bodies.[2]

Although these enquiries have been beset by difficulties of planning and timing, since the whole Civil Service field could not be looked at simultaneously, it is already clear that the Unit has made a valuable contribution to the effectiveness of pay negotiations in the Civil Service, where the two parties to a claim can now be sure that they are arguing from a similar factual basis, whereas in the past the Treasury and the Departments derived inestimable advantage from having control of the official machine in assembling their evidence. The surveys have now been regularized through an arrangement that the Unit shall cover the main Civil Service classes in four year periods.

### THE STAFF ASSOCIATIONS

After the First World War the range of membership of the staff associations in the Civil Service greatly extended. Usually they are bodies set up to deal with the interests of a specific class, or of a

[1] *Report*, para 136, p. 36.
[2] *Civil Service Pay Research Unit: First Annual Report, 1957*, para 6 (b) p. 4.

series of allied classes. It is a law of their inner being that they should wish to continue to expand, even to the extent of covering interests that are not essentially assimilable, and in the minds of many an association leader is the dream-picture of the all-comprehensive Civil Service association that will offer a united front to the authorities. Usually the association begins as a small voluntary group with elected representatives who carry out all the necessary work in their spare time. Eventually the job passes beyond the scope of the voluntary official and full-time officials are appointed: sometimes from outside the Service. The larger Civil Service associations today have professional officers and some of them constitute very powerful organizations in the trade union movement.

There are certain restrictions on these Associations which affect their drive and effectiveness compared with outside trade unions. First there is the restriction, by custom though not by law, upon the use of the strike weapon as not being compatible with the spirit of public service. Strikes, even unofficial ones, are rare and when they do occur their participants may be subject to disciplinary action. In the words of the then Attorney General, when moving the Second Reading of the Trades Disputes and Trade Unions Bill in 1946:

'this Government, like any Government as an employer would feel itself perfectly free to take any disciplinary action that any strike situation that might develop demanded.'[1]

Secondly, there is the aim of the Civil Service to keep clear of political activities. While the policy of the associations varies in this respect, it would in the main be true to say that association workers are persons of strong political views who sometimes find it difficult not to confuse their own personal inclinations with the interests of their constituents. The tendency is certainly for the larger and more influential associations to take a more active interest in political affairs. Many associations have now affiliated to the Trade Union Congress, as they are again entitled to do under the 1946 legislation just mentioned.[2]

There is no closed shop in the Civil Service, but it is administratively desirable that associations should achieve as near to one hundred per cent membership as possible. It is the official attitude,

---

[1] Quoted from *I.P.C.S. Handbook*, 1962, para. 74, p. 21.

[2] Repeating the Trade Disputes and Trade Unions Act of 1927. This Act, passed as a consequence of the General Strike of 1926 to which certain Civil Service organizations gave support, made it illegal for a civil servant to be a member of an association catering for outside members or having political interests.

therefore, to encourage the civil servant to belong to his appropriate association and new entrants particularly are made aware of the advantages of staff co-operation. The point is made in the introductory booklet for new entrants to the Civil Service issued by H.M. Treasury. As will be stressed later modern large-scale administration depends very much for its efficiency upon being able to gauge the views of its personnel. This will ensure an encouraging attitude to trade unionism on the part of the official interest but the fact that Whitleyism depends upon complete staff co-operation in itself presupposes such an attitude.

In the main the associations have made good use of the Whitley system. Had such a scheme not been devised with official sanction it is clear that some sort of Civil Service staff council would have had to be formed to deal with matters of common interest to associations. Thus the National Staff Side as the voice of all civil servants serves a very special purpose in its own right. There have of course been disagreements and for periods some associations have not co-operated. This has usually happened at the departmental level where on a few occasions an association has left the Staff Side rather than continue to agree to differ with its co-members. On the National Staff Side associations representing the higher staffs withdrew as a consequence of the policy of the Staff Side during the General Strike in 1926. This was in many ways a pity, but hardly a wounding blow in light of the small size of the associations concerned. However, since the Second World War the common front has been restored and the Staff Side is to-day representative of all non-industrial civil servants.

Its membership at present is divided between:

(1) Post Office Group (including Union of Post Office Workers, Post Office Engineering Union, Association of Post Office Controlling Officers, Society of Telecommunication Engineers, Federation of Sub-Postmasters, Head Postmasters' Association, Postmasters Association, Telephone Contract Officers' Association, and Telecommunications Traffic Association);

(2) Civil Service Alliance (including Civil Service Clerical Association, Inland Revenue Staff Federation, and Ministry of Labour Staff Federation);

(3) Executive Group (including Society of Civil Servants, Customs and Excise Federation, Association of Officers of Ministry of Labour, and Association of H.M. Inspectors of Taxes);

(4) Association of First Division Civil Servants;

(5) Institute of Professional Civil Servants;

(6) Federation of Civil Service Professional and Technical Staffs;

(7) Civil Service Union.

The grand total of National Staff Side's representative capacity as at 31st December 1964 was approximately 641,000, compared with 484,000 in 1945 and 327,000 in 1939. (Quoted from *Whitley Bulletin* Vol. XLV p. 90, June 1965).

## ARBITRATION

Remuneration is a constant subject of staff agitation. It is the first task of the associations to press on behalf of their membership claims for improved salaries. Disagreement with the Department or the Treasury is not an unusual outcome of such negotiations. It was thought at the introduction of the Whitley system that such difficulties would be solved by the new machinery, but success in this sphere depends largely upon compromise and where, in the public interest, the Official Side feels itself compelled to refuse concessions which involve expenditure there is bound to be deadlock between the two sides. To solve such deadlocks arbitration under the Industrial Courts Act of 1919 was applied to the Civil Service in 1925. There had already existed, largely as the outcome of wartime conditions, a Conciliation and Arbitration Board for Government employees, which had sat between 1917 and 1923. This Board had done effective work and its discontinuance by the Government on the score that it was no longer necessary was received critically by the staffs, whose agitation was instrumental, after strong Parliamentary pressure, in inducing a change of policy on the part of the Government.

Under the new arrangement a division of the Industrial Court, appointed to cover Civil Service cases, was authorized to deal with claims affecting the emoluments, weekly hours of work, and leave of any well-defined category of civil servants who, for the purpose of a particular claim, occupy the same position, or have a common interest in the claim', but the cases of individual officers are excluded. The need for this arbitration machinery is demonstrated by the fact that between 1926 and 1936 the number of Civil Service cases considered by the Industrial Court was approximately 44 per cent of all cases brought before it. In October 1936, when it was decided to separate the Civil Service side from the Industrial Court, the present Civil Service Arbitration Tribunal came into being. The Tribunal consists of a chairman appointed by the Crown, together with one member representative of the official interests and one member representative of the Staff Side of the National Whitley Council, drawn respectively from panels specially set up for the purpose by the Minister of Labour. The Tribunal does not adjudicate upon claims from grades whose salary range rises above the maximum of the Principal's scale. Proceedings are conducted with a minimum of formality in accordance with flexible rules lad down by the court itself. Cases for the staff are usually presented by leading officials of the associations concerned, while the official viewpoint is put forward by a representative of the Department or the Treasury. Although hearings are open to the public there is no place for rhetoric. The Tribunal considers its findings in private and issues its award within a few days of the sitting.

There can be no doubt that the Civil Service Arbitration Tribunal serves an essential purpose. It has afforded aggrieved sections of the staff the opportunity to air their grievances and, on sustaining their case, to obtain redress. It is true that the findings of the court cannot, over a period in which so many changes have taken place in the national situation, be interpreted in relation to some unswerving standard of equity, for in fact the influences of the current economic situation and the overriding considerations of national economy can be clearly detected in decisions reached over the years. But after all no servant of the State can ask for more than that his just aspirations shall be weighed in relation to the needs and resources of the community that he has chosen to serve. During 1949-50 when the Tribunal, while showing sympathy with the staffs, refused in accordance with the Government's policy of a national wage freeze, to adjudicate for the time being on the claims laid before them, it was considered both within the Civil Service and in wider circles that the whole principle of arbitration had been negated.

Similar repercussions followed the Government's announcement in 1961 of a pay pause to grapple with current economic difficulties. The Government's immediate steps meant a pay standstill in the public sector and alteration of the terms under which disputed claims could be taken to arbitration. As a further instance of the Government's use of the Civil Service as an example—or stooge, as civil servants themselves preferred to regard it—was bound to evoke resentment within the Service, but there were much more serious considerations. The very nature of the new system of pay adjustment, by fair comparisons, meant that such a pay pause would deprive public officials of advances already achieved outside. There was a spontaneous feeling of injustice throughout the Civil Service and the associations had no difficulty in stimulating opposition. Apart from the immediate protests by the Staff Side through normal Whitley channels, protest meetings were widely organized by the various staff associations and reactions from the rank and file were on a scale and publicity level that took one's mind back to similar upsurges way back in the 'twenties.

Economically there was a good deal of common sense in the Government's general policy, if it could be universally applied, but the authorities were in a dilemma. By operating the pay pause in the only area over which they had any sort of direct control they stigmatized the new policy with a flavour of injustice that ensured its failure from the outset. Within a matter of months failure had to be recognized, and normal arbitration arrangements were restored.

One effect the existence of the Tribunal has certainly had. It has enabled H.M. Treasury to divest itself of some of the characteristics of the stern and heavy father and at the same time freed it to press with all its resources the case for public economy. On the other hand the shifting of the immediate responsibility to the Tribunal, even if ultimately the responsibility of implementing the Tribunal's findings must rest upon the Government, had undoubtedly enabled a more friendly attitude to develop between the Treasury and the rest. This is of course to a great extent due to the success of Whitleyism, but it is difficult to feel confident that that success would have been so evident had the last word on salary matters devolved upon the National Whitley Council.

### ACHIEVEMENTS IN STAFF CO-OPERATION

Opinions on this or that aspect of staff co-operation differ and for long the success of Whitleyism was held to be in the balance. In the Departments its efficiency has varied both in place and time. At the time of the Tomlin investigation, for example, some heads of Departments advocated the abolition of the system, and Staff Side enthusiasts have not infrequently raised their voices in disappointment at the meagre results achieved.

There can be little doubt, however, that on balance there have been considerable gains both to the staffs and to the Administration in the development of staff co-operation in the Civil Service since the First World War. The whole atmosphere has changed from a situation in which the master-servant relationship predominated to one in which the official elements are first and foremost in encouraging co-operation and condemning those who stand aloof. It is understandable that there was an interim period during which this was not universally so and that for some time there were areas of the Service in which administrators of the old school placed a black mark against the names of those who devoted themselves to their colleagues' interests. As late as 1939 the decision on this point may well have been still in the balance, but events since then have surely turned the scale in favour of the new system. In fact it is no exaggeration to claim that the introduction of Whitleyism has been the only fundamental change in the Civil Service since the Treveylan–Northcote reforms of 1853–70.

From the very outset the National Whitley Council was responsible for essential reforms in the general administrative field. Not only did it sponsor the new Reorganization of 1920, to which ample reference has already been made, but it continued steadily through joint co-operation to improve personnel methods in many directions, such as promotional procedure, consideration of suggestions by the staff, organization of training schemes, and in keeping many bread and butter matters in close adjustment to changing facts. The staffs were keenly concerned in protecting the interests of their temporary colleagues, in obtaining due adjustments in the war bonus system that caused so much heart-burning after the First World War and, when the Tomlin Commission had reported, in co-operating closely in the implementation of its report which, if it made no spectacular proposals, threw out a number of suggestions that led to improvements in detail, e.g. with regard to superannuation.

Possibly the most serious criticism is that the associations and Whitley councils have been too much concerned with bread-and-butter matters. Until recently too little attention was paid to improving the efficiency of their constituents, to furthering the more purely professional interests of civil servants. It has already been made plain that even in staff training, in which field the Staff Side was for long undoubtedly ahead of the Official Side, interest was very moderate until the Select Committee on National Expenditure came upon this particular scene in 1942. Civil servants have never been eager to equip themselves professionally nor has any Civil Service association vied in this with such an organization as the National and Local Government Officers Association, whose activities in a parallel public administrative field are so worthy of emulation.

During the Second World War the National Whitley Council gained greatly in reputation and prestige. The Whitley councils and the associations had co-operated closely with the Administration in the war preparations that had been going forward steadily since the *démarche* at Munich in 1938. In particular, their participation in the planning of the evacuation schemes for the Departments in the event of intensive bombing of the centres of administration, especially Whitehall, or of invasion was to be of great importance in the months ahead; for it soon became apparent that the average official viewed with concern the radical dislocation of his home life that evacuation made inevitable, and in the absence of an immediate and obvious threat—upon which the smooth operation of such a scheme of administrative dispersal could not wait—the individual member of the staff could not easily be convinced that his enforced evacuation was really necessary. This and many other wartime problems were co-operatively faced by the National Whitley Council, working through special standing committees. The Civil Service was called upon to set an example in relinquishing peacetime privileges—especially with regard to leave and hours of work—in face of the dire national emergency. The staff representatives, naturally eager to voice the views of the majority in patriotic response to the Government's calls, did not always find it easy to convince some of their constituents that these sacrifices by example would not eventually constitute a heaven-sent excuse to take away from the Civil Service advantages that some official elements had always grudged.

The contribution of the Whitley and staff organizations to the running of the wartime administration was of great importance and deserves a study of its own. Not only did the normal problems continue, frequently with aggravated acuteness, but new ones were created by the need to organize and to serve the crowds of temporary officials who entered the Service, often from a very different occupational environment, and also by the creation of a number of brand-new ministries containing but a nucleus of permanent civil servants. Later on there were the problems of post-war resettlement to be faced and, as we have already seen, plans were put in hand well in advance to deal with such matters as recruitment and training. The staff associations greatly expanded their membership. They were therefore called upon to strengthen their own organizations, often by additions to their professional appointments.

### CO-OPERATION IN ADMINISTRATION

Had the Civil Service staff movement not arisen in its present form on a surge of spontaneous enthusiasm in the years following the First World War and become consolidated into the effective system of joint consultation that now exists, it is no exaggeration to suggest that the Administration itself would have had to introduce some such system. The fact is that when an administrative organization develops large-scale characteristics, so that it is no longer possible for contacts between the administrators at the top and the rank and file to be conducted on a paternalistic basis, some effective form of consultation becomes an absolute necessity to administrative efficiency. Administration is a human activity depending upon a high degree of co-operation between all who are engaged in it. The highest success of administrative processes can only be achieved where the minds of administrative workers are receptive and friendly to the processes they are called upon to operate. There is something intangible about administration that renders the least obstruction, which may often be unconscious, not only difficult to discover but disproportionately destructive of the efficiency standards that the leader has in view.

In a large-scale administrative organization staff or personnel management is an art that assumes an ever-increasing importance and the administrative leader cannot achieve the best results in this field unless he has an easy means of discovering the views of his subordinates and of preparing their minds at all times to the acceptance of new methods whose introduction they may often be disposed at first to resent. In a small organization such matters can be talked over in a friendly informal atmosphere; in a large one the administrator has need of properly constituted channels of communication. This, however, is merely one side of the problem. The administrative leader who does not recognize that his most promising ideas spring as bright particles in the minds of a hundred colleagues is already doomed to sterility. It is only by making full use of the ideas and experience of all who are in direct contact with the day-to-day activities of the organization that the most efficient administration can be achieved, and this depends upon the existence of a communications system on the lines of Whitleyism in the British Civil Service.

### RECENT TRENDS

Much more attention is now being given by the staff to the improvement of efficiency, due partly no doubt to the recent upsurge of interest in management inside the Service and partly to an increasing realization that even in so-called non-productive spheres improved remuneration[1] must depend largely upon increased productivity. The assessment of administrative efficiency may well be difficult but it is a problem that has to be tackled. Here again the 'fair comparisons' principle, despite—or perhaps because of—its empirical approach has had a positive impact upon Civil Service thinking.

As in so many other matters which have been touched upon in this book, there is in fact little that is new in this interest in efficiency methods, except perhaps in its widening basis of recognition.

[1] It should be understood that this term is not taken to include pay increases designed to offset the erosion of the value of the money paid, which is a continuing accompaniment of inflation.

In particular, suggestions by members of the staff to improve their work have always been welcomed by enlightened seniors, and it has long been standard practice for officials with bright ideas to minute them in writing and pass them up the line to the head of the office for consideration. Often, it is to be feared, good ideas emerging through such processes have been pigeon-holed by supervisors who could not be bothered or who, selfishly, disliked any credit of this sort going to a junior, while others, with greater vision but even less integrity may have sought ways of taking the credit for themselves! As a by-product, formal suggestion schemes had the advantage of eliminating some of the normal outcomes of weak human nature.

Even when the staff associations were still too immature to bother themselves about such matters and before the advent of Whitleyism, the Post Office, which after all could be considered a productive Department, had introduced a formalized suggestions scheme for its numerous manipulative staffs, to whom modest monetary awards were made for meritorious proposals. Before 1939 that Department's clerical staffs had already been brought into this scheme and other Departments, under Whitley aegis, had introduced schemes of their own which were widely available to their staffs. For example, excellent schemes had been introduced by the Departmental Whitley Councils of the Customs & Excise and the Inland Revenue Departments.[1]

Since 1945 there have been many further developments of this sort and the Treasury itself has become sufficiently convinced of the value of formal suggestions schemes to underwrite the payment of more generous awards if Departments choose to embody such in the arrangements. The scheme introduced by the forerunner of the Ministry of Social Security is of particular interest in this connexion. Organized under close Whitley supervision, it is open to all members of the staff, is not restricted to matters of purely technical substance and detail (although obviously it is here that there is most scope for the deployment of the staffs' peculiar experience and skills) and its awards are not purely nominal, as was the case of earlier schemes. As much as £100 has been awarded for a suggestion of originality and merit, while annual payments have totalled over £1,000.[2] A note of an award is made on the official's personal file.

An interesting development of the Whitley idea took place in the

---

[1] See E. N. Gladden *Civil Service Staff Relationships* (1943) pp. 124/7.

[2] During the period from the scheme's inception in November, 1948 to December, 1964 a total of 1651 awards had been made, totalling to date £6,353 10s.—(*M.P.N.I. Report for 1964* (1965), p. 62).

Post Office towards the end of 1949, when it was decided to set up the Post Office Joint Production Council, consisting of members from the Headquarters Administration, the Regional Directors, and representatives of the staff associations, and supported throughout the Department by a series of Joint Production Committees, similarly based at the local level Joint Production Committees have the same membership as local Whitley Committees though they work quite separately. The aim of this new machinery was to discuss and approve means of increasing productivity in the Post Office. Contrasting the two types of joint consultation it can be said that, whereas the approach of the two sides of the ordinary Whitley bodies is in the main an endeavour to reconcile what may be opposed points of view, the Production Committee members work as individuals, without 'sides'.

In practice this machinery is used to consider staff suggestions and to encourage efficiency through local discussion and publicity on problems of service, inefficiency and waste.

To deal with the many problems, which are generally of a specialized nature, four Panels were introduced to advise the Council on suggestions falling within their respective provinces: namely, a Postal Panel, a Telecommunications Panel, a Clerical Panel and an Internal Relations Panel. The latter specializes in matters of internal publicity, which is an important factor in any productivity campaign.

In an interim assessment in 1958 the Production Committee itself observed:

The direct savings achieved so far have not been spectacular, but the care and thought devoted by individual members of the staff to produce 30,000 suggestions, and the further interest stimulated by consideration of these suggestions, while they cannot be measured, are of the greatest value. The regular meeting together, at offices throughout the country, of representatives of local management and staff as one team, intent on exploring ways and means of improving efficiency, is creating a much closer spirit of co-operation, greater pride in craft at all levels, and a keener interest in, and a greater acceptance of, responsibility for the efficiency of the service. These factors give the true measure of the success of Joint Production in the British Post Office today and of its promise for the future.[1]

This experiment has been confined to the Post Office, which has a special status and different technical needs from the normal run

[1] Extract from an article contributed by the Post Office's Joint Production Committee to an American journal. By the beginning of 1966 the number of suggestions was approaching the 59,000 mark.

of Departments, but the problem of achieving maximum efficiency in administration is a perennial topic of discussion. More recently, arising largely from increased interest in Civil Service management, which has already been mentioned,[1] the matter has again come to the fore in Whitley spheres. As a result of the new national incomes and prices policy, worked out in consultation between Government, management and the trade unions and embodied towards the end of 1964 in a *Joint Statement of Intent on Productivity, Prices and Incomes,* the general theme was taken up inside the Civil Service between the Treasury and the Departments. Special Efficiency Committees have been set up both by the National and the Departmental Whitley Councils, by whom the matter is now under active consideration.

[1] See page 95 above.

# CHAPTER VIII

## CIVIL SERVICE MORALE AND OBLIGATIONS

In Chapter I emphasis was placed upon civil service as the manifestation of a special type, an *esprit de corps* and a sense of self-dedication of the official to the service of the common weal. Civil service in this sense has been an essential balancing factor in a developing democracy, which as a form of government has throughout history demonstrated an ingrained tendency to become distorted and corrupt. The need in the circumstances for such a balancing factor in the shape of the professional administrative corps of the modern state is universally accepted if not so widely achieved. This accounts to some extent for the worldwide interest that has been taken in the British Civil Service and its methods.

As a matter of fact, although democracy needs the impartial conduct of a civil service in the management of its administrative business, its inherent principles do not necessarily lead in this direction. The outstanding modern example of a civil service born and bred in the atmosphere of democracy, that of the United States of America, demonstrates clearly the dangers of pressing democratic principles in spheres in which they are not necessarily applicable. The practice of rotation in office, which assumed that every citizen was capable of conducting every citizen's business, and the spoils system which gained such an impetus from this practice were logically based on Jefferson's democratic principles and have persisted to the present day despite the successful attritions of many reformers who have recognized that however good democracy may be in the political sphere it is less appropriate where the techniques of administration reign. Other modern civil services have grown out of aristocratic institutions with much more efficient results. In France, for example, the traditions of the Civil Service go back to the *ancien régime,* as remodelled by the Napoleonic drive for administrative efficiency: in Germany the Civil Service, even under the degenerate regime of a Hitler, was still inspired by the ideals of the state services of seventeenth and eighteenth century Prussia.

Even in Britain it was the example of the aristocracy, which had so long been habituated to conducting the administration of the country through the unpaid appointments of Justices of the Peace, that triumphed, first by substituting a non-patronage service for the exploitative bureaucracy of the East India Company, last by transmuting the patronage system of the central government in Britain into an intellectual *élite* inspired by the classical philosophies of Plato and Aristotle. As Gladstone had foreseen when controverting the foolish prognostications of the anti-reformers in 1854,[1] under the new open competition system the rag-tag and bobtail of the patronage-mongers were to be replaced by the highly educated sons of the upper and middle classes.

In the early days of open competition, when entry to the Civil Service was for the first time freely open to all, it was in fact only the sons of those who could afford to pay for an education at Oxford or Cambridge who could hope to enter the top class of the Civil Service. It was this leadership group, who came to occupy most of the leading posts in the Departments, that set the high standards of conduct and determined the particular morale of the Victorian Civil Service. They were of the same breed as the temporary politicians whom they served. They thought in the terms of the public schools where most of them had studied: they lived the same sort of lives and knew the same people. Their standards of conduct were determined by the Royal Court and the aristocracy, whose very obedient servants they were.

These new officials did not enter the Civil Service for gain. Even the poorer sons of the aristocracy who chose the Civil Service as a career, chose it with their eyes open. Scales of pay were better then than they are now, but they were never lavish and under the new system there were to be no perquisites. These civil servants were, and indeed their successors continue to be, dedicated men who preferred the service of their Sovereign and country to the struggle for money and power that went on mightily around them in the hey-day of Victorian capitalism.

This new leadership group, based upon an intellectual superiority proved both in the halls of the ancient universities and in the examination room at Burlington Gardens, set the example of high devotion, impartial achievement and great integrity for which the British Civil Service is still esteemed. The other classes, the Second Division and the rest, accepted their pre-eminence without question and followed their example. The educational gulfs between the classes were wide enough to prevent any challenge of the Administrative Class's superiority coming from below. But the conditions of service offered by the State, if not lavish were sufficient to distinguish the Civil Service career at most stages and to place it in a category of its own. Public esteem did the rest.

[1] Letter to Lord John Russell, January 20th, 1854. Quoted in John Morley's *Life of Gladstone* (1903), Vol. I, p. 649.

M

Of course the situation was not static. The great drive towards universal education that characterized the half century following the Civil Service reform of 1870, changed the relative position of the classes. Natural brain-power allowed youths of the lower middle and working classes gradually to climb the educational ladder, but these elements were well assimilated by the time they sat their examination—otherwise they were not likely to have chosen this particular career. The politicians too changed even more rapidly under the impact of an expanding democracy to which the aristocratic British Constitution adapted itself with remarkable success. Different types began to sit in the ministerial chairs in Whitehall. The men changed, the system changed; but the spirit of service continued and was even strengthened. This has been the real miracle of British government during the hundred years following the Trevelyan-Northcote reforms, which we may without exaggeration term the Civil Service Century.

### RULES OF CONDUCT

The special nature of official employment imposes certain duties on the civil servant, whose conditions of service therefore include important obligations, apart from the advantages and disadvantages discussed in Chapter III. It is a matter of grave concern to the community that its public servants should maintain high personal standards of conduct and carry out their official duties with high integrity. This is not the situation in some countries, where holders of public office are not prevented from taking advantage of their official positions to offset inadequate remuneration from public funds: nor was it always the case in this country before the patronage system was brought to an end. The morale of a public service, it need hardly be emphasized, depends upon other things besides monetary rewards and the perquisites of office. A minor official on a comparatively low salary, such as a postal or Customs official, may often be exposed to considerable temptation when carrying out his ordinary duties and it is necessary that the discouragement to submission to such a temptation should be sterner in his case than in that of the ordinary citizen who succumbs to a similar fault. This is the reason why legal penalties imposed for minor defalcations in which petty officials are implicated often appear to be out of all proportion to the misdemeanour committed, particularly as they may involve also the loss of all earned pension rights.

In fact official morale depends to no small extent upon the general standards of the community in which the particular service operates, for it is clear that even if we have a right to expect the official to set an example, it would be unrealistic to insist that the gap between the two spheres should be a wide one.

Much depends no doubt on the degree of enthusiasm with which the civil servant approaches his work. A person who devotes himself to the service of the State knows that he is inevitably sacrificing certain marginal opportunities. He will not grow rich and, even if the risk of utter poverty is absent, to sacrifice such a chance of wealth has a discouraging effect upon the spirit of the energetic person. To be really efficient the public official must, therefore, believe in his life's work with almost religious devotion. But if this high endeavour necessarily springs within the soul it can be maintained and matured, except in the heart of the exceptional individual, only by a system that proffers justice to its servants. Hence the need for the good conditions of service that have already been discussed in this book.

Public criticism has it contribution to make in the building of this high morale in the Civil Service. For even the official who is inspired by the ideal of service will soon lose his enthusiasm if he feels that this contribution is consistently depreciated by those whom he serves. Reasonable criticism will help to keep the ordinary official up to the mark. Constant vigilance on the part of the public is the only safeguard against the growth of bureaucracy. On the other hand a tendency to make the Service a scapegoat for everything that goes amiss and to hold up the official as an inferior sort of human being will gradually undermine the highest morale, rendering the average official despondent and apathetic in the performance of his daily tasks.

It is by no means certain that ill-informed and unfair criticism in the press in Britain has not had some influence in this direction. In a democracy some of this criticism is understandable, even when it includes an element of irresponsibility. There may be political reasons for attributing to a civil servant's incompetence the failure of some particular policy, and in every community there are individuals who through enviousness or other undesirable motives will join in the hunt for an official scapegoat, but there can be little doubt that the main cause is ignorance. The public are woefully ignorant of the working of public offices and of the many intricate problems of public administration. To remove some of this ignorance is not the least of the useful functions that the public relations officers of the Departments are called upon to perform. But a much more energetic offensive against this particular form of ignorance needs to be underaken and on a much wider front.

The British Civil Service recognizes the need to maintain specially high standards of personal conduct. There are few specific vetos—and these will be discussed in the following sections—but the civil servant is expected to conduct his private affairs in such a way as to avoid bringing discredit upon the Service. Normally there is no official inquisition into a civil servant's private life, which is not the concern of his Department. His personal activities—for example, with regard to matrimonial difficulties—will be considered only so far as they may affect the efficient performance of his official duties and this will to a large extent depend upon the type and responsibility of the work that he performs. The more flexible attitudes of society in such matters since the war have had their effect inside the Service.

In one direction, however, official rules are stringent. Any personal applications made by a civil servant on matters affecting his salary and conditions of service must be made to the head of his Department.[1] Any attempt to manipulate outside influences—for example, through Parliament—to obtain preferment within the Service, and this applies particularly to advancement by promotion, will be met by official disfavour and thus defeat the object in view.

### USE OF OFFICIAL INFORMATION

The public official often has access to secret information: even subordinate officials become aware of information whose communication outside official circles might prove detrimental to public policy, and there are occasions when an official by using information obtained in the course of his normal duties could gain advantages that might well be substantial. It is obvious, therefore, that the civil servant, in so far as he is aware of facts that if published might affect public policy, is under a special obligation to use official information with the utmost discretion. He is subject in this matter to the Official Secrets Acts, to special Departmental pronouncements and to a code of conduct that is generally recognized as correct Civil Service practice.

The Official Secrets Acts of 1911[2] and 1920 impose special penalties for the disclosure of official information. Their operation is not, of course, confined to members of the Civil Service nor is it restricted to secret information.

The Acts make it an offence for an official to disclose, without

[1] The normal procedure is to make such applications collectively through the appropriate staff association, but the individual civil servant's right to make personal application by memorial though rarely used nowadays has not been rescinded.

[2] The former replaced the original Act of 1889.

permission, to an unauthorized person any information acquired in the course of his official duties, unless it has already been made public. This covers materials published in any way; in the press, in printed form, in lectures, or in radio and television broadcasts, and so on. The veto covers non-secret as well as secret information and continues after the official has left the Service or retired.

These statutes are wide in scope, covering at once activities that are highly treasonable and disclosures that might be considered little more than indiscreet, but they are not a complete guide to a civil servant's conduct in such matters. Communication of information to the Press, for example, may be covered by departmental rules under which an official is forbidden to make an official communication to the newspapers except under proper authority, and prohibited from corresponding with them in his personal capacity on any official subject.

The publication by civil servants of articles and books that have a bearing upon official matters is not, however, forbidden providing the Official Secrets Acts are not contravened. It is not the object of the rules to prevent the reasonable dissemination of information or to discourage the scientific approach of officials to matters of professional interest. Permission to publish must be sought from the Departments concerned or from H.M. Treasury. If the information contained in the work comes primarily from official sources and it is considered that copies would be of value to the Administration the right is reserved of placing publication in the hands of the Stationery Office or alternatively, where the author is allowed to retain responsibility for publication, to ensure that copies are available for official use at an agreed price. There is no evidence that these rules are ungenerously administered. If, therefore, the Civil Service as a profession is disinclined to discuss in print the problems of its operation the cause must be sought elsewhere than in rules by which matters of official secrecy are rightly hedged.

Long before the Official Secrets Acts the doctrine of the inherent secrecy of Cabinet business, reinforced by the development of the principle of collective responsibility, had become established, thus placing a special responsibility upon civil servants to ensure such secrecy. Without the Queen's consent such documentation, however unimportant, could not be made available to the public for a period of fifty years. This 'fifty year' rule, comparing unfavourably with the practices of some administrations abroad, was much resented by scholars and others concerned with research into and the writing of recent history, but the position has been changed by the Prime Minister's statement in the House of Commons on 9th March, 1966, that the rule would be altered to reduce the period of veto to thirty years, which should be much more widely acceptable. This could affect civil servants by inclining them to be more reticent in their written comments and recommendations, in the knowledge that their views will be open to public comment within the span of their own official 'lifetime'. They are of course concerned also as guardians of the public records which is an important responsibility, even if until recently Ministers were in the habit of claiming confidential documents relating to their own Departments as personal property, no doubt mainly to protect themselves from their successors!

Civil servants are under special obligations with regard to the patenting of inventions made by them in the course of their official work. It is left to their Departments to decide whether the inventor should be allowed controlling rights or required to assign all rights in the invention to the Crown, possibly reserving to himself a share in any commercial proceeds. He may apply to a Departmental Awards Committee for an award, with the right of appeal to the Central Committee of Awards, which consists of nominees of those Departments that are most concerned with inventions, under the presidency of a high legal authority. Much will depend upon the nature of the invention and the circumstances in which it has emerged. It may be a by-product of the official's activities or of little official value, in either of which cases few difficulties will arise in the assignment of the patent to the official. On the other hand many inventions are the result of team work. Specific assignment is difficult and if the work is carried out by officials specially devoted to experiment and research—an expanding category—there will normally be no claim to patent rights, although the latter may be considered in cases of exceptional brilliance and utility.

There are, no doubt, many circumstances in which a civil servant could use official information to his own advantage, for example, by anticipating the results of official action that may be contemplated, such as the imposition or raising of controls and changes in the tax schedule proposed in the Budget or estimating the effect of official policy on foreign exchange rates. A case of the latter type, which had received a good deal of publicity in the press and the courts, was investigated by a Board of Enquiry set up by the Prime Minister, Mr. Stanley Baldwin, on February 1st, 1928. The closing paragraphs of the Report[1] are so illuminating that they are printed as an Appendix to the present chapter. It had been alleged in the course of the case of *Ironmonger and Company v. Dyne,* heard in the Kings Bench Division of the High Court, that three officials of the Foreign Office had been using their official

[1] Cmd. 3037. February 1928. See Appendix, pp. 167/9.

knowledge in speculative transactions in foreign currency for the purpose of private profit. While concluding, after examining all the
available evidence, that neither of the officers concerned had used, or
endeavoured to use, any official information for the purpose of their
transactions, the Board of Enquiry were justly critical of the activities of the officers concerned, which were of a gambling nature and
inconsistent with their obligations as civil servants. This case clearly
illustrates how necessary it is that civil servants should not merely
avoid breaking the law or contravening the rules of their department, but should also refrain from conduct that merely raises
suspicions incompatible with their official positions. This is indeed
a high standard in an erring world!

During the period shortly following the Second World War, when
the central administration was expanding rapidly and it had become even more difficult than usual for members of the public to
understand the workings of the Departments, there was a good
deal of public discussion of the emergence of a new type of agent
or 'contact' man, who was specially skilled in bringing interested
members of the public into touch with the official most likely to be
in a position to deal expeditiously with applications for licences and
suchlike matters. Bribery and corruption were rather more than
hinted at. A tribunal under the chairmanship of Sir George Justin
Lynskey, a judge of the High Court of Justice, was therefore
appointed by the Home Secretary to enquire whether there was any
justification for allegations that payments, rewards or other considerations had been 'sought, offered, promised, made or received
by, or to Ministers of the Crown or other public servants in connection with licences or permissions required under any enactment,
regulation or order or in connection with the withdrawal of any
prosecution and, if so, in what circumstances the transaction took
place, and what persons were involved therein'.

In its Report[1] the Tribunal, although critical of the attitude of
certain political officials, completely exonerated the civil servants
whose activities they had been called upon to investigate. Once
again the high reputation of the Civil Service had been completely
upheld. The Lynskey Report, however, deserves study, since
it shows how easily powerful temptations may assail the public
official who comes late into the official sphere, after experiencing an
easier code outside, and how thinly drawn in modern society may
be the dividing line between the path of official rectitude and the
incline to venality.

[1] Cmd. 7616 (1949).

## PARTICIPATION IN NON-OFFICIAL BUSINESS

Restriction of the civil servant's participation in outside activities is not completely determined by rules guiding his use of official knowledge. Speculation in foreign currency, as in the case just mentioned, may be unwise in any circumstance, yet only culpable if the official is working in a Department in which he has access to useful official information. Nevertheless, the civil servant's outside business activities are subject to certain definite rules. Generally he can engage in lawful business providing his personal attendance is not required by it during official hours. This is laid down as a minimum for universal application which Departments may supplement to meet any special circumstances attaching to their own activities. The rule[1] reads:

(i) No officer may at any time engage in any activity which would in any way tend to impair his usefulness as a public servant.

(ii) No officer may engage in any occupation or undertaking which might in any way conflict with the interest of his Department or be inconsistent with his position as a public servant.

(iii) It is the duty of any officer, who may have any doubt as to the propriety of undertaking any particular work, to consult the Head of his Department, or the Establishment Officer.

Outside business activities may give a civil servant an interest in contracts with Government Departments. Such participation is stringently regulated and an official is bound to disclose fully any interest of this type to the Head of his Department, who has discretion to permit the transaction. In this case steps will be taken to ensure that the officer concerned does not participate in the transaction on the Department's behalf. Failing such authority no government contract may be let to an officer of the contracting Department or to a partnership or company of which an officer of such a Department is a partner or director.

One of the circumstances considered likely to impair the efficiency of a public servant is serious pecuniary embarrassment. There are long-standing rules dealing with the bankruptcy and insolvency of civil servants. A civil servant becoming bankrupt or insolvent must report the fact immediately, on pain of dismissal, to the Permanent Head of his Department, to whom he is called upon to submit with the least possible delay a full statement of the position. The Head has discretion to decide whether disciplinary action is called for, dismissal being the penalty in cases of dishonesty or

---

[1] Quoted from Order in Council of January 10th, 1910, Clause 17.

discreditable transactions. In the meantime, unless there is evidence of the latter, the officer concerned is allowed to continue in his post providing that his duties do not involve the handling of public moneys.

There are numerous rules in the Departments with regard to borrowing, gambling or resort to a moneylender. All are designed to maintain the integrity of the public service and are important, since financial difficulties can lead to other unsatisfactory situations. For example, a senior officer borrowing from a subordinate could place himself in the position of being pressed to grant favours in other ways in order to liquidate his obligation.

There can be no doubt that the general standards of the Civil Service in this connection are very high. The rules are strict, as indeed they should be, and strictly administered in the public interest, but there is humanity in their application, every case being treated on its merits. In at least one large Department, which handles considerable sums of public money, the Departmental Whitley Council has operated a scheme to aid, with tact and in confidence, officers who find themselves, not dishonestly, in financial difficulties. Under the scheme a staff committee administers the official's salary while the debt is being liquidated. Nor are the departmental regulations dealing with this subject always devoid of humour as the following quotation shows:

'Finally, I would like to advise members of the staff on the actual experience of the cases that have come before me that resort to a moneylender is fatal. However bad an officer's financial position be it cannot but be made worse by resort to a moneylender. There are bad moneylenders and very bad ones. *There are no good ones,* and those who write the nicest letters and have the kindest faces are the worst.'

There is one problem that has a close bearing on this and the previous section, namely, the acceptance by the civil servant of outside appointments. The services of a public official may, by virtue of his inside knowledge and official contacts, be of special value to a business concern, which may make it worth his while to transfer his services to the new field of activities and, in view of the gap between the salaries of highly placed individuals in the official and non-official spheres, it is not difficult for the business concern to make a very favourable offer to the official whose services they want. There is, of course, nothing to prevent a civil servant resigning his post and taking up an outside appointment, although usually he will think twice of relinquishing his pension rights unless adequate compensation is offered. Many, however, do so every year. It is, nevertheless, a grave fault for a high official to seek to use his official position to obtain preferment outside the Civil Service and any such action may lead to dismissal.[1] The question of imposing some restrictions on the civil servant who wishes to transfer his activities to another sphere has often been raised.[2] It is difficult to solve this problem without doing injustice to the individual and possibly the only effective way is to ensure that the counter-attractiveness of outside service is not too pronounced. For officers holding high rank in the Civil Service and the Armed Services the Government has imposed a two-year embargo following retirement upon the taking up of appointments in firms concerned with government loans, subsidies or contracts, or in which the Government is closely interested in any way financially.

Since the war the position has been considerably eased by permitting civil servants to transfer to posts in the public corporations, academic institutions and international agencies, without sacrificing their pension rights.

## RESTRICTIONS UPON CITIZENSHIP

The civil servant, who is in many ways by the very nature of his duties made more than usually conscious of his citizenship, is bound by his official obligations to be something less than a citizen. As an individual he has a right to his own political views, and in his private capacity he can support his own party and vote for the candidate of his choice. Publicly there are restrictions upon the degree of his participation in political affairs.

In this country policy is determined by the political parties and imposed by the Ministers of the Crown, both corporately and individually. The civil servant acts in a professional capacity and the less he airs his personal views the better. There has been some falling away from this ideal of recent years especially among the lower grades of the Service, whose political activities as trade unionists cannot with confidence be said always to have advanced their own professional interests. It has to be admitted, however, that political participation is much less important in the lower reaches; although, with the expanding participation of the State in social fields, even the most junior officers may become involved in matters that have important political implications. It is impossible, for example, for a junior clerk in an employment exchange to handle the registration of an unemployed person without being

[1] See *Report of Board of Enquiry* (1936), Cmd. 5254 and *Minute of the Prime Minister* (1936), Cmd. 5255.

[2] See, for example, *Statement relating to Report of the Royal Commission on the Private Manufacture of and Trading in Arms*, 1935–6, Cmd. 5451, para. 15.

brought into contact with situations in which the political aspects of public policy may be criticized or appraised. He must always be on his guard against incurring the charge of partisanship and, even when his sympathies are involved, he must not forget that there are other aspects to the question which the next Parliament may call upon him officially to implement.

Nevertheless, with the rapid growth in the size of the Civil Service it has come to be recognized that there are grave disadvantages in excluding such a large body of citizens from the full rights of citizenship and that the rules appropriate to a compact leadership group may no longer be suitable to a much larger group. From August 1925 the industrial staffs under the Defence Departments had been exempted from the general embargo upon Parliamentary candidature. In response to pressure from the staffs to extend the area of exception the Chancellor of the Exchequer, Sir Stafford Cripps, set up in April 1948 a special committee under the chairmanship of Mr. J. C. Masterman to inquire into the wider problem of political participation. The Masterman Report of June 1949[1] was received with great disappointment by the Civil Service. It proposed the extension of the area of exemption to all industrial and minor and manipulative grades, but refused to include any of the clerical grades. In some directions it even recommended a tightening up of existing practices. Under the new arrangements, in order to comply with the provisions of the Succession to the Crown Act, 1707,[2] all civil servants would have to resign before nomination day, but members of the exempted grades who were not elected would be reinstated on application within a week of declaration day. Reinstatement after ceasing to be a Member of Parliament would be granted subject to certain conditions.

The Government accepted the principles set out in the Masterman Report but, after protracted discussions with the staff representatives, the proposal that the Civil Service should be divided horizontally in two groups, a politically free and an excluded group, was modified by the introduction of an intermediate group with restricted rights.[3] Political activities in the national sphere are defined as (i) adoption as a Parliamentary candidate, (ii) holding in party political organizations offices impinging wholly or mainly on party politics in the national field, (iii) speaking in public on matters of national political controversy, (iv) expressing views on such matters in letters to the press, books, articles and leaflets, and (v) canvassing on behalf of parliamentary candidates. A similar list

---

[1] *Report of the Committee on the Political Activities of Civil Servants,* Cmd. 7718 (1949).
[2] Now House of Commons Disqualification Act, 1957.
[3] Cmd. 8783.

covers local political activities. The politically free group comprises broadly all industrial civil servants and the non-industrial staffs in the minor and manipulative grades as proposed by the Masterman Committee. These may participate in any of the activities listed. The intermediate group covers broadly the typing and clerical grades and those of equivalent status, manipulative supervisory grades and other senior grades of equivalent status who are not actually members of the Executive class. Subject to receiving the Department's permission, which will depend largely upon the extent to which their personal duties are compatible with such activities, these officers may be allowed to participate in any of the activities listed except adoption as Parliamentary candidate. The politically restricted group, which can participate in none of these activities at the national level, includes the Administrative, Executive, Professional and all other senior classes not definitely included in one of the other groups. Permission may still be granted by Departments to members of this group to participate in local political activities depending upon the Department's particular responsibilities in the localities. Their position has not therefore been modified by the new rules.

## SECURITY ARRANGEMENTS

It is a matter of great importance as well as of considerable interest that the high standards of morale and public service, for which the Civil Service in Britain is universally recognized, were built up during the period following the introduction of open competition in 1870. At a time when the general philosophy of the nation endorsed with enthusiasm the principles of the open market and the doctrine that the devil was welcome to the hindmost, a special enclave was being created in the employment field, within which the public official was exhorted to place the public weal before his own personal advantage. The Civil Service existed as a neutral non-competitive group within the capitalist system and as such undoubtedly had a steadying influence upon the rest of the national economy.

There were, of course, a number of factors conspiring to produce this situation and the nation had reason to be pleased that this was so. Revulsion from the inefficiences of patronage was the impetus, but there can be no doubt that the *noblesse oblige* of an aristocratic ruling class had an imponderable influence upon the new official corps. As the educational system expanded, widening year by year the basis of the leadership group, the time-honoured principles of public service were inculcated in the souls of those who chose public administration as their life's work. If they held other views they were unlikely to seek within the Government Departments life's unrestricted excitements. It speaks volumes that the prestige of State service should have continued to attract in abundant measure sufficient talents to cope with the increasing complexities of the work. The general rule that the civil servant should be politically neutral in approaching his work served to reinforce the solidarity of the Civil Service.

We have already mentioned in Chapter III the effect of the recent economic and social changes on the position of the Civil Service in the community: the changing attitude of the official to politics is likely to have equally radical repercussions. In a democratic world the State should have no concern with its servant's political views. The public official who, on entering his profession, signs away his personal right to disagree with the political views of the regime has already become a slave. An expanding bureaucracy is then synonymous with a slave state. Yet with the advent of totalitarianism in politics the strain on the allegiance of some officials becomes too great and the temptation of the State as employer to examine the political credentials of its servants becomes stronger and stronger. A stage may be reached when it feels that it can no longer afford to regard with impartiality the views of those who do not accept the principles upon which its whole existence rests. In the last resort the Democratic State is no more bound to accept the service of those who publicly proclaim that they will not on the 'appointed day' honour their bond, than to accept the allegiance of the criminal who rejects the moral law of the community.

It is, nevertheless, a matter for regret if the State is called upon to face the problem of the servant who does not accept the assumptions upon which it works. Witch hunting is never a happy pastime for the democrat and in an atmosphere of suspicion intolerance is liable to expand until justice becomes a farce. Victimization thrives wherever totalitarian philosophies have currency.

Even before the Second World War, when totalitarianisms of the Right were in the ascendant, the political integrity of the Civil Service was considered by some to be threatened and accusations of victimization were made. There were cases where sympathizers of Fascism were alleged to be under observation and although the Government denied that it had any concern with the political views of its servants, it is difficult in such a situation for it so to control its subordinate authorities that undue precautions are not taken. The spirit of the times, fear-ridden with incalculable consequences, favours the suppression of the unorthodox.[1]

[1] As for example in the case of Major Vernon in the Air Ministry; see *The Strange Case of Major Vernon* (National Council of Civil Liberties).

Since the war the Government has discarded its attitude of non-concern. Events in the wider world have had no little influence in bringing this about. Thus in his statement to the House of Commons on March 15th, 1948, the Prime Minister, Mr. Clement (now Earl) Attlee, stated categorically:

'Experience, both in this country and elsewhere, has shown that membership of, and other forms of continuing association with, the Communist Party, may involve the acceptance by the individual of a loyalty which in certain circumstances can be inimical to the State. It is not suggested that in matters affecting the security of the State all those who adhere to the Communist Party would allow themselves thus to forget their primary loyalty to the State. But there is no way of distinguishing such people from those who, if opportunity offered, would be prepared to endanger the security of the State in the interests of another power. The Government has, therefore, reached the conclusion that the only prudent course to adopt is to ensure that no one who is known to be a member of the Communist Party, or to be associated with it in such a way as to raise legitimate doubts about his or her reliability, is employed in connection with work, the nature of which is vital to the security of the State.

'The same rule will govern the employment of those who are known to be actively associated with Fascist organizations.

'I should emphasize that this action is being taken solely on security grounds. The State is not concerned with the political views, as such, of its servants, and as far as possible alternative employment on the wide range of non-secret Government work will be found for those who are deemed for the reason indicated to be unsuitable for secret work. It may, however, happen that it is impossible to find suitable employment elsewhere in the Civil Service for individuals with specialist qualifications and in such cases there may be no alternative to refusal of employment or dismissal.'

It was made clear that the decision in such cases would not rest with the security services, whose function was only to provide information. In accordance with constitutional practice the final decision was left with the Minister, but an Advisory Body of three eminent retired civil servants (who came to be known as the Three Advisers) was appointed to examine on appeal the evidence in all cases where the Minister decided that a *prima facie* case had been made and the person charged disputes the charge. In the meantime the officer concerned was to be suspended and placed on leave with pay while the case was under consideration.

It was not completely clear, in view of the constitutional position of the civil servant within the Service, why this new procedure and machinery were really necessary. The Minister is finally responsible for the officials within his own Department. Except in the case of specialists for whom there were no alternative posts available, normal staff control should have prevented unsuitable persons from holding specific posts or made it possible to change them, without challenge, as soon as it was discovered that they were not suitable. Such changes, whatever the position of the officer, would in normal course be little more than of a routine nature. The explanation presumably is that an unhealthy situation had already developed in certain reaches of the Service and that the integrity of the Civil Service was being threatened by the attitudes of certain individuals whose hearts were less concerned with the practice of public administration than with the building of some New Jerusalem that they conceived it to be their business to impose upon their less enlightened brethren. It may be concluded that authoritative action by the Government was necessitated by the fact that the political heads were not equally enthusiastic to preserve the political neutrality of the Civil Service and also that some such publicity was needed to make the Service as well as the community alive to the seriousness of this development. Otherwise there appears to have been little in the situation that could not have been dealt with in the course of ordinary Civil Service management. One consequence of all this is that the Civil Service Commission bring to the notice of all candidates the regulations relating to the exclusion of members of Communist and Fascist organizations from certain security posts. Such exclusion is not of course within the jurisdiction of the Commissioners but will be provided for by the individual Departments to which candidates are assigned.

It is hardly surprising that the staff associations have viewed these innovations with concern and have done everything possible to safeguard the interests of their members. A number of individual cases were reported in the Press and some comparatively obscure civil servants obtained a notoriety that they would not otherwise have earned.

In a sense these developments were little more than the curtain raiser to the disclosure of a much more serious state of affairs, through a series of espionage cases in which civil servants were involved. The first of these was the Maclean–Burgess affair of 1951,[1] when two Foreign Office officials disappeared behind the Iron Curtain in suspicious circumstances, later to become self-declared traitors. As a consequence the Government on November

[1] *Report concerning the disappearance of two former Foreign Office Officials* (Cmd. 9477), 1955.

23rd, 1955, set up a Conference of seven Privy Councillors[1] 'to examine the security procedures now applied in the public services and to consider whether any further precautions are called for and should be taken'.

While concluding that there is nothing organically wrong with the Government's security arrangements, the Conference, in a Report to the Government early in 1956[2], state that 'the chief risks are presented by Communists and by other persons who for one reason or another are subject to Communist influence', and that one of the main problems today is 'to identify the members of the British Communist Party, to be informed of its activities and to identify that wider body of those who are both sympathetic to Communism, or susceptible to Communist pressure and present a danger to security.' They go on to state that while the problem is a general one it is recognized as of special importance in certain areas of the public service, such as the Foreign Service, the Defence field and the Atomic Energy Organization.

'Character defects as factors tending to make a man unreliable or expose him to blackmail or influence by foreign agents' are of great importance and it is the duty of 'Departments to inform themselves of serious failings such as drunkenness, addiction to drugs, homosexuality or any loose living that may seriously affect a man's reliability'. Consequently the Conference state that it is not only the responsibility of the Heads of Departments, but of supervisory officers generally 'to know their staff' and not fail 'to report anything which affects security'.

'A serious character defect may appropriately be the determining factor in a decision to dismiss a particular individual or to transfer him to other work.' 'The fact that a public servant is a Communist not only bars his employment on secret duties, but may also in some departments have an unfavourable effect on his prospects of promotion.' The Conference go on to recommend that no individual should be employed on secret work who is living with a wife or husband who is a Communist or Communist sympathizer.

A significant pronouncement in the White Paper runs: 'The Conference is of opinion that in deciding these difficult and often borderline cases, it is right to continue the practice of tilting the balance in favour of offering greater protection to the security of the State rather than in the direction of safeguarding the rights of the

[1] These were the Lord President of the Council; the Lord Chancellor; the Secretary of State for the Home Department; Lord Jowitt; Members of Parliament for Lewisham, South, and Vauxhall; and the Permanent Secretary to H.M. Treasury.

[2] *Statement on the Findings of the Conference of Privy Councillors on Security* (Cmd. 9715), 1956.

individual.' Further, it may sometimes be necessary to decide against so employing a person 'because after the fullest investigation doubts about his reliability remain, even although nothing may have been proved against him on standards which would be accepted in a Court of Law'.

It can be assumed that such serious deviations from normal constitutional practice would not have been recommended without good cause. The proposals, nevertheless, have serious implications for the future of the Civil Service. It must be clear to all but the wilfully blind or the sentimentally doped that support for the policy and methods of the Communist Party is incompatible with membership of the British Civil Service. Yet it is equally certain that the change in attitudes implicit in the measures proposed to counter this threat is incompatible with the inherent spirit of civil service. This is of course a dilemma of our modern society which is not peculiar to the public service and glib answers on the basis of political theory or mere sentiment will not provide the certain solution for those who have to take responsibility for results.

The Conference recommended that the Tribunal of Three Advisers previously appointed should continue to hear appeals under the more stringent measures now proposed and that the whole matter should first be discussed with the representatives of the staffs concerned. This was done and, naturally, in the Civil Service press and elsewhere a good deal of concern was manifested at the further threat to the individual civil servant's liberty, however much the increased strictness might be deemed necessary. Criticism was concentrated upon the vague wording of the White Paper, which was but a summary of the Privy Councillors' findings. As a result greater precision was evident in the new security regulations which were issued by the Treasury during 1957.

Events were not to allow matters to rest here. Espionage was in the air. On 11th May 1961 the Government announced the appointment of an independent Committee under the chairmanship of Lord Radcliffe, whose terms of reference were:

'In the light of recent convictions for offences under the Official Secrets Acts, to review the security procedures and practices currently followed in the public service and to consider what, if any, changes are required.'[1]

A comprehensive survey was certainly undertaken by the Radcliffe Committee but again the text of the White Paper, issued in April, 1962, itself applying security consideration's to the Committee's investigations, provided only a summary of the proceedings.

---

[1] White Paper on *Security Procedures in the Public Service*, Cmnd. 1681 (1962).

N

Yet it presents a valuable general picture of the existing security organization and procedures of the Central Administration, with a good deal of detail on specific aspects not hitherto available elsewhere, and it is interspersed with the Committee's recommendations for improvement.

From our point of view the Committee's animadversions on the general tendency of civil servants not to take security matters seriously are of particular interest since in such situations the psychological reactions of officials is of primary importance. It could well be asked whether this particular viewpoint arises from a feeling on the part of the inside expert that the outside 'politician' (using the term in its widest sense) is inclined to overdo the security aspect and to over-emphasize the effect of espionage, serious as no doubt it can sometimes be. As a parallel the working official is vividly aware of the antics of the, not uncommon, cautious top-executive who marks all his files 'urgent' or 'confidential' and defeats his own objective by reducing all his activities to one dead level.

More serious altogether was the Committee's allegation that the staff associations had become assembly points of Communist sympathizers from both outside and inside the Civil Service. They stated:

'We enquired into the penetration of Communists of the Civil Service staff associations and trade unions and were disturbed at the number of Communists and Communist sympathizers who are holding positions in those bodies either as permanent full-time paid officials or as unpaid officers or members of executive committees. We undertand that there is no evidence that the Communists have made any exceptional effort to gain control of these unions, but they appear in fact to have achieved a higher degree of penetration here than in almost any other sector of the trade union movement. No evidence has been brought to our knowledge that Communist union officers, whether serving on a paid or unpaid basis, have been detected in any form of espionage. Nevertheless, we regard this presumably deliberate massing of Communist effort in the Civil Service unions as most dangerous to security, however one defines it.

'We suggest, therefore, that it would be reasonable to establish the right of any Department in respect of establishments or staff employed on secret work to deny access to or to refuse to negotiate (whether by correspondence or face to face) with a named trade union official whom it had reason to believe to be a Communist under the definition used in the purge procedure. We envisage that the Department would be required to challenge the union official formally, as in the purge procedure, and that he would have a right of appeal to the Three Advisers'.[1]

Before proceeding to tighten up internal security arrangements on the lines proposed, the Government, through the ordinary Whitley channels, discussed the findings of the Radcliffe Committee with the staff associations who were understandably concerned to protect the interests of their representatives and officials. In the process of revision which followed an interesting change in procedure was the arrangement whereby a civil servant whose case was considered by the Three Advisers should have the right to be accompanied by a 'friend', who might be an association official, while he was presenting his opening statement in reply to the allegation against him.

At this very time a particularly disturbing espionage case was being conducted in the Courts, which led to the conviction of an Admiralty clerk at the Naval Attaché's office in Moscow, and to the demand for an inquiry by resolution of both Houses of Parliament on 14th November 1962. While the detailed report[2] of the special Tribunal, set up under the chairmanship of Viscount Radcliffe, found little to criticise in the actions of the officials concerned in the case, it was again made abundantly evident that the procedures were still inadequate.

To improve current means of supervision of the Departments' security arrangements, early in 1964 the Government set up the Standing Security Commission under the chairmanship of a judge of the High Court 'to investigate and report upon the circumstances in which a breach of security is known to have occurred in the public service, and upon any related failure of departmental security arrangements or neglect of duty . . .' The Commission's first report in July 1965 followed the convictions of an official of the Ministry of Aviation and an N.C.O. attached to the Ministry of Defence (Army Department).[3]

After examining critically the actions of the two convicted men the Security Commission went on to comment upon the security arrangements in general and to make further recommendations. They felt in the main that the Radcliffe Committee's recommendations were being put into effect, but they considered that the importance of the security staffs were not being fully appreciated in all Departments. They emphasized the importance of instruction

---

[1] *Op cit* Paras. 33 and 34, p. 9.

[2] *Report of the Tribunal appointed to Inquire into the Vassall Case and Related Matters* (Cmnd. 2009) 1963.

[3] *Report of the Standing Security Commission. June, 1965,* Cmnd. 2722 (1965).

being provided in security responsibilities. In this connection it is interesting to note that the Central Office of Information had already produced a lively booklet entitled *Their Trade is Treachery*, as part of the educational campaign to improve the awareness of middle and lower grade officials and of members of the Armed Forces of their responsibilities in regard to security matters.

As a result of the Security Commission's Report it was considered necessary to set up a Board of Inquiry to examine the conduct of the four civil servants mentioned in the Report, two of them by name. The Staff Side of the Civil Service National Whitley Council had taken strong exception to the naming of officials in the Standing Security Commission's Report before they had had an opportunity to appeal and have their case examined by an appropriate body. The Report of the Board of Inquiry[1] vindicated the Staff Side's attitude. With certain practical modifications the Government have substantially accepted the Security Commission's proposals, and so the matter rests at the moment.

It is easy to overdramatize the position. In a world of emotional ideologies where the older patriotisms have not yet been replaced by a higher loyalty, security standards are bound to be weakened. The limelight recently played upon the Civil Service tends to emphasize its own high standards and its desire to preserve them and the high expectations of the public that this shall be so, rather than the actual falling away that has taken place of recent times. That this falling away from the old standards is an universal phenomenon, which some would interpret as good rather than bad, and not therefore peculiar to the Civil Service, where indeed the decline may well be less than elsewhere, does not preclude us from searching out causes that may be peculiar to the Civil Service. One wonders, for example, whether some of the persons implicated in these cases would ever have got into the Civil Service under pre-1939 recruitment conditions, or whether management skills are as good as they were. There seems to be among Civil Service supervisors today an inadequate awareness of what is going on inside the Service but outside the range of their own limited sphere of control. The problem of insufficient supervisory awareness needs further consideration. But in suggesting such possible shortcomings in the Civil Service it is necessary to remember that the task of control has been rendered difficult by the increasing complexities of official business. Better management and supervision are needed today to avoid a deterioration of previous standards.

[1] *Report of a Board of Inquiry appointed by the Prime Minister following the Report of the Security Commission on the Bossard and Allen Cases* Cmnd. 2773 (1965).

## APPENDIX TO CHAPTER VIII

*Extracts from Report of the Board of Enquiry[1] appointed by the Prime Minister to investigate certain Statements affecting Civil Servants. (Cmd. 3037, 1928.)*

54. We think in conclusion that we shall not be travelling outside our terms of reference if, as three Civil Servants of some experience and jealous for the honour and traditions of the Service, we indicate what we conceive to be the principles which should regulate the conduct of Civil Servants—whether engaged in Home Departments or in diplomatic missions—in their relation to the public.

55. His Majesty's Civil Service, unlike other great professions, is not and cannot in the nature of things be an autonomous profession. In common with the Royal Navy, the Army and the Royal Air Force, it must always be subject to the rules and regulations laid down for its guidance by His Majesty's Government. This written code is, in the case of the Civil Service, to be found not only in the Statutes but also in Orders in Council, Treasury Circulars and other directions which may from time to time be promulgated; but over and above these the Civil Service, like every other profession, has its unwritten code of ethics and conduct for which the most effective sanction lies in the public opinion of the Service itself, and it is upon the maintenance of a sound and healthy public opinion within the Service that its value and efficiency chiefly depend.

56. The first duty of a Civil Servant is to give his undivided allegiance to the State at all times and on all occasions when the State has a claim upon his services. With his private activities the State is in general not concerned, so long as his conduct therein is not such as to bring discredit upon the Service of which he is a member. But to say that he is not to subordinate his duty to his private interests, nor to make use of his official position to further those interests, is to say no more than that he must behave with common honesty. The Service exacts from itself a higher standard, because it recognizes that the State is entitled to demand that its servants shall not only be honest in fact, but beyond the reach of suspicion of dishonesty. It was laid down by one of His Majesty's Judges in a case some few years ago that it was not merely of some importance but of fundamental importance that in a Court of Law justice should not only be done but should manifestly and undoubtedly be seen to be done; which we take to mean that public confidence in the administration of justice would be shaken if the

[1] Consisting of Sir Warren Fisher, G.C.B., G.C.V.O., Sir Malcolm Ramsay, K.C.B. and Mr. M. L. Gwyer, C.B.

least suspicion, however ill-founded, were allowed to arise that the course of legal proceedings could in any way be influenced by improper motives. We apply without hesitation an analogous rule to other branches of the public service. A Civil Servant is not to subordinate his duty to his private interests; but neither is he to put himself in a position where his duty and his interests conflict. He is not to make use of his official position to further those interests; but neither is he so to order his private affairs as to allow the suspicion to arise that a trust has been abused or a confidence betrayed. These obligations are, we do not doubt, universally recognized throughout the whole of the Service; if it were otherwise, its public credit would be diminished and its usefulness to the State impaired.

57. It follows that there are spheres of activity legitimately open to the ordinary citizen in which the Civil Servant can play no part, or only a limited part. He is not to indulge in political or party controversy, lest by so doing he should appear no longer the disinterested adviser of Ministers or able impartially to execute their policy. He is bound to maintain a proper reticence in discussing public affairs and more particularly those with which his own Department is concerned. And lastly, his position clearly imposes upon him restrictions in matters of commerce and business from which the ordinary citizen is free.

58. Between the regular investment or management of a private fortune on the one hand, and speculative transactions in stocks, exchange or commodities on the other, there are obviously numerous gradations, and it may often be difficult to draw the precise line of demarcation between what is lawful and what is prohibited; it may even be inadvisable to make the attempt, because many things, though lawful, may yet be inexpedient. But some transactions fall indubitably on one side of the line rather than upon the other. It might well be desirable for a Civil Servant in all circumstances to avoid transactions wholly speculative in character; but where he is employed in any Department to which, whether rightly or wrongly, the public attribute the power of obtaining special information, such as the future course of political or financial events likely to affect the rise and fall of markets, then we assert unhesitatingly that participation in such transactions is not only undesirable or inexpedient, but wrong. The knowledge that Civil Servants so employed are engaged in them could not fail to shock public confidence at home, and, especially if matters of foreign exchange are involved, to produce a deplorable effect upon opinion abroad.

59. We content ourselves with laying down these general principles, which we do not seek to elaborate into any detailed code, if only for the reason that their application must necessarily vary

according to the position, the Department and the work of the Civil Servant concerned. Practical rules for the guidance of social conduct depend also as much upon the instinct and perception of the individual as upon cast-iron formulas: and the surest guide will, we hope, always be found in the nice and jealous honour of Civil Servants themselves. The public expects from them a standard of integrity and conduct not only inflexible but fastidious, and has not been disappointed in the past. We are confident that we are expressing the view of the Service when we say that the public have a right to expect that standard, and that it is the duty of the Service to see that the expectation is fulfilled.

# CHAPTER IX

# EXTERNAL CONTROL

The Civil Service in Britain is not a separate government power. It is the professional staff of the offices of government and is largely concentrated in the Executive, which has the greatest need for its administrative services, but civil servants also serve the Judiciary, a function which they share with local government officials. The administrative services of the Legislature are independently organized, as we shall see in Chapter XI. The Civil Service is as completely subordinate to the Executive as any other administration is to its parent body, yet it is distinguished for its professional independence of the political part of Government. Here we have a separation of function as distinct from a separation of power.

In spite of its unique status and its complete subjection to the control of the Ministry-of-the-day the general question of Civil Service control is a complex one, to which the present and following chapters are devoted. It is to be understood that 'control' is used here in a very broad sense to include various degrees of control, shading into the many influences that are bound to impinge upon, and to some extent mould, such an important national institution. In the present chapter we are concerned not only with the normal constitutional controls operating through the Machinery of Government, but also with wider community influences that are so important in a democracy.

## LAW OF THE CIVIL SERVICE

We are told that there is no Administrative Law in Britain, except insofar as the ordinary law dealing with purely administrative matters may be so classified, as it often is in the text-books. But the fact is that the Civil Service is still shaped and regulated by enactment under the Royal Prerogative, which is most certainly not a part of the ordinary law. Its limits are determined by common law and may be restricted or indeed eventually displaced entirely by statute law if Parliament so decides. Regulations under the Royal Prerogative are surely a separate sort of law, a remnant of the Crown's original executive power, and to the extent that it still operates to shape the Administration, which is still considerable in the case of the Civil Service, it is a distinct administrative law, although something of an anachronism in our system of Government.

The Civil Service is still largely shaped and its domestic procedures laid down by regulations under non-statutory Orders in Council, and upon such regulations the individual civil servant has no recourse to the ordinary courts. He is subject to the discretion of the Crown. Even appeals against dismissal cannot be taken beyond the responsible Minister of the Crown as the legal appointing authority. Of course the Sovereign no longer initiates such law-making, which is made on ministerial authority through the Privy Council. These Orders in Council confer general powers, the actual detail of Civil Service organization and operation being embodied in regulations issued by the Treasury under the Order.

Thus there exists no comprehensive Civil Service Statute as is to be found under most modern systems of government. However, largely because of the involvement of money, Parliament has from the first legislated on questions of superannuation, on which there is a continuous series of statutes going back to 1834.[1]

In earlier days the public official as a servant of the Crown was appointed by Royal Warrant or Patent[2] in accordance with which he operated, or he might be the personal servant to a holder of such an appointment which included the right to delegate part or all of his duties to deputies and assistants. It is significant that Trevelyan and Northcote in their Report of 1853 visualized a switch of authority for personnel control to Parliament when they recommended that their proposals should be embodied in an Act. In face of opposition the Government of the day, after foreshadowing such legislation in the Queen's Speech early in 1854, decided to legislate for the Civil Service by Order in Council under the Royal Prerogative. Following the two important Orders in Council of 1855 and 1870 establishing the Civil Service Commission and introducing open competition, a series of such Orders were issued laying down rules applicable to the Civil Service and its conditions of service. These were consolidated in an important Order in Council in 1910, but after the First World War two Orders in Council of 1920 gave H.M. Treasury the power to make regulations to modify these

[1] An earlier Act of 1822 providing for a contributory scheme was repealed in 1824.

[2] The practice still survives for appointment by the Crown of certain officials holding high posts, members of administrative boards in control of Departments and some inspectors, who hold office under Letters Patent, Orders in Council or Royal Warrant. There is also the case of the Special Commissioners of Income Tax who are appointed under Treasury Warrant.

arrangements, and this has since been replaced by the Civil Service Order in Council, 1956. Thus we see that even the Royal Prerogative has been subjected to the process of delegation, albeit necessarily in face of the growing complexity of the task of administrative regulation.

There are in fact a number of statutes that affect the civil servant and few modern Acts of Parliament fail at least to define tasks for which the Civil Service is to be responsible. Thus the Trade Disputes and Trade Unions Act of 1927 (subsequently repealed) affected the civil servant's right to belong to a trade union with outside affiliations or political objectives. The Official Secrets Acts place him under special obligations with regard to the communication of official information. Numerous statutes define the authority of specific officials, such as inspectors who may, for example, be given special powers of entry and the right to demand the disclosure of specific information. Most modern Departments operate under a statute which creates a Ministerial office and gives its occupant power to appoint such officials and servants as he may need, subject to the consent of the Treasury. The staff numbers of the several Departments and offices of the Central Government are set out in the annual estimates, which are eventually covered by the Appropriation Act, although only the vote figures actually appear therein.

### GOVERNMENT AUTHORITY

The Civil Service is under the direct control of the Government, whose servant it is and within whose sole authority it operates. But 'the Government' is a somewhat woolly term for which 'the Executive' or 'the Administration' are often substituted, possibly with a rather varying emphasis, the former when the activating source is intended, the latter when the Government's day-to-day operations are borne in mind, though there is really little consistency in such usages.

What we are actually concerned with is the centre of power and that surely in the British system is the Cabinet under the leadership of the Prime Minister. The Cabinet as such is a policy-making and decision-reaching body and not an executive. Executively it works, to some extent through the Privy Council of which it forms a part, but mainly through the offices held by its members as Ministers of the Crown. The Prime Minister himself may operate through the Privy Council, where this is constitutionally appropriate, but otherwise he exercises direct executive power only through such office as he may personally occupy. Traditionally the Prime Minister, otherwise without formal status, had fallen into the practice of taking the post of First Lord of the Treasury. This arrangement was purely conventional up to 1937, and sometimes other posts had been chosen, for example the Foreign Secretaryship,[1] but under the Ministers of the Crown Act of that year the Premiership was coupled statutorily with the post of First Lordship for salary purposes.

At this level co-ordination of business common to more than one Department is carried out through Cabinet Committees dealing with specific subjects to which (unlike to full Cabinet meetings) civil servants and other experts are invited as may be necessary. But the Cabinet as such does not direct the Civil Service, except in the limited sense now to be mentioned, although of course it decides the policy by which it is shaped and governed. It does have a secretariat of its own, the Cabinet Office, under a Secretary who ranks with the Joint Permanent Secretaries to the Treasury and has a Civil Service staff on normal lines, but predominantly of the Administrative Class, with Special Advisers on Science and Economics as well as Military and Technical staff. The organization includes the Central Statistical Office, under a Director with a graded staff of Statisticians (co-ordinating statistics for the Departments) and an Historical Section, with a staff of honorary and professional Historians (concerned mainly with the Histories of the Second World War).

It must be emphasized that, as at present constituted, the Cabinet Office is a high-level secretariat to provide advice and information and office services for Prime Minister and Cabinet, and not a Presidential or Prime Minister's Department as exists under some other systems of government. A Prime Minister's Office, in so far as it exists as an executive body, is to be found inside the Treasury, where the Prime Minister works through the Head of the Home Civil Service on matters relating to machinery of government and the Civil Service.

The Cabinet works out Government policy as a continuing process, but it is left to the individual Ministers (some of whom are not members of the Cabinet) to carry out, through their Departments, that part of the policy relating to their own sphere. Each Minister must accept responsibility for the Cabinet's broad policy, in accordance with the principle of collective responsibility, and at

---

[1] During the Second World War, Churchill as Prime Minister and First Lord also held the post of Minister of Defence. For a short period over 1957–9 an Atomic Energy Office operated under the direct control of the Prime Minister.

the same time he is held individually responsible for the activities of and results achieved by his Department. As we have already seen, it is at this point where the Minister meets his chief administrator, in the guise of Permanent Secretary as head of the Department's professional staff, that the vital control of the Civil Service in its day-to-day operation manifests itself. At this point Minister-Politician becomes Minister-Administrator, and it is here that we should let the matter rest until we consider the subject of 'Internal Management' in the next chapter.

PARLIAMENTARY CONTROL

Parliament, as we have seen above, can, when there is need, legislate for the Civil Service and here, therefore, is the ultimate control, but in the main this function is left to the Government, or Ministry, who, under the parliamentary system, are also members of one of the Houses,[1] which in effect means that the State's administrative business is confided to a group of legislators upon whom any criticism is conveniently concentrated. The convention that a Minister is responsible for his administration even in detail means that he cannot publicly disown such responsibility and blame his officials. Consequently it is through criticism of the results of a civil servant's activities and not of him as a person that Parliament is able to maintain some control over the Central Administration. This arises not from some restriction on the legislature's competence, but from the fortunate fact that the conduct of officials is not usually the point at issue. If professional integrity and morale were low no doubt the position would be very different. As it is, the Cabinet system ensures that Parliamentary criticism of the Civil Service shall operate indirectly through the criticism of policy and interrogation of the responsible minister.

This may take place at various stages in debate and on the adjournment, but question time is undoubtedly the most effective of the Parliamentary means of administrative control. Ministers are called upon to answer questions on the day-to-day detail of their administration. Such questions may be *bona fide* searchings after illumination, or artfully designed probings into weak spots; frequently they are based upon complaints put forward by an M.P.'s constituents. In any case the Minister, who has due notice of the question, cannot plead ignorance. He must find out what has happened. For this purpose an urgent inquiry is directed from his

[1] Not legally necessary but conventionally so, except under the emergency conditions of wartime when senior statesmen may hold Ministerial office without becoming Members of Parliament or Peers of the Realm.

Private Office[1] down the line to the spot where the alleged incident occurred: written explanations are forwarded and official interpretations are provided, together with such additional information as may in the experience of the officials be considered likely to anticipate the supplementary question which the Minister may be asked. This procedure is well calculated to elicit the truth, for the senior officials will not accept excuses from their subordinates or risk their reputations by misleading the Minister. If he, by manipulating the evidence, tries cleverly to evade the issue and fails, the blood will then be on his own head. There can be little doubt that this system works and has a salutary effect inside the Departments, where every official is constantly aware that a mistake on his part affecting the rights of a member of the public may have political repercussions. It is sometimes argued that this type of interrogation tends to excessive red tape methods, but the time actually involved in propounding answers to Parliamentary questions is not relatively so great and the value of the method is not easily overestimated. The main element of red tape, which is an inevitable expense of any system that involves public accountability, rests in the need for the Civil Service to document its activities to a degree that a businessman would consider excessive. This would still be necessary without the particular institution of question time. The appointment of an Ombudsman, referred to in the next section, will no doubt modify these procedures.

Parliament's other method of controlling administration in the Departments is through its Select Committees, which have power to interrogate responsibile officials and to examine work processes. However, the three Select Committees in question, namely on Public Accounts, Estimates and Statutory Instruments respectively, are each concerned with a specialized sphere and there are wide administrative territories in the Departments that are not under their purview. It is significant that these committees are not supposed to be concerned with policy but with the way the Departments have carried out Parliament's wishes within the respective spheres. The Public Accounts and Estimates Committees are concerned with matters of finance, forming part of the structure of financial control. From this influence the civil servant is never released. It is in fact important to the success of any system of financial control that public officials at all levels should be daily conscious of guarding the public purse and treating all costs as though they were to come out of their own pockets. In the operation of this particular control the position of the Comptroller and Auditor General is important. Although himself a public official, subject very much to the general

[1] Title of small staff of civil servants responsible for his personal business.

conditions of the Civil Service from which he is usually selected, he stands in an independent category as a servant of Parliament, appointed by the Crown and removable only on an address from both Houses of Parliament.

It is important that Members of Parliament, and others of course, should be well-informed on the workings of the Central Administration and the Civil Service, but for many reasons, including traditions of official reticence strongly reinforced of late by security requirements[1] and the inherent complexities and obscurity of administrative activity, such information is not easily come by. Special machinery is needed for this purpose and numerous proposals have been made to introduce a system of committees in the House of Commons to specialize on the work of specific Departments, or groups of Departments, similar to those figuring in the American Congress, only to be rejected on the grounds of unsuitability for our system and particularly of incompatibility with maintaining the principle of full ministerial responsibility. In view of the accepted effectiveness of the existing Select Committees, notably the two finance committees just mentioned and the Select Committee on Nationalized Industries (Reports and Accounts), all of which have probed pretty widely into the Departments, despite the curb on policy questions, this argument seems to be pretty thin. No one has yet determined when policy ends and execution begins. Moreover such committees are purely advisory and not designed, nor should they be, to erode the Minister's unique authority. On the contrary it can often be helpful for him to have an independent source of information about what is happening in his own parish. Understandably senior civil servants do not like such enquiries for many reasons but this is one of the facts of administrative life in the second half of the twentieth century to which they must learn to accustom themselves.

During the war the Select Committee on National Expenditure recommended the introduction of a similar Committee on 'the Machinery of Government with special reference to the economic use of personnel', to be assisted by a permanent Assessor as an Officer of the House.[2] This was rejected by the Government, no doubt with full approval of their professional advisers. As a matter of fact the Estimates Committee, rehabilitated and much more successful since the war, has gone some way to providing the sort of survey of the Departments which its wartime substitute had done so effectively. Since 1945 the Estimates Committee enquiries have

[1] See page 158 above.

[2] *Sixteenth Report from the Select Committee on National Expenditure* (*Session* 1941/42), *Organization and Control of the Civil Service*. (1942) p. 41.

covered most of the major Departments, and some have dealt specifically with the Civil Service, notably in the session 1947-48 on 'The Civil Service Commission', in 1963-64 on 'Treasury Control of Establishments', and in 1964-65 on 'Recruitment to the Civil Service'.[1]

Recently the adoption of such a system of specialist committees has been recommended by the House of Commons's Select Committee on Procedure[2] but the Government again did not agree and the Estimates Committee are going ahead with a scheme of grouped surveys by means of their existing sub-committees. It is of interest in the present connection that criticism of the public corporations had similarly been found difficult by Members of Parliament in the absence of detailed inside information and the Select Committee already mentioned was set up in consequence, accompanied inevitably by the serious misgivings of pundits who are always very good at prognosticating why suggested changes in our system of government cannot possibly work, either because they are against tradition or do not go far enough! In fact their growing shelf of informative reports has been widely welcomed for doing just what the Select Committee on Nationalized Industries was designed to do.

COMMUNITY INFLUENCES

In a democracy the public have particular interest in the Civil Service and it is right and proper that civil servants should in a special sense consider themselves servants of the people. This not only arises essentially from the basic civil service idea but is the logical consequence of the continuing extension of a State participation in the social services and in many other ways that increase daily contacts between officials and citizen. The civil service image is therefore of vital importance, for the Central Administration cannot work effectively without the maximum attainable citizen participation. To illustrate this point it is only necessary to refer to the importance of form-filling as a stage in many administrative procedures. The Civil Service is bound to recognize that undue complexity in form design and demanding more information than the specific transaction demands places an undue strain upon members of the public, who on their side need to know enough about public administration to appreciate how far the form-filling is necessary and its efficient fulfilment to their own advantage.

The Civil Service is becoming much more aware of the need for

[1] I.e. the *Ninth, Fifth and Sixth Reports* of the respective sessions.
[2] *Fourth Report from the Select Committee on Procedure* (Session 1964–65).

public understanding of their work and the Departments' information services are designed with this as a major objective, and certainly not for purposes of propaganda, as ill-disposed critics have sometimes alleged. It must be admitted that such criticisms have usually been directed against the general principle of Government publicity rather than against the specific activities of the Central Office of Information. The latter is a Government Department with a Civil Service staff, which functions as a provider of information materials for other Departments as a common service, and not as a propaganda agency.

The real problem here is involved in the achievement of an informed democracy and it has to be admitted that our present civilization is rapidly becoming so complicated that the citizen's task is already overwhelming. When it is remembered that, within the larger informational field, the sphere of public administration is itself extremely complex and not very easy to understand, it is hardly surprising that civil servants themselves do not find that understanding easy to come by. While the Government and the Departments must continue to do all they can to ensure that the public is properly informed upon the State's activities their efforts will not be fully effective without the constructive support of the schools, the press and the wireless services.

The schools have always had a close relationship with the modern Civil Service. From the outset the Civil Service Commissioners have maintained step by step relations with the educational authorities. The adoption of the liberal literary subjects as the mainstay of the system of higher examinations had an important influence upon the development of the universities and public schools in the second half of the nineteenth century, when the interplay between the examination demands and the build up of studies, especially at Oxford and Cambridge, was vital in the formation of the Administrative Class. At the same time headmasters at the public and new secondary schools were deeply involved in ensuring that the type and standards of the examinations for the middle and lower levels of the Civil Service should keep in step with their own curricula. Individually competition among themselves was directed to ensuring that they obtained fair shares of the highly competitive and usually restricted successes. Right up until 1914 the Commissioners felt themselves bound to listen carefully to the schools' views on this subject.

Between the wars the schools maintained their interest, but the tardy return to open recruitment, due to the establishment of numbers of temporary ex-Service officials, coupled with a high degree of stagnancy in the Civil Service, restricted the effect of their influence and the Commission's interest in their guidance. Recently the widespread substitution of the General Certificate of Education in place of the written competitive tests has virtually meant that the schools have taken over a part of the Civil Service Commissioners' function without need to accept much responsibility. The greatly widened field of equivalent, or even better, career openings available to the same class of candidate, which has greatly contributed to removing the substantial competitive margin which formerly existed, has meant that the schools are now much less concerned with the actual impact of the Civil Service examinations. The schools' proper aim is to produce the good citizen. Whether it is their job to produce the good official is another question. This is what the G.C.E. is now expected to guarantee, without insisting upon anything more specific than a minimum qualification in English.

The press, if less responsibly involved, can be quite as influential as the schools in its impact upon the Civil Service. But journalists are busy people who have to react quickly without always having time to check the facts. Unless they are already well-briefed they are liable to jump to all sorts of not-quite-right conclusions, and this they do not find difficult with regard to the Civil Service, whom the public tend to look upon as unmitigated bureaucrats addicted to non-stop tea-drinking, a caricature which would be worthy of Parkinsonian laughter were its general effect not so serious, not merely upon officialdom itself but upon the community which inevitably suffers the loss of efficiency accruing from the lowering of the Civil Service's public esteem. How far this caricature rests upon a healthy dislike of official interference, which has a pedigree going back at least as far as Ancient Egypt, and how far upon modern anti-socialist propaganda, which is as ably supported by the press of the left as of the right, is not easy to determine. Within the focus of the modern Welfare State it is a positive duty of the press to understand better what public administration is all about and to provide its readers with a reliable interpretation. It is hardly an exaggeration to suggest that in its successful accomplishment of this the future of our complex society could ultimately rest!

The various wireless broadcasting services have an important part to play and, since they are mainly run by public officials, they should have a better understanding of the problems involved. In the main the image of the official put over both by sound and vision is never much more than humorously critical and therefore not essentially unacceptable, but these new communications services could contribute so much more constructively in explaining the public services to the people, without making such an amateur job of it.

LEGAL CONTROL

The civil servant is individually responsible to the ordinary courts for his acts in the performance of his official duties, irrespective of any orders he may receive, which must be legal to be valid. In other words there is not in Britain a *droit administratif* which, in the public interest, subjects the official to a special administrative code when carrying out his public duties. As we have already seen[1] the civil servant is to some extent subject to greater legal restrictions or disadvantages that the ordinary citizen—for example under the Official Secrets Acts and through loss of official privileges, especially accrued pension, as a consequence of criminal conviction—and he has no recourse to the courts on matters authorized by Royal Prerogative. The recent case of *Dudfield v Ministry of Works* illustrates the position. An industrial civil servant, employed by the Ministry of Works, claimed arrears of wages, or damages in respect of breach of contract, for non-payment of an increase held up by the imposition by the Government of a pay pause in August 1961. In the course of a detailed judgment[2] it was held that the official had no legal right to the sum claimed nor was there any legal obligation on the part of the Department to pay it. The claimant was entitled only to such sum as was authorized by the Treasury.

Until the passing of the Crown Proceedings Act, 1947, immunity of the Crown from being sued for tort or under contract meant that a civil servant causing damage or injury in the course of his official duties could be held personally responsible and—failing a Petition of Right which was a very difficult procedure, within the discretion of the Crown—such a case had to be taken against the individual. Such cases frequently arose against Post Office van-drivers for damages suffered in road accidents and it had become the regular practice of the Department to meet all costs. Liability in such cases is now placed squarely upon the Departments.

Another interesting legal situation, affecting the work rather than the official, is the Crown's privilege in the course of legal proceedings, whether it is itself involved or not, to withhold documents in the public interest. In such cases the Court requires a certificate, claiming immunity, signed by the responsible Minister. This is a matter he cannot delegate to his civil servants.

[1] See page 150 above.
[2] See *'Times' Report* of 24.1.64. The case merely illustrated what was already generally accepted as the legal position.

## PUBLIC INQUIRIES

Public inquiries of a general nature have been initiated from time to time to examine, on behalf of Parliament and Government, the state of the Civil Service and to suggest changes should they be necessary. Such inquiries are in the tradition of English government, going back to William the Conqueror's Domesday Book, and in our particular field they have gone a good way to neutralizing the difficulties and disadvantages of access to inside information about the Departments and the Civil Service. They have certainly provided a much more impartial picture of the Central Administration than insiders can be trusted to produce. A favoured means has been to establish a Royal Commission with specific terms of reference and wide powers of interrogation and of calling for documents. They have usually included notabilities from various fields of activity. But just as frequently other forms have been adopted. Thus the Trevelyan-Northcote Report of 1853/54 was produced by two insiders, the Select Committee's Report of 1860 by parliamentarians, the so-called Playfair Commission's Report of 1874/75 by a special committee which was not a royal commission, while the Reorganization Report of 1920 was again produced by insiders. It has to be admitted that the two insider committees, equipped as they were with invaluable experience of the actual working of the Departments, have to date had by far the greatest impact upon the Civil Service. Now (1966) we have a new Committee under Lord Fulton, consisting of both outsiders and insiders, which is not a Royal Commission, upon whose findings the verdict of history will be awaited anxiously by some, hopefully by many, for the time for a radical revision is surely ripe.

For special investigations, in which the employment of strict judicial procedures are necessary, the practice has been followed of setting up special tribunals under the Tribunals of Inquiry (Evidence) Act, 1921.[1] Of this type the Lynskey inquiry *Reflecting on the Official Conduct of Ministers of the Crown and Other Public Servants*[2] and also the Radcliffe inquiry *Into the Vassall Case and Related Matters,*[3] covering the activities of Ministers, Naval Officers and Civil Servants on the question of Official Secrets, have already been mentioned in the appropriate context and do not call for further discussion here.

There is also the proposed introduction of a Parliamentary

[1] Reviewed by Royal Commission in Cmnd. 3121 (1966).
[2] See page 153 above.
[3] See page 165 above.

Commissioner for Administration[1] to scrutinize on Parliament's behalf grievances of the citizen not otherwise fully catered for. At the outset it is proposed that the Commissioner should deal only with complaints of personal injustice suffered by the complainant, sent via a Member of the House of Commons who will decide whether it is an appropriate one for reference to him. Such complaints are to be confined to the Departments actually listed and there are to be so many exclusions that the White Paper needs to be quoted:

'The exclusions which we propose to make from the Commissioner's field of investigation are those where there are dominant considerations of national or public interest—namely, the exercise of powers to preserve the safety of the State; matters which Ministers certify as affecting relations with other countries; matters relating to the administration of colonial territories; and the exercise of powers in relation to investigating crime or determining whether a matter shall go to the courts. The Commissioner will not normally pursue matters which are within the competence of the courts; he will have discretion to act if he thinks that the remedy open in the courts is not one which the complainant could reasonably be expected to use, but this will not affect anyone's right of access to the courts. He will not pursue issues already covered by tribunals or other quasi-judicial bodies, or by the Council on Tribunals and the Scottish Committee—of both of which he himself will be an *ex-officio* member. Nor will he look into the exercise of the Prerogative of Mercy or into the exercise of the personal authority of the Sovereign in conferring honours and privileges, or into appointments by the Crown or by Ministers. He will be excluded from investigating actions of Departments in personnel matters, including orders and discipline in the Armed Forces. Finally, purely commercial relationships of Departments with customers or suppliers will not come within his purview.'[2]

Such a formidable list of exclusions makes it difficult to be impressed by the real need of such an institution. The innovation seems at best to be an anaemic version of the Ombudsman, introduced successfully by the Scandinavian countries, by whose experience the particular development has been inspired.[3]

It is generally agreed that, in the absence of a complete system of administrative law whose introduction would presuppose a radical upheaval in our system of government, some additional

[1] White Paper on *The Parliamentary Commissioner for Administration*, Cmnd. 2767 (1965).

[2] *White Paper*, para. 8, p. 5.

[3] New Zealand has also introduced the system with success.

means are needed to deal with complaints about the Administration that are not already cared for by existing methods. One would have thought, however, that the Departments themselves could have devised suitable machinery for dealing with the general run of complaints to the satisfaction of the public—and of course some already do this rather better than others—leaving to Parliament, mainly through Question Time, to close the gap. Even the notorious Crichel Down case, from which so many erroneous conclusions have been drawn, would have been avoided by more effective communications inside the Department concerned. There is a widespread opinion, especially among legal people, whose own particular procedures do not predispose them to understand the very different needs of efficient administration and the importance of keeping it fluent, that civil servants are always doing things calculated to erode the freedom of the individual. In truth, the trouble is often too much law and the need for complex internal codes to operate it. In practice the Departmental authorities lean over backwards to ensure that the rules are interpreted with the maximum of leniency to the citizen compatible with the general interest. Too many additional brakes could soon bring the machine to a halt and automatically increase the tide of complaints!

Nevertheless it is not likely that civil servants will be much bothered by the new machinery: in fact it is more likely to bring them exoneration than blame. The public will certainly have a new safety valve for their understandable if somewhat old-fashioned anger at official interference and perhaps some of their habitual misjudgements of officialdom will receive an impartial airing not readily available through other channels. It is as well to remember in this context that institutions eminently suitable for smaller states are not necessarily suitable for really larger ones, and vice versa.

## RECRUITMENT CONTROL

Here we reach the overlapping boundaries of the two types of Civil Service control. Under some systems recruitment of the Civil Service is carried out inside the Administration, but the setting up of an independent Civil Service Commission in Britain in 1855 marked a radical change in this respect. This development was one of the most perspicacious mid-Victorian reforms and one that was to be widely followed throughout the world. Control at this stage is specifically designed to set and maintain proper standards of recruitment, i.e. at the official's point of entry into his career and to exclude the otherwise inevitable patronage which has undesirable effects upon the general efficiency of the Administration.

Suggestions, therefore, that the maintenance of the autonomy of such an agency is now outdated must be treated with great caution, however authoritative the source. We have not yet evolved a society in which the natural urges to achieve private gain at public expense have been replaced by a spontaneous devotion to public service. Patronage and nepotism are social diseases endemic in all human societies. The quasi-judicial certification of an autonomous Civil Service Commission or Public Service Board remains an urgent necessity at the selection stage of all public appointments. It is not only a matter of efficiency but of justice to the rest of the community. Currently this requirement is being progressively weakened in our system by the delegation of so much of the selection process by the Commissioners to other agents.

Organized as an ordinary Department, with Civil Service staff under the direction of the Commissioners, the Civil Service Commission has always been located structurally inside the Central Administration, although the appointment of the Commissioners by the Crown has enabled a proper independence to be maintained. The practice of so organizing the individual Commissioners that they act also as the senior executives of the Department, like any other senior Administrative Class officials, is administratively economical but tends to confuse the outsider, who must judge institutions at their face value. Furthermore the practice of permitting these Commission posts to become stepping stones to highest Civil Service positions is certain to influence the attitudes of their occupants, who are of course only human! No one denies that in actual practice the Civil Service Commission operates with Complete impartiality and in full accord with the spirit of the regulations, but here too it is important that justice should not merely be done but be seen to be done. In what has been one of Britain's valuable institutional exports this is an imperative condition.

# CHAPTER X

# INTERNAL MANAGEMENT

When we move over from external control to internal management we move into the true sphere of the Civil Service, but not completely out of the sphere of the politician who, under the Cabinet has distinct administrative responsibilities. Apart from his specific functional task—the specialism of his Department—the Minister, as administrator, is responsible for the Department's internal management, in the accomplishment of which the Civil Service is his professional instrument.

## ADMINISTRATIVE REALM OF THE POLITICIAN

Management of the Central Administration operates at two levels—Treasury and Departmental—and it can hardly be denied that the emergence of the Treasury as the focus of Civil Service control has gone a long way in restricting the managerial initiative of the individual Minister. From the earliest days of English Government, finance, through the Exchequer, has operated as the most powerful, and at the same time most flexible, of administrative controls, first in the hands of the King and later as an instrument of Parliament. The present division of Civil Service management into two layers has largely come about through the development of Treasury control, a term which today covers both financial and establishments control. It was hardly chance that led prime ministers to prefer the First Lordship of the Treasury as the most suitable executive post to give reality to their constitutionally nebulous position. The Chancellor of the Exchequer's membership of the Treasury Board also rendered it easy and convenient to hand over the working headship of the Department to him. Under the Cabinet, as the supreme co-ordinating instrument of the Executive, the Treasury constitutes the only comprehensive co-ordinating body at administrative level. Through this influential Department all lines of executive and administrative action operate and converge upon and from the individual Departments, within each of which they form a series of vertical channels of executive action completely separate from one another. To explain how in practice the individual Ministerial realms are meshed into a single administrative entity is the main theme of the present chapter.

There is in fact nothing to prevent a Minister from participating in any of his Department's activities; nothing, that is to say, but the physical impossibility of carrying such intervention very far and the constitutional practice of leaving to the Permanent Secretary full responsibility for running the Department and producing the results required of him. From being, within the last century, mere secretarial offices of the Minister, equipped with secretaries and clerks skilled in the processes of report and letter-writing, the copying of documents and keeping of records, the Departments to-day have become complex regulatory, executive and, sometimes, service-providing organizations, in which the clerical processes, often much more complicated than they then were, have come to comprise but a minor part of a Department's administrative activity.

It is maintained by some that a Minister can no longer shoulder such an extensive responsibility and that the doctrine of ministerial responsibility is therefore outdated. 'How can he know,' the critic asks, 'everything that is being done within his administration in his name?' Surely this is the position of most leaders in our complex society! It is one of the important factors that renders their task so difficult and leads to indifferent accomplishment. Today the figurehead is no longer enough. It is the leader's job to take responsibility, to see that he has administrators who are competent and adequately equipped to adopt the methods required to achieve the desired objectives. To be effective statesmen Ministers must have the capacity to test whether their administration is working satisfactorily and to know whether the administrators are on top of the job. They must also have the means and power to act whenever they even suspect that this is not the case. The political machinery enables them to share, up to a point, their burdens with their subordinate political colleagues, holders of the office of Minister of State and Parliamentary Secretary[1], and the Government as a whole can help considerably by seeing that the State's machinery is properly organized and geared to achieve the best results. Any idea that the overall responsibility can be, or ought to be, passed down to the officials leads inevitably in the direction of bureaucracy, a system in which the administrative tail wags the political dog.

The best of Civil Services will not do its best unless it is directed by competent Ministers. Clearly the Minister's job is among the most responsible, most burdensome and most highly skilled in the land. Perhaps too little attention has been given to the quality and training of Ministers in our highly administrative society? But this is not a matter which falls within the scope of our study.

[1] Under the Secretary of State the latter is known as 'Parliamentary Under-Secretary of State'.

## TREASURY CONTROL

Treasury control has become a complex concept which is not easily unravelled.[1] It covers a complexity of financial influences and controls which in themselves run, far beyond administrative realms, out into the community in all directions. It also includes Civil Service control which itself has both financial and establishment aspects. Financial control is not our concern here, except as an operation in which civil servants of all ranks are intimately involved in the course of their duties.

Even in the days before reform, when a Minister's autonomy was at its highest, the Treasury had already acquired a special authority in such general staffing matters as existed: for example, taking the initiative in abolishing sinecure offices and the employment of deputies, and providing general advice and regulation on matters affecting the Administration as a whole. At the time the scope of Treasury patronage was so wide that the Department's Parliamentary Secretary was known significantly as Patronage Secretary[2], his task being to dispose of the patronage of the Treasury, the revenue-collecting agencies, and certain other offices among nominees proposed by members of the Government.

The great influence of Sir Charles Edward Trevelyan at the time of the mid-nineteenth century reforms has already been emphasized.[3] Apart from his outstanding personal contribution, there can be little doubt that his occupancy of the top permanent post under the Treasury Board was vital in ensuring that his influence should percolate through the strong walls of patronage and custom which still hedged round the central offices of the State.

As the importance of establishment work grew the participation of the Treasury in this field extended more and more. The Order in Council of 1870 gave them powers to make rules in certain matters of staff organization not directly associated with finance and subsequently their influence over establishments expanded as the modern Civil Service structure gradually emerged. The new position was recognized after the First World War when establishments work was separated from departmental finance, with which it had hitherto been associated inside the Treasury and reorganized upon a separate basis within the Department. At the same time the Treasury's regulatory powers over the Civil Service were extended and consolidated.

[1] See particularly *Sixth Report from the Select Committee on Estimates*, Session 1957/58, 'Treasury Control of Expenditure' (1958).

[2] Today he acts as Chief Government Whip.

[3] See page 19 above.

This development of the Treasury as influential establishments agency has been an important factor in the Civil Service's history. It meant that, in virtue of the massive size and variety of the tasks of the new Service, the Treasury became the depository of a vast experience in personnel matters, to which no one else had such a comprehensive access and at a time when the art of personnel management was hardly recognized outside the governmental field. The contribution made by the Treasury and the British Civil Service as forerunners in this specialist sphere of management is still not widely appreciated.

As a consequence of this development the autonomy of the Departments has inevitably been modified on the management side. They have to conform to general Treasury rules and advice, unless a special case can be made for acting otherwise. Yet they retain a certain initiative in a number of matters on which they have the power to issue their own instructions. As an example of these may be cited regulations restricting the right of members of a Department to carry on spare-time activities that may impinge upon its specific sphere of responsibility.

Following upon more recent reorganizations within the Treasury the establishment and finance aspects of the work, while still closely interrelated at the estimates stage when staff members are inseparable from manpower costs, have become even more distinctly organized. In 1956 the single Permanent Secretary was replaced by two Joint Permanent Secretaries, one of whom holds the title of 'Head of the Home Civil Service' and is responsible for all questions of machinery of government, Civil Service management (including advising the Prime Minister on senior appointments[1]) and internal Treasury organization, while his colleague has oversight of finance and economic matters. It is at this point therefore that the Prime Minister, operating through the Head of the Home Civil Service, maintains direct contact with and control of the Central Administration.

## CENTRAL MANAGEMENT

Through its control functions the Treasury has emerged as the one general management body over the Departments. This management is not confined to financial and establishment activities, however important they may be. Other management services have been added and a wider concept of management in the Government field

[1] In particular this includes promotions to the rank of Permanent Secretary, Deputy Secretary and the posts of Principal Establishment Officer and Principal Finance Officer in the Departments.

has appeared, hesitantly and with little premeditation, largely under the pressure of events. Similar trends are discernable in other systems. The importance of this development was rightly stressed in the Plowden Report, already mentioned.[1] Summarizing the several channels or instrumentalities through which this central management is achieved it will be convenient to look at them briefly under the following headings: (1) Regulation, (2) Staff Consultation, (3) Management Services, (4) Common Services, (5) Inter-departmental Committees, and (6) Establishments Liaison.

(1) *Regulation* H.M. Treasury is authorized to regulate the Civil Service under the principal Orders in Council. These rules cover structure, procedures, conditions of service, such as are often elsewhere embodied in a Civil Service statute, as well as more detailed regulations. They include the important general rules and standards for the examinations by which the Civil Service Commissioners are guided. In their making the views of the Departments and the staffs are taken into account. The regulations are collected together in *Estacode,* a loose-leaf publication, which forms the Civil Service's bible throughout the Departments, although they do not of course extend to those subjects over which the individual Department has discretion and for which it can make its own regulations.

(2) *Staff Consultation* It has already been seen in Chapter VII how this important managerial function, through the Whitley Councils and staff associations, enables both the experience and the support of the staff to be obtained before regulations are finally promulgated. Of course, where such agreement cannot be achieved within the limits of efficiency desired by the authorities, decisions may be imposed by administrative action. This is not frequently necessary in the Civil Service today.

Although the active participant in the Whitley system has usually been the Staff Side it would be a mistake to underrate the importance of the system in facilitating closer co-ordination among the Departments through their representatives on the Official Side. For some time the early Whitley system was looked upon by many departmental heads as an obstacle to effective control—a sort of fifth wheel—but it has since become clear to everyone that it meets a real management need and has contributed outstandingly to the gradual shaping of the system which we are outlining here. It is obvious that had not such a formal system of consultation existed in this modern era an effective substitute would have had to be invented.

[1] See Report pp. 16–19, and page 95 above.

(3) *Management Services* Foremost among the management services for which the Treasury have taken general responsibility are staff training and organization and methods. The need for training, in the Civil Service as elsewhere, made its initial impact at the desk, the bench and the counter. It was therefore in such Government organizations as the Post Office and the Inland Revenue Department that training was formally organized, largely because the time had arrived when the daily tasks could no longer be effectively accomplished by individual supervisors without central advice and aids and, possibly, classroom facilities. As we have already seen,[1] the Treasury came into the picture following the enquiry of 1943/44, conducted significantly under the chairmanship of the Financial Secretary of the Treasury, Mr. Ralph Assheton, M.P., with the establishment of a Training and Education Division to determine general training policy, provide guidance and materials on training for the Departments, organize special courses including the training of departmental instructors in the techniques of teaching, and in trying out and disseminating information on training developments and methods. The importance of this innovation merely as a potential channel of control is obvious.

Training is very much an establishments responsibility, which is concerned with the improvement of the skills of the individual and the quality of his performance, but it has an important technical side which takes it into every field of activity within the Administration. There it is concerned with the work and its techniques.

The Sixteenth Report from the Select Committee on National expenditure of Parliamentary session 1941/42 (1942), out of which the Assheton enquiry arose, also had an important outcome in the sphere of work processes. Marking the birth of the modern Organization and Methods ('O & M') movement, which has spread far and wide since the War, its development by the Treasury has drawn to it the interest of experts from many lands.

The Select Committee were advocating the systematic study of organization as applied to the Departments, which they considered had hitherto been unduly neglected, despite proposals made by a number of previous enquiries[2] that the Treasury should become a clearing house of this sort of expertise. Between 1919 and 1939 they had mainly concentrated their attention on the introduction of office machinery and in this field important advances had been made.

Soon after the outbreak of war the staff of the Investigation Section, who had hitherto been responsible for this development,

[1] See page 91 above.
[2] *Op cit*, pp. 15–18.

was increased and reorganized with the title 'Organization and Methods Division'. Similar investigations were being conducted by the Departments, a few of which, by mid-1941, had set up their own O & M branches. The Select Committee strongly recommended the extension of this service and the outcome was the raising of the status of the work and the appointment, for the time being, of an outside expert to guide its development. O & M has become a firm Treasury responsibility which has added to its controlling capacities.[1]

The larger Departments were encouraged to maintain their own O & M branches, H.M. Treasury's resources being made generally available, but mainly concentrated upon the smaller Departments. The Treasury's position is really one of mentor and guide. Its services are advisory and provided at the invitation of Heads of Departments. Training is provided at the Treasury for O & M officers throughout the Civil Service. Even within the Departments O & M is advisory, the decision whether its findings and advice should be followed being left to the executive heads. Of course, pressure can always be exerted from higher levels, especially where obstructionist attitudes are in evidence, but it is the firm policy of O & M investigatory teams to get over their ideas by taking the executive staffs into their confidence as they go along. O & M is not to be confused with inspection.

There are few specific rules in the practice of O & M. It represents more an attitude of mind than an array of accepted techniques. Its important objective is to inculate in officials a habit of objective examination, a capacity to stand outside and look impartially into the organization and processes in which they are involved. O & M men are not experts: they are selected officials who, after serving a term on the work, are expected to return to normal duties, taking with them their new knowledge and experience and disseminating the new attitude as widely as possible. O & M is really the application of common sense to the examination of day-to-day experience. It is none the less difficult to implement because its need is so obvious. It has all the inertias of routine and the prejudices of the lazy mind to break down.

This new approach has increased the civil servant's awareness of the work processes, which become more complex and therefore more difficult to cope with, and certainly need to be looked at more analytically by their operators. In the same direction there has been the impact of automation, and particularly of automatic data processing (ADP), which has called for a new propensity both to see the picture as a whole and to assess the precise position of

[1] See H.M. Treasury's *The Practice of O & M* (H.M.S.O., 1965).

the individual official's activities in the changing scheme. The natural conservatism of the administrator has received a new challenge, the effect of which will be cumulative. These changing techniques, affecting as they must widening fields of public activity, are bound to operate as controlling factors in their own right and reinforce the need for a more consciously co-ordinated management.

(4) *Common Services* The centralization, for reasons of economy and efficiency, of the procurement and provision of supplies and services required by a number of branches or departments is an important need of all extensive administrative systems, though some have been tardy in developing these common services, as they are usually called. The principle is well developed in the Civil Service, since each Department, in the very nature of its activities and structure, has a need for its own internal common, or housekeeping, services to achieve effective management. Such matters as establishments, legal advice, statistics, staff training, information, library and so forth fall under this heading, and within each Department their provision is centred at headquarters. For the Central Administration as a whole some important common services, available to all Departments, are organized in specialist Departments, or distinct branches of large Departments. Prominent among these are (i) H.M. Stationery Office (office supplies, printed forms and publications), (ii) Central Office of Information (information media), (iii) Parliamentary Counsel's Office (bill drafting), (iv) Public Record Office (centralization and preservation of records), (v) Central Statistical Office (statistics) and (vi) Ministry of Public Buildings and Works (equipment and accommodation). Of these the first three are specialist Departments under individual executives subject to the oversight of the Chancellor of the Exchequer. The fourth and fifth are also Specialist Departments, respectively responsible to the Lord Chancellor and the Cabinet Office; while the last is a ministerial Department which also exercises important general functions, although historically its predecessor, the Office of Works, was a Common Service Department of the ordinary type.

Treasury control over the first three of these services is very close and this is desirable since they are essential management factors. The concentration of the supply function facilities the provision of such goods and services to smaller organizations who might have to expend disproportionate time and resources in obtaining and maintaining small stocks. It also facilitates a more widespread use of resources and ideas through standardization, although there is bound to be some loss in variety and experiment, especially to smaller units who may have less influence in deciding the final product. Standardization is itself a means of managerial control through which pressures and influences can be subtly projected by the unit which has the final say.

(5) *Inter-departmental Committees* To bridge the communications gap between individual Departments numerous inter-departmental committees are set up at Civil Service level. Some of these are constituted on a more or less permanent basis, as for example for the co-ordinating of Government contract procedures, but the majority are of an *ad hoc* type set up to deal with specific matters at a juncture when co-ordination is of particular importance. They do not form a co-ordinated network and responsibility for their origination will usually rest with the Treasury only when such matters as finance and establishments are involved. Inter-departmental committees operate at different levels to bring together the officials who are involved in activities in which the several Departments are involved. Thus, in the Central Administration the committee system is spontaneous and flexible, does not constitute a co-ordinated network and is not a built-in method of administration as it sometimes is in other branches of public administration.

(6) *Establishments Liaison* This brings us to what is the most important management link, namely the establishments liaison between the Treasury and the Departments, a process to which activities under all the preceding headings contribute.

Each Department has its own Principal Establishments Officer, in larger units usually ranking as Under Secretary and possibly bearing some such title as 'Director of Establishments and Organization'. He is responsible to the Permanent Secretary for all personnel matters and usually for such allied subjects as organization and methods, inspection, supplies, premises library, records, internal instructions, typing, staff welfare, etc. His is one of the most important of the headquarter divisions. It maintains close liaison with the Establishments side of the Treasury and direct contact with the Department's own establishment officers in the regions and other detached branches, to whom such responsibilities are delegated as is necessary to deal with staff matters expeditiously on the spot. The staffs of all these establishment branches are members of the Department's normal Civil Service gradings, varying with the level of the work involved. They are not specialists, but spend a period of duty on establishments work and then pass on to other work, for it is considered desirable for such experience to be disseminated widely throughout the Administration.

The several establishment units are inter-related on a staff rather than a line basis, but the establishments network is by its very nature an effective channel of management control. The Departments' Establishment Officers keep close contact with the Treasury through both formal periodical meetings and informal talks. Directions have to be issued on occasion but in the main Treasury Control operates through discussion and agreement reached by officials who understand the general situation and appreciate each other's points of view. It is important to understand that the Treasury does not plant its agents inside the Departments, although this is sometimes suggested by outside exponents! Such an arrangement would soon come up against the principle of ministerial responsibility. It is true that at one time there was a good deal of antagonism between the Departments and the Treasury but with the steady growth of Whitleyism and the creation of general management liaison this has largely dissolved. Of course there are ex-Treasury officials in the senior ranks of the Departments and there is an equivalent interflow in the opposite direction. It is not hard for such people to see each other's points of view, and civil servants of all ranks who are transferred from one Department to another find no difficulty in transferring their allegiance to their new Department. This is certainly one of the virtues of the departmental system.

## DEPARTMENTAL MANAGEMENT

Each Department has its own functional responsibilities in which H.M. Treasury has no concern, except through its finance function. Departmental management is a large subject which can be only briefly outlined here. It is shared by the Permanent Secretary with his senior administrators (Deputy Secretaries and Under Secretaries) who control the several functional Divisions of the Department's Headquarters, some of which are concerned with the policy, regulatory and general administrative aspects of the major functions for which the Minister is responsible to Cabinet and Parliament, while others are concerned with those housekeeping or common service functions which are needed in the running of the Department in its entirety. Headquarters' policy-making may be divided between assistance to the Minister, through experienced advice and the provision of essential informational, statistical and research services, and administrative policy-making in shaping and managing the Department to achieve its overall objectives. Under the Minister the Permanent Secretary has virtually three distinct responsibilities: (1) advising the Minister and providing him with information needed in policy-making, (2) personal responsibility for the Department's finance, as its Accounting Officer (under appointment by the Treasury), and operating direct to the Comptroller and Auditor General and the Public Accounts Committee of the House of Commons, and (3) overall management of the Department on the Minister's behalf.

Over the years a Department may acquire an image and a life of its own, but it has to be remembered that it exists to fulfil that part of the Executive's function which has been entrusted to its Minister and has no right of existence as a mere preserve of the Civil Service.

The operation of Treasury Control within the Department is the particular responsibility of the Divisions under the charge of the Principal Establishment Officer and the Principal Finance Officer in whose activities the Permanant Secretary is bound to evince a special interest. In a sense Treasury Control is shared with the Department on a co-operative basis and these officials adopt an attitude to the other branches of the Department very similar to that adopted by the Treasury in relation to the Department. The Establishment Officer has responsibility for such staff activities as appointment, allocation, promotion, discipline and discharge in which the Minister is still the final authority. He works in close liaison with the Departmental Whitley Council which is established independently to deal with staff matters that relate to the Department as distinct from those concerning a number of Departments or the Service as a whole.[1] The Principal Finance Officer (probably with some such title as 'Accountant General') is responsible for internal accounting and audit, for co-ordination of the estimates, finance statistics, and for liaison with the Exchequer and Audit Department, whose officials in the case of the larger Departments may be domiciled within the Department to facilitate their checking of the Appropriation Accounts as the basic transactions are completed. They are there as a matter of convenience and have no power to intervene in the Department's executive business. Being themselves civil servants they are fully aware of their proper position, and relationships between the two groups are co-operative and amicable. In fact their on-the-spot advice can often be of value to the departmental authorities, whose one concern is to ensure that in this sphere Parliament's wishes are carried out to the letter.

Where the Department has a distinct executive element, in the shape of separate establishments or an inspectorate, or in a service-providing organization of Regional Offices and Local Offices (as in the Post Office, Social Security Departments, Revenue Departments and the Ministry of Public Building and Works) executive and managerial authority is delegated to Regional Controllers

[1] See page 133 above.

P

and other Executives, varying somewhat in scope from Department to Department, and to the Managers of Local Offices, ranking from Executive Officer in the smallest to Chief Executive Officer in a few of the largest but, in an average size office with a staff of from fifteen to fifty, under a Higher or Senior Executive Officer.

Within each Department authority is passed down the line through general regulations, specific instructions and files, personal contacts, staff conferences, Whitley discussions, common service provision, financial regulation, audit and inspection, organization and methods, circulation of information, publication of a house journal, staff training and so forth. Interdepartmental committees may be set up at any level, and personal contacts are maintained with officials in other bodies where their activities contact and overlap and such liaison is obviously desirable to get the job done.

Here then is a real complexity of management, ranging from the higher management at Headquarters to the middle management further down, to all of which many of the principles of general management apply. In this field of management there is now a general Civil Service pattern which has grown up to a large extent spontaneously over a long period and as the result of inter-conflict and co-ordination between the Treasury and the Departments, to some extent assisted by the interflow of staffs between the Departments. Today it is realized that it generally works very well, although it often calls for more foresight and a greater co-ordinative effort than it usually receives. There is a prospect that automation will simplify the communications network and concentrate the web of control but not remove the need for more conscious attention to management than in the past.

### PROFESSIONAL RELATIONSHIPS

Under this heading will be considered three important professional factors: (1) Leadership of the Elite, (2) Opposite-number Contacts, and (3) Professional Activities.

(1) *The Elite* The gradual emergence of the Administrative Class, which did not take its final form until the Reorganization of 1919/ 20, and the establishment of this class as an elite has been well authenticated in the literature of the Civil Service and is clearly explicable by the facts of the situation. With the elimination by the reforms of 1853/1870 of the favourites of the politicians and the place-seeking 'failures' of the aristocracy, and their progressive replacement by the highly intellectual Oxbridge products of the Upper Middle Class, the leadership group of the Civil Service became something of a closed shop, mainly recruited at the university-

leaving stage and only occasionally, until recent post-war decades, receiving outsiders by promotion from within the Service. This 'eliteness' did not rest solely upon the selectness of their appointment: they were also highly competent, in virtue of the eminent suitability of their classical literary education, to meet the administrative needs of the pre-Social Service State. Their essentially academic outlook on life made them admirable foils to their more forthcoming political masters, who were nevertheless imbued with similar prejudices.

These Victorian politicians, themselves members of a compact ruling group, found staunch supporters in their new administrative aides and had not the slightest wish to return to the bad old patronage days. After all, the two groups—political and professional—even though they tended to come from rather different strata of the bourgeoisie, had in general been to the same public schools, grappled with the same Latin texts which they continued to quote throughout their lives, and met each other at the country house parties so admirably described by Anthony Trollope, who was in a position to observe them at close quarters with acute, if critical, understanding. They read *The Times,* frequented the same clubs and saw eye to eye on the things that mattered! Even if brilliance of scholarship had lifted some of these scholars rather higher in the world than perhaps their beginnings warranted they were not backward in assuming the colour and manner of their new society. As H. E. Dale writes in what is still one of the best interpretations of the Higher Civil Service in its heyday:

'The question how far the men who rise to the top in the Civil Service take on the 'tone' or 'colour' of a class other than that to which they belong is delicate and difficult. The only definite information bearing on the question is the figure relating to membership of the great London clubs. More than three-quarters of our high administrative officials belong to one or more clubs of high status and considerable luxury, where the entrance fee might be twenty guineas or more, and the annual subscription from twelve to twenty guineas. These institutions are of the upper class (not even of the upper-middle) in their premises, their equipment, the style of living practised there, their whole atmosphere. Though many of the members would not be described as wealthy, only a wealthy man could unaided provide for himself and his family space, food and drink, service, and other amenities of life to the same standard as he will find at the Union, the Travellers', or the Reform. It is a fair presumption that a civil servant who joins such an institution ranks himself socially with the opulent classes of the community, if he does not belong to them by origin. The figures and inferences set out above suggest that nothing like three out of every four high permanent officials belong by origin to those classes. It follows that a large proportion of the Higher Civil Service, having gained by their talent a right to enter a social class above that to which they were born, have more or less deliberately exercised the right. That proportion, and the proportion who belong by birth to the upper and upper-middle class, together include nearly all the chiefs of the Service'.[1]

With the growth of the Civil Service towards the end of the nineteenth century and after, the dual division of labour recommended by Trevelyan and Northcote was no longer adequate to the administrative needs of the Departments. An Intermediate Class had already begun to appear to deal with the superior, but rather uninspiring, work of the new audit and accounting branches. For these it was deemed that the highest classical scholarship was not essential and recruits with lesser degrees could be accepted. It was an astute move at Reorganization to see that these new middlemen should constitute a class of their own with the rather confusing title of Executive, and thus in a much expanded Serevice to ensure the preservation of the selectness of the leadership group! The system in fact worked admirably up to 1939, with so many other national institutions, and was accepted, despite occasional mutterings from those frustrated by the exiguousness of the bridges between the Administrative Class and the rest. The Administrators had no difficulty in maintaining their leadership prestige within the Service.

In the meantime the working class politicians came to occupy the seats of power in growing numbers, boys from working class families had risen through scholarship and competed successfully in the examinations, although not in numbers in any sense proportionate to that class's size or intelligence potential. Yet in neither case does the system seem to have since been greatly modified. The old traditions continue in both the political and the administrative spheres. The influence of the elite is still hardly challenged, except perhaps by external changes which could well reduce its function to the status of the human appendix.

It is little mitigation of the situation to suggest that today half the present Administrative Class have been recruited from below. Few of those who came up from the middle grades occupy the leading positions, which are still largely the monopoly of the

[1] H. E. Dale in *The Higher Civil Service of Great Britain* (Oxford Univ., 1941) pp. 50–51. Today the figures quoted for club fees must be radically revised in light both of the great decrease in the value of the £ and also of post war changes in income levels, taxation and social relationships. By 'Higher Civil Service' Mr. Dale meant the equivalent of Assistant Secretary and above.

higher university element. These others belong to two broad types. Those who have come up at an early competition stage and those who have been selected at later stages in their careers. The former are a special feature of the post-war Civil Service and there is no reason to suppose that they will not be as effectively assimilated to the Administrative Class as were their forerunners. With regard to those selected at later stages in their career the element of chance has no doubt entered into the process to a high degree. Before the war there were very few, but the war created a need that the authorities were unable fully to meet from other sources. With regard to the individual much depended upon his having the right opportunity in the right place at the right time, and even in such instances, the decision having been made by a member or members of the Administrative Class, it is likely that the generally held conception of the sort of person fitted to be a member of that select corps will have had an important influence on the result. Among the competent, even brilliant, type of civil servant in the other ranks there are those who are always on the side of authority and quite exceptionally adept at formulating the answer that will be most acceptable to those at the top. It is no secret that they get on better than those who are outspoken and speak their minds on matters on which their opinions are sought. It is less that the administrator will consciously eliminate such types than that their own chiefs will see that they do not even appear in the running. Thus, in the final reckoning all who are selected from within the Civil Service to enter the Administrative Class will have had to conform to tests laid down by members of that class. They must be *persona grata,* and it is rarely that a mistake is made.

The present organization of the Civil Service, coupled with the intellectual predominance and the social homogeneity of the Administrative Class, thus places an almost overwhelming controlling power in the hands of that Class. The Administrative Class is in fact one of the most powerful oligarchies in existence. It has ruled over its own particular sphere for the best part of a hundred years almost without challenge. Its quiet, impersonal and highly responsible exercise of its great power, springing from a great sense of duty, has so obscured the realities of its position as to disarm criticism. Yet despite its efficiency, devotion to duty and sense of mission this power is no less pervasive. The rest of the Civil Service exercises initiative only by its good graces. In this sense the only will in the Civil Service is the will of the Administrative Class. On its record of public service it stands unchallenged, setting an example that the lesser breeds of official strive, almost hopelessly, to emulate.

(2) *Opposite-number Contacts* General control within the Service is aided by the pattern of general classes (as opposed to individual postings or independent departmental hierarchies) which operates horizontally across the vertical divisions created by the system of autonomous Departments and enables officials in one Department readily to identify their opposite numbers in other Departments, and thus to facilitate informal contacts in the conduct of business. Thus it is not only the general acceptance of the elite that helps to create the image of the Civil Service as an entity, but also the recognition at lower levels of the relative equivalence in authority and competence of officials in one Department by their opposite numbers in another.

Normal administration (some would say 'bureaucracy') insists that questions to be cleared at certain levels of authority must pass up the line to the appropriate point for decision, although in everyday practice competent subordinates are able to take, what may be called routine, decisions without such referring. In the case of questions of this type affecting two Departments this would mean passing the question up the line in one Department to the appropriate level, bridging the gap between the Departments at that level, and then passing the question down the line in the second Department for advice before the whole process is gone through in reverse. To operate in this way would mean working to rule with a vengeance! Officials learn to assess how far a matter for decision needs to be passed up the line and to know at what point in another Department the required decision or information is likely to be forthcoming. They can usually designate their opposite number in another organization and they get into the habit of making informal contacts by telephone or personal call which will cut down the normal bureaucratic process to a minimum. Such opposite-number contacts are important in all administering, but they are greatly facilitated by the system of classes and grades whereby an official in one unit can readily assess the point of contact in another at which a successful issue can be anticipated.

(3) *Professional Activities* The Civil Service is in a sense a profession and indeed a noble profession, for it has a high tradition of service and self-effacement, which distinguishes it from a mere occupation, a means of earning a living. It is in this special civil service spirit, which has no taint of bureaucracy, that Lord Bridges, in his *Portrait of a Profession*,[1] discovered the professional attitudes of the British Civil Service. Otherwise the Civil Service lacks certain characteristics that are essential to a profession, namely,

[1] See Sir Edward Bridges's Rede Lecture *Portrait of a Profession* (Cambridge, 1950).

autonomy and powers of self-regulation, often in other fields legalized by statute. The Civil Service in its subordination to the political organs of the State could never achieve the autonomy of a profession without becoming bureaucratic. Its standards of competence have been so closely determined by the system of competitive recruitment that so far no strong urge has been felt to take steps consciously to improve these standards. The multifarious nature of the Civil Service tends also to act against a single professional unity. Indeed the content of his lecture suggests that Lord Bridges had the Administrative Class mainly in mind and it is common practice to consider the other reaches of the Civil Service as being of small professional importance, an attitude that is usually strenuously resisted only by those civil servants who are also members of other professions.

There is no autonomous body solely concerned with the strictly professional interest of the Civil Service. The Staff Side of the National Whitley Council and the individual staff associations, usually to a much lesser degree, are the only bodies with aspirations in this field and they are much more actively concerned in the trade union than the wider professional interests of their clientele. It is not that professional matters are outside their scope, but that bread and butter problems must take priority under a sort of Gresham's Law in staff relationships that relegates purely professional problems to a subsidiary position.

It is doubtful whether a wider conception on Civil Service professionalism can develop unless and until more interest is shown by the individual civil servant in the study of the techniques of public administration. The only existing body in Britain that has such an objective in view is the Royal Institute of Public Administration,[1] which, however, is concerned with all branches of public administration and is constitutionally not designed to encourage a purely Civil Service viewpoint. It may well be that the recent introduction of a professional Diploma in Government Administration[1] specifically for civil servants (as counterpart to the Diploma in Municipal Administration previously introduced for local government officials) will help to change the situation, but the relatively modest success of the innovation to date gives little room for optimism on this score.

## CONCLUSIONS ON CONTROL

Simply stated, control of the British Civil Service can be summed up as a straight-forward minister–civil servant relationship. The

[1] See page 99.

former decides, the latter administers: but, since the former's decision depends to some extent upon the latter's advice, based upon his professional knowledge and experience, this initial simplicity soon assumes an appearance of confusing complexity. The present and preceding chapters have attempted to map these complexities, which lead in many directions and emerge as a web of control operating both from without and within the Administration. No one activates the administrative system from one point, no one occupies a position from which complete control can be operated. As the Cabinet system is a co-operative enterprise at political level, so is the supporting administrative system a co-operative enterprise, not responsive to one controlling impulse. In this sphere we are confronted by an intricacy of routes and cross-routes, of controls and influences operating over these routes, of checks and balances preventing either an excess or a failure of power at any particular point. It may seem highly illogical, but it is largely the result of natural growth, and it works!

# CHAPTER XI

## OTHER CIVIL SERVICES

As we saw in Chapter I the Civil Service comprises the staffs of the Central Administration whose salaries are paid out of funds authorized by Parliament at Westminster. So far this book has been largely confined to discussion of the problems of the non-industrial sectors and one of the topics of the present chapter will therefore be the Industrial Civil Service. But there are a number of other separate government administrations operating in the islands, if not all strictly within the United Kingdom, which should also be mentioned. These are the Civil Services of Northern Ireland, the Channel Islands and the Isle of Man, which will be briefly described.

Even within the Central Administration the line is not always easily drawn and there are a number of organizations which have a decidedly civil service flavour. Such, for example, are the Corporation of Trinity House, dating back to 1514, and the more modern British Council (1934) and Arts Council (1940), types of public corporation. In the same category is the United Kingdom Atomic Energy Authority, which retains the staffing pattern of the Civil Service out of which it grew and whose finances are still closely controlled by the Treasury. The Post Office, on the other hand, whose finances are now separated from the Treasury is still staffed by civil servants although its status is at present under active reconsideration. However, in the main the public corporations, particularly those responsible for the nationalized industries in the power field, are independently staffed and not therefore within the scope of the present discussion.

Among other interesting organizations there is the Royal Household from which the Civil Service originally sprung, but today, although it still retains certain public functions, this is essentially the private staff of the Sovereign and may be regarded as beyond the borders of our field, as may the administrative staffs of the Church of England, which nevertheless, as an established church, stands close to the government field. In fact the Church Commissioners, concerned with certain organization and finance matters, are certainly in the quasi-Civil Service category. The staffs of the

Houses of Parliament are also separate, yet they are so closely related in form and attitudes to the Civil Service that a section is being specially devoted to them.

Local government officials are often confused by the public with civil servants, a confusion which becomes more and more understandable with so many civil servants operating in the localities. Nevertheless their allegiance to their separate local authorities and their terms of service differentiate them from the Civil Service. It is only latterly that these officials have begun to emerge as a specific Local Government 'Service'. Despite their undoubted separateness it is felt that their function and outlook are so close to that of the Civil Service that it is appropriate to include a brief section about them.

In addition, there are the country's Oversea Services to which the following chapter is being devoted.

### INDUSTRIAL CIVIL SERVICE

The Industrial Civil Service, whose importance, even existence, is often overlooked in the discussion of Civil Service matters, includes all the industrial workers—craftsmen, tradesmen, labourers and others—who are employed in the workshops and factories and on various constructional works under a number of Departments, among which the most important (with approximate totals at present employed) are: Aviation (14,000), Defence (169,000), Home Office (4,000), Public Building and Works (39,000), Stationery Office (4,000), Technology (1,000) and Royal Mint (800). Until the beginning of 1965 over a hundred thousand industrial workers were so graded in the Post Office, but from 1st April of that year these have been re-graded non-industrial, with consequent changes in the overall totals for the two sectors. The total of 235,800 industrial civil servants employed on 1st April, 1965, indicates the importance of this field and represents a considerable increase in such public activity since 1939, when the figures were already inflated by war preparations.

Apart from the essentially non-administrative nature of the work performed by the industrial grades, the main distinction between them and the non-industrial civil servants formerly centred around their different terms of service. While the very nature of official employment gave them certain advantages, industrial civil servants were employed on the same general conditions as their opposite numbers in outside employment, with the Fair Wages Provisions being one of the main determining factors (see below). They enjoyed no privileges in regard to tenure and such matters as the payment of wages during sick absences, although there were some established posts in this occupational field carrying the privileges of the permanent civil servant to which unestablished industrials could be recruited by nomination to the Civil Service Commission in the normal way. Since the war, however, under the influence of the substantial changes in the status and advantages of the ordinary industrial worker and a much modified social outlook, considerable improvements have been made in the position of the Industrial Civil Service, which is now much more closely assimilated to the general Civil Service pattern discussed in the earlier chapters of this book.

The standards of the equivalent outside employment have always been applied to the industrial grades but the great improvements in that field have rendered it less difficult to raise the standards and status of the latter. Many of them have been conceded establishment, although claims to complete establishment have been rejected on the grounds that the State needs a substantial margin of temporary workers to meet the wide fluctuations in manpower demands that are liable to arise from changes in governmental policy. Agreeing just where the line should be drawn has been among the most important responsibilities of the trade unions in this field. Members of the industrial grades have been represented not by special Civil Service staff associations but by the appropriate general trade unions for their particular occupations. The inclusion of workers in both public and private employment in the same trade unions has led to modifications in the staff consultation systems. Thus, during the currency of the Trade Disputes and Trade Unions Act, 1927/1946, the restrictions imposed upon the Civil Service[1] did not apply to industrial civil servants.

Whitleyism was introduced into the Government's industrial establishments as a matter of course in 1919, ahead of its application to the Non-Industrial Civil Service,[2] and by the end of the following year Joint Industrial Councils had been established on the lines proposed by the Reconstruction Committee,[3] in the existing Office of Works, Admiralty, Ministry of Munitions, Air Ministry, War Office and Stationery Office, while separate Joint Trade Councils had been brought into existence for government employees in the engineering, shipbuilding, building and miscellaneous trades.

The interests of these industrial civil servants continue to be looked after by these two types of council. Departmental Joint

[1] See page 135 above.
[2] See page 129 above.
[3] See page 129 above.

Councils have been maintained in the major employing Departments, supported where necessary by joint committees for the separate establishments on a factory, works, shop or local basis. The actual scheme varies from Department to Department. The Official Side consists of departmental representatives and one member appointed by the Minister of Labour, while the Trade Union Side is appointed by those unions which have members within the Department. The function of the Departmental Joint Councils is to consider and discuss matters other than trade questions which are of mutual and domestic concern to the Department and its industrial employees. These include such matters as the interpretation of departmental regulations, welfare, hours and holidays, provision of tools, staff transfers, and so forth.

Trade questions are dealt with by separate Trade Joint Councils, of which there are three covering severally the Shipbuilding, the Engineering and the Miscellaneous Trades. They are particularly concerned with wages and other conditions of service. The Official Sides are appointed by Ministers of the Departments concerned and include also representatives of the Treasury and the Ministry of Labour. The Trade Union Sides are appointed by unions having members in the establishments covered by the Council. By a special arrangement the Forestry Commission have a Joint Council which combines the functions of both the departmental and the trade councils.

These several councils are not linked in any way with the Civil Service National Whitley Council, but general service questions affecting the Industrial Civil Service are looked after by a Joint Co-ordinating Committee for Government Industrial Establishments, under the chairmanship of a senior Treasury official. The Official Side consists of representatives of the several employing Departments, the Treasury and the Ministry of Labour, while the Trade Union Side is composed of three representatives of each of the three Trade Joint Councils.[1]

The pay principles recommended by the Priestley Commission[2] do not apply to the Industrial Civil Service. The Government had for a long time made it a practice to include Fair Wages clauses in its contracts, imposing upon outside contractors the obligation of paying proper wages in accordance with current market conditions, and discountenancing any attempt to undercut prices by paying low wages. It could hardly have conceded less favourable conditions to its own workers. The present arrangements are based upon

[1] See Ministry of Labour's *Industrial Relations Handbook* (H.M.S.O., 1961) pp. 119–120.

[2] See page 49 above.

the Fair Wages Resolution, endorsed by the House of Commons on 14th October, 1946, under which the Government in its relations with its own industrial employees undertook to pay rates of wages and to observe conditions of employment not less favourable than those established for the trade or industry in the district where the work is carried out. It is thus clear that while the standards of remuneration of industrial civil servants are safeguarded by public policy the wage structure is not a purely Civil Service arrangement but remains geared to the industrial market. One of the consequences of this is that the Industrial Civil Service has since the war maintained its relativity with industry according to practice already existing and has enjoyed the advances in remuneration made by workers in general during recent years.

Obviously these advances have not come as a matter of course, and the system of joint consultation has made an important contribution here as in the Civil Service more generally, notably in the introduction of sick pay and improvements in general conditions of service, as well as in the planned extension of establishment with superannuation rights to an agreed total of industrial workers spread over the Departments to a number which they could reasonably expect to employ permanently in the future. Under these arrangements each industrial official designated for establishment has to be nominated to the Civil Service Commission for completion of the usual formalities and issue of a Civil Service Certificate.

It should be emphasized in conclusion that the Industrial Civil Service is separate only in a functional sense. It forms an integral part of the Departments' staffs and is subject to the overall direction of the Minister and his senior administrators.

There has recently been an important development which is bound to change the whole position of the Industrial Civil Service as described in the foregoing paragraphs. In considering the question of *Pay of Industrial Civil Servants,* put to them by the Government, the National Board for Prices and Income (in their *Report No. 18* (Cmnd. 3034) of June 1966) strongly recommended that the nation wide distinction between staff and workers should be discarded as completely out of date in the present circumstances. Since the distinction between the Industrial and the Non-Industrial Civil Services has been based upon this wider convention the adoption of this policy would end the distinction between the two 'services'. The Board conclude their proposals with the recommendation that "the Government should make it its aim, over a period of time, to build on what is common to the industrial and non-industrial civil services with the ultimate objective of according all Government workers equality of status."

NORTHERN IRELAND

Between 1801 and 1921 Ireland formed part of the United Kingdom, retaining to some extent its own administrative system centred upon Dublin. In the Government of Ireland Act, 1920, which provided for the creation of separate parliaments in Southern and Northern Ireland, with powers to unite, the present Government of Northern Ireland had its origin. The outcome was that, when Southern Ireland accepted a Free State with Dominion status, Northern Ireland opted out of the all-Ireland proposal in December 1921 and accepted partition. The existing system of government has federal characteristics, although the legislative supremacy of the United Kingdom Parliament in certain matters means that 'quasi-federal' is probably a more apt label.

The Sovereign is represented by the Governor appointed, for six-year terms, by the Crown. There is a separate Parliament in Belfast consisting of two chambers. The House of Commons has 52 members, 48 of whom are elected in single-member constituencies while the other four represent Queen's University, Belfast. Its maximum term is five years, subject to dissolution earlier by the Governor on the recommendation of the Prime Minister. The Senate has 24 members, who are elected for eight years by the House of Commons under a system of proportional representation, plus the Lord Mayor of Belfast and the Mayor of Londonderry, *ex officio.* Half of the Senators retire every four years. Generally the procedures of both Houses are moulded on Westminster. Northern Ireland also sends twelve elected members to the United Kingdom House of Commons. There is a separate system of law courts under a Supreme Court of Judicature for Northern Ireland, from which on certain conditions appeals may go to the House of Lords.

The Northern Ireland Parliament is empowered to legislate for the six counties, except on (1) matters of Imperial concern, which include the Crown, making peace or war, military, naval and air forces, treaties, titles of honour, treason, naturalization, domicile, external trade, submarine cables, wireless telegraphy, aerial navigation, lighthouses, coinage, etc., and (2) matters 'reserved' to the United Kingdom Parliament, i.e. postal services, post office and trustee savings banks, designs for stamps.

Executive powers are exercised by the Executive Committee of the Northern Ireland Privy Council, or Cabinet, consisting of Ministers appointed by the Governor. A Minister, if not already a Member of Parliament, must become one within six months, although a Minister without Portfolio may be excepted. The present Cabinet consists of the Prime Minister and the Ministers of the following Departments, together with the Minister in the Senate: Finance, Home Affairs, Health and Social Services (formerly Labour and National Insurance), Education, Agriculture, Commerce, and Development Planning. Apart from these Ministries there are the Cabinet Office, Public Record Office, Office of the Parliamentary Draftsman, the Exchequer and Audit Department (under the N.I. Comptroller and Auditor General), the National Assistance Board, and the Civil Service Commission.

The Civil Service, originally taken over from the Imperial Departments is regulated by Orders made by the Governor and organized on the British pattern, except that in the Administrative Class there is a Deputy Principal between the Principal and Assistant Principal grades and the Executive and Clerical Classes have been combined and regraded Staff Officer, Junior Staff Officer, Senior Clerk, Clerk and Clerical Assistant. The total Civil Service staffs on 31st March, 1965 (excluding industrials and part-time employees) was 10,130. These were employed in the Departments just mentioned and the Houses of Parliament.

Recruitment is the responsibility of three Civil Service Commissioners appoined by the Governor. The principle of open competition is accepted, although, as in the case of Britain, its original objectivity has been eroded. Today educational suitability is generally assessed on the basis of successes in the General Certificate of Education examinations, but the actual choice is made by Selection Boards constituted from a panel of officials, which includes the Permanent Secretaries of the Ministries of Finance and Education and the Secretary of the Civil Service Commission, together with officers of Deputy Principal rank and above in the several Departments who have experience of establishment work. In the case of recruitment to the Administrative Class (Assistant Principals) examinations are undertaken, by Method I and Method II,[1] on behalf of the Northern Ireland Government by the Civil Service Commission in London.

Civil Service regulations are made under the authority of the Minister of Finance, in consultation with the Departments and the staff through their representatives. General procedures are similar to those of the Home Civil Service, except that the compactness of the individual Departments and of the Service as a whole facilitates management and the achievement of maximum co-ordination and deployment of abilities.

Civil Servants organize their own staff associations, and there

---

[1] See page 72 above.

is a Whitley Council for the non-industrial staffs, with a membership of twenty. This consists of an Official Side of ten senior officials nominated by the Governor, including one from each of the Ministries of Finance and of Health and Social Services, and a Staff Side of ten representatives of approved staff associations. The Chairman comes from the Official Side and the Vice-Chairman from the Staff Side, and each side selects a secretary from its membership.

The Excepted and Reserved Services are undertaken by United Kingdom Departments through their own offices and officials in Northern Ireland. Thus the Northern Ireland and United Kingdom Civil Services work side by side in the same territories similarly to the State and Federal Civil Services in the United States.

### THE CHANNEL ISLANDS

Arising from their history as the only surviving territories of the Dukedom of Normandy and their geographical proximity to France, the Channel Islands enjoy a high measure of self-government. Matters of diplomacy, defence and post office services are handled by the Home Government, but statutes passed at Westminster apply to the Islands only when specific reference is made therein. Otherwise legislation is enacted on the spot. Contacts between the Crown and the Islands are made through the Privy Council and the Home Secretary.

The Channel Islands are divided into the separate Bailiwicks of Jersey and of Guernsey, the latter including Alderney and Sark each of which has its own governmental institutions. For each Bailiwick there is a Lieutenant-Governor and a Bailiff appointed by the Crown. Each has its own legislature, known as the States, and system of law courts, over each of which the respective Bailiff acts as President. Administration is carried on through a series of boards, committees and councils appointed by the States. There are separate Civil Services for each Bailiwick, whose duties, because of the diminutive size of the two communities, partake of the functions of both central and local government.

### JERSEY

*Constitution*[1] The States of Jersey consist of 12 Senators, elected for six years with half retiring every three years; the 12 Constables of the twelve Parishes of the island; and 28 elected Deputies, all retiring every three years. All elections are based upon universal

[1] Recently codified in *States of Jersey Law,* 1966.

suffrage. The Dean of Jersey, the Attorney-General and the Solicitor-General, appointed by the Crown, sit and speak in the States but cannot vote. The officers of the States are the Greffier of the States who is the clerk of the States, the Deputy Greffier of the States who is the clerk-assistant of the States, and the Viscount who is the executive officer of the States. Administration is supervised by the States through a series of committees made up of their own members. The following list of committees existing in 1966 indicates the wide range of such administration:

Agriculture, Ann Alice Rayner Fund Delegation, Channel Islands Air Advisory Council, Common Market, Cottage Homes, Defence, Deux Greffes, Education, Elizabeth House, Essential Commodities, Establishment, Etat Civil, Finance, Gambling, Harbours and Airport, Housing, Industrial Disputes, Island Development, Joint Advisory Council, Judicial Reform, Legislation, Prison Board, Public Health, Sewerage Board, Social Security, Tariff Council, Telephones, Tourism, War Department Properties and Watersplash Petition.

*Administration* This is carried out by civil servants employed in several departments which, as in the case of the local government system in England and Wales, do not necessarily coincide with the committees of the States. The present departments are:

Agriculture, Airport, Aliens, Bailiff's, Civil Defence, Education, General Hospital, Harbour Master's, H.M. Prison, Housing, Impôts, Income Tax, Judicial Greffe, Land Officer's, Law Officer's, Motor Traffic, Office of the Lieutenant General, Official Analyst's, Pathological Laboratory, Planning Officer's, Police Headquarters, Probation Officer's, Public Health, Public Markets, St. Saviour's Hospital, School Dental Officer's, Sewerage Board, Social Security, States' Engineer's, States' Greffe, States' Treasury, Superintendent Registrar, Telephones, Tourism, Viscount's, and Weights and Measures.

The Civil Service of Jersey is regulated by *Actes des Etats,* confirmed by Orders in Council. The present system is legalized in the *Acte* entitled 'Civil Service Administration (Jersey) Law, 1948', amended by similar *Actes* of 1953 and 1961. Detailed Rules are issued from time to time under these *Actes*.

Control of recruitment and other matters of personnel management are placed in the hands of a Committee of the States, originally known as the Civil Service Board but now the Establishment Committee. Up till 1953 acutal appointments and dismissals remained within the discretion of the several committees of the States and other administering authorities, but the new *Acte* converted the

Board into an employing body for the States which now, as Establishment Committee, makes all appointments and dismissals, but regard must still be had to the views of the authority to whom the officer is, or is to be, allocated. The Committee is also responsible for determining remuneration and other conditions of employment of all officers.

Employees of the States are classified as 'officers' and certain other categories, only the former being usually included in the term 'civil servant'. The legal definition reads:

" "Officer" means an employee of the States or of any administration of the States, whether established or unestablished, whose duties are wholly or mainly administrative, professional, technical or clerical, but does not include any person employed wholly or mainly as an industrial or manual worker, any member of the States of Jersey Police Force or the States of Jersey Fire Service, any school teacher, any member of the staff of the public prison or any of the persons specified in Article 5 of the Civil Service Administration (Supplementary Provisions) (Jersey) Law, 1950'.[1]

The Civil Service is organized in three broad categories and a number of specialist groupings. The main categories are (1) the General Grade, divided into Lower, Intermediate and Higher Divisions, (2) the three Executive Grades, B, A and Higher, and (3) the Administrative Grade, divided into six Groups from F up to A. The General Grade includes typists, machine operators, junior clerks and several other types of junior posts, but not messengers. To each of these specific divisions, grades and groups, a short salary scale is allocated. The specialist groupings are similarly graded, but some professionals and technicians are included in the Executive and Administrative Grades. The salary scales are adjusted from time to time by the Establishment Committee, after consultation with the administering authorities and representatives of the staff. Increments according to the service scale may be deferred by the Committee where the administering authority certifies that the service of the officer has been unsatisfactory.

The Establishment Committee is responsible for promotional appointments, on recommendations upon officials' performance from the administering authority, which set up Appointments Boards for the purpose. These have a similar function to the promotion boards in the United Kingdom. The rules provide that:

(1) The principle governing all questions of promotion shall be the efficiency of the civil service, and promotions shall depend on the fitness of the candidate for the grade to which promotion is

[1] *Civil Service Administration (Jersey) Law,* 1961, Art. 1.

contemplated. In promotion to a post in which the work is of a routine character, seniority shall carry more weight than in the case of promotion to a post carrying greater responsibilities.

(2) An officer who so desires may submit to the Establishment Committee a brief statement of his educational record, including the studies and examinations undertaken since leaving school and generally of any information illustrating qualifications, experience and inclination.[1]

The rules also cover such matters as annual leave, special leave and sick absences, and include a comprehensive scheme of pensions. Probably the most interesting enactment is embodied under the sub-heading 'Rules for the Conduct of Staff'.[2] This covers not only the usual veto of personal influence, political participation and the publication of official information without prior permission, but also extends to such matters as private conduct, punctuality and even smoking on official premises, which in the Home Civil Service are left to convention and local regulation. An important right is conferred upon the individual official to make submissions in writing to the Establishment Committee, providing they are addressed through the head of the department or other administering authority, and the staff also have the right of direct approach to the Establishment Officer without having to obtain prior permission from the head of the department. In 1966 the total strength of the Jersey Civil Service was 700.

## GUERNSEY

*Constitution* In Guernsey the States of Deliberation is broadly similar in membership and function to the States of Jersey. In place of the Senators of the latter there are 12 Conseillers, elected by a special body known as the States of Election. There are also 33 People's Deputies, elected by popular franchise, and 10 Douzaine Representatives, of the ten Douzaines or Parishes, each of which has its council of 12 persons. The States of Election is an electoral college consisting of the Bailiff, Conseillers, People's Deputies of the States of Deliberation, as well as the 12 Jurats, the 12 Rectors, H.M. Attorney General, H.M. Solicitor General and 34 Douzaine Representatives. For the election of Conseillers 4 representatives of the States of Alderney are added.

Guernsey is generally responsible for the islands of Alderney and Sark, but Alderney has its own elected President and States of nine

---

[1] *Civil Service Administration (Salaries) (Jersey) Rules,* 1964, para. 6.
[2] *Civil Service Administration (General) (Jersey) Rules,* 1949, paras. 10 and 26.

members and its own Court, while Sark has a system which is a mixture of feudal and popular government. At the head of the latter is the Seigneur—at present *La Dame de Serq*—who is assisted by the Chief Pleas, an assembly consisting of 40 Tenants and 12 elected Deputies, presided over by the Seneschal.

In Guernsey Her Majesty's Greffier acts as Clerk of the Court, Clerk of the States and Registrar of Births, Marriages and Deaths. Administration is supervised by the States through a series of Boards and Committees, made up of members of the States, but in some cases including also non-members. The following were operating during 1966:

Accident Law Reform Committee, Advisory and Finance Committee, Agriculture Committee, Ancient Monuments Committee, Appointments Board, Arts Committee, Bailiff and Law Officers Salaries Investigation Committee, Bathing Places Committee, Board of Administration, Board of Health, Cadastre Committee, Central Outdoor Assistance Board, Children Board, Civil Defence Committee, Civil Service Board, Civil Service Pensions Committee, Dairy Committee, Ecclesiastical Committee, Education Council, Electricity Board, Elizabeth College Board of Directors, Emergency Council, European Free Trade Association and Economic Community Committee, Fort George Development Committee, Gambling Investigation Committee, Horticultural Advisory Service Committee, Horticulture Committee, Horticultural Industry Investigation Committee, Hospital Board, Housing Authority, Income Tax Authority, Insurance Authority, Island Development Investigation Committee, Joint Guernsey-Alderney Advisory Council, Labour and Welfare Committee, Ladies' College Board of Governors, Law of Succession Committee, Legislation Committee, Liberation Religious Service Committee, Lifeboat Committee, Military Service Committee, Non-Contributory Pensions and Outdoor Relief Investigation Committee, Parochial Outdoor Assistance Boards, Passenger Transport Licensing Authority, Pilot Board, Police Committee, Post Office Advisory Committee, Preservation of Natural Beauty and Control of Agricultural Land Committee, Priaulx Library Council, Prison Board, Public Assistance Authority, Public Thoroughfares Committee, Reception Committee, Sea Fisheres Committee, Stranger Poor Assistance Committee, Subsidies Investigation Committee, Telephone Council, Tourist Committee, Trading Stamps Investigation Committee, and Water Board.

*Administration* Administration is undertaken by civil servants, who are responsible to the several Committees of the States. The main departments in which they serve are:

Agriculture, Horticulture, Board of Administration, Board of Health, Cadastre (i.e. valuation for rating), Civil Defence, Civil Service Board, Education, Horticultural Advisory Service, Housing, Income Tax, Labour and Welfare, Police, Public Assistance, Island Development, Social Insurance, Public Thoroughfares, Tourist and the Trading Departments for Electricity, Water Works, Telephone and the Dairy.

The Board of Administration deals with a wide range of subjects which include the Treasury, Harbours, Airports (Guernsey and Alderney), Parks and Gardens, Markets, Slaughter House, Cold Stores, Customs and Excise, Immigration, Engineers and Architects, Public Works Department, Maintenance Department, Stamp Revenue Office, Weighbridges, Weights and Measures, Sewage Collection from Cesspools, Refuse Disposal, Fire Brigade, Foulon Cemetery and Crematorium, Automobile Registration and Taxation, the Committee Secretariat, and the States Office, Alderney. There are also separate offices for the Bailiff, the Law Officers of the Crown, the Greffe, H.M. Receiver General, H.M. Sheriff and H.M. Sergeant.

Under an Order in Council, entitled the *Loi Sur La Constitution D'Un Conseil De Nomination* (1932) an Appointments Board was established to appoint certain of the most senior officers of the Civil Service. Otherwise the Civil Service is regulated by Resolutions of the States which do not require confirmation by Order in Council. Apart from the exception just mentioned establishment matters are dealt with by the Civil Service Board, which is responsible to the States for all matters relating to the remuneration and conditions of service of all staff employed by the States, excluding (i) appointments of officers by the Appointments Board, of teaching staff by the Education Council and of nursing staff by the Board of Health and the Public Assistance Authority, and (ii) the numerical establishment and conditions of service, other than pay and emoluments, of the Island Police Force. The Civil Service Board's wide-ranging function includes the fixing and keeping under review, after consultation with the appropriate Committee, of the establishment for every department other than such technical posts as may be agreed between the Board and the employing committee concerned. The Board is involved in decisions on rates of pay, conditions of service and the filling of vacancies. It appoints members of the Official Side of any Joint Negotiating

Committee dealing with salaries and wages and conditions of service of all staff for which the Board is responsible and in negotiating and signing, on behalf of the States, general agreements on salaries and wages.

The Civil Service is organized broadly into (1) a General Grade, which includes typists, machine operators, Clerical Officers and Higher Clerical Officers, and (2) a series of Executive, Administrative, Professional and Technical grades each of which is divided into a number of groups and to each of which a short salary scale is allocated. In 1966 the total strength of the Guernsey Civil Service was 653.

### JERSEY AND GUERNSEY

From this rather summary account of the two island services it is clear that the two systems, although independent of each other, are strikingly similar. While adopting general civil service principles they combine the methods of both central and local administration. The use of committees for executive control is favoured and one cannot help remarking upon the high degree of functional differentiation—one might almost say 'proliferation'—which, if it appears excessive in view of the size of the administrations concerned, no doubt has the great advantage of ensuring that official and citizen co-operate intimately in the conduct of the public business.

### THE ISLE OF MAN

*Constitution* The Isle of Man, although subject to the general control of Parliament at Westminster, is not part of the United Kingdom and has a governmental system of its own. This consists of the Governor (ranking as Lieutenant-Governor), appointed by the Crown, and the ancient Tynwald, which is made up of (i) a Legislative Council of high dignitaries, two appointees of the Governor and five members elected by the House of Keys, and (ii) the House of Keys of 24 members, elected by the people.

*Administration* Administration is shared between the central services of the Governor, acting through his senior permanent official, the Government Secretary, and the several Boards of Tynwald. There is also an Executive Council which advises the Governor on all matters of policy and legislation. Its members are the Chairman of the Finance Board, the chairman of four of the Boards of Tynwald, as elected by the Tynwald, and two other members of

Tynwald, excluding *ex-officio* members, appointed by the Governor. The Governor's contact with Whitehall is through the Home Secretary, who is responsible for advising the Crown on the affairs of the Isle of Man as of the Channel Islands.

The interesting characteristic of this system from our viewpoint is the method of administration through a number of separate boards, to which members of both the Legislative Council and the House of Keys are appointed. Thus members of Tynwald act in both a legislative and an administrative capacity, and in fact their membership of the Boards to which they are assigned is compulsory.

Some Boards are composed entirely of members of Tynwald (usually five) and these are the following: Board of Agriculture and Fisheries, Assessment Board, Board of Education, Government Property Trustees (three members), Harbour Board, Health Services Board, Highway and Transport Board, Local Government Board, and Tourist Board. The Finance Board consists of a Chairman and two members, one of whom may belong to any other Board of Tynwald.

Other Boards, and bodies classified as such for various purposes, have outside members as well as members of Tynwald. These are the Airports Board, Civil Defence Commission, Civil Service Commission, Electricity Board, Forestry Mines and Lands Board, Gaming Board of Control, Local War Pensions Committee, Manx Electric Railway Board, Manx Museum and National Trust, Police Board, Board of Social Services, and Water Board.

From their titles it is clear that the functions of these bodies cover subjects that could fall under central, local or public corporation control in the United Kingdom.

The Central Services under the Governor's control handle specific subjects and also deal with any residuary matters which do not fall within the province of any Board or similar body. The departments concerned include: Government Office, Treasury, Employment Division, Income Tax Assessment Division, Meat Grading Division, Reprographic Department, Industrial Division, Attorney General's Department, General Registry, High Bailiff's Office, H.M. Prison, and Public Analyst's Department.

*The Civil Service* The Civil Service comprises the staffs of all Boards and Departments, and officers are interchangeable where the work is similar. This applies more particularly to the Administrative and Clerical grades. Co-ordination is effected through the Isle of Man Civil Service Commission (comprising three members of Tynwald, one other member appointed by the Governor, and the Government Secretary) which fixes establishments and arranges appointments and transfers. Practices and conditions are to a large extent modelled upon those of the Home Civil Service and salaries are in general related to posts which have been agreed as being analogous, mainly in the Home Civil Service or in local government service in the United Kingdom. Pensions for all civil servants are non-contributory, awarded by analogy with the U.K. Superannuation Acts. Staff interests are looked after by the Isle of Man Government Officers' Association and Whitley arrangements also operate. In 1966 the Isle of Man Civil Service totalled 472.

Only to a limited extent do United Kingdom Departments function in the Isle of Man. The General Post Office administers the postal and telegraph services and officers of H.M. Customs and Excise operate under a mutual arrangement between the two Governments. The Ministry of Defence has a few officers operating communications services and the B.B.C. runs a station amplifying radio and television reception.

### PARLIAMENTARY STAFFS

The House of Lords and the House of Commons each has its own staff of officials and employees who are appointed as servants of the respective Houses to provide them with the necessary administrative and other services. Appointments are made by senior officers of the Houses and the officials are not civil servants, although their terms of service are modelled more or less on those of the Civil Service. In 1966 these staffs totalled 117 in the House of Lords and 305 in the House of Commons, figures that are certainly not inflated when it is realised how much business is involved today in running the chambers. A good deal of the actual day-to-day management is carried out by Peers and Members of Parliament organized as committees, which are themselves serviced by senior members of the respective staffs.

### HOUSE OF LORDS

The general management of the House of Lords is the responsibility of one of the Great Officers of the Realm, the Lord Chancellor—or to give him his full title 'Lord High Chancellor of Great Britain and Keeper of the Great Seal'—who is selected as member of the Government by the Prime Minister. He acts as Speaker of the House of Lords, albeit with somewhat less authority than the Speaker of the Commons, from whom he differs in actively participating in the debates of the House. He is at the same time head of the Judiciary and member of the Cabinet. The Officers of the House also include the Chairman of Committees, selected by the House from its own membership.

The officials of the House of Lords are organized as separate departments: namely, Department of the Lord Chancellor, Department of the Chairman of Committees, Department of the Clerk of the Parliaments, Department of the Gentleman Usher of the Black Rod, Librarian's Department, and the Department of the Lord Great Chamberlain and Serjeant-at-Arms.

The most important of the senior officials is the Clerk of the Parliaments, who is appointed by the Crown by letters patent and is removable only upon address of the House. His stature is similar to that of a Permanent Secretary, although he has direct control only of his own department, and he acts as Accounting Officer of the House. He is assisted at the Table by the Clerk Assistant and the Reading Clerk, both of whom are appointed by the Lord Chancellor with the approbation of and subject to removal only by order of the House. The Clerk of the Parliaments himself appoints and may remove the other Clerks. He is responsible for the preparation of minutes and proceedings, advising members on points of order and appeals, the custody of records and documents (including the manuscript records in Victoria Tower) and for other matters in connection with the House's legislative and judicial business.

The Department of the Clerk of the Parliaments is organized into the following divisions: the Public Bill Office (which includes the Printed Paper Office), the Private Bill and Committee Office, the Judicial Office, the Journal Office, the Record Department and the Accounting Department.

The office of the Gentleman Usher of the Black Rod, dates back to the reign of Henry VIII. He holds his appointment by letters patent and is assisted by the Yeoman Usher and a working staff. He has certain administrative duties, such as issuing tickets to the Strangers Gallery in the Lords and the maintenance of order there. The Serjeant-at-Arms, another ancient office, holds his appointment from the Crown by letters patent under the Great Seal. He attends upon the Lord Chancellor personally with the Mace and is responsible for order in and execution of the orders of, the House of Lords. The House also appoints an Examiner of Petitions for Private Bills to act in conjunction with a similar appointee of the House of Commons. Shorthand Writers to the Houses of Parliament, to assist the committees and so forth, are jointly appointed by the Clerk of the Parliaments and the Clerk of the House of Commons.

## HOUSE OF COMMONS

The Speaker, whose office dates back at least to 1377 and who was once the Sovereign's representative in the House of Commons, is today its presiding officer with the function of regulating debate and enforcing observance of its rules. He is the guardian of the privileges of the House and executes all its orders. He still holds his appointment from the Crown but is elected from among its own members by the House of Commons. He does not vote, except in the event of a division being equal, and does not take part in debate. He has wide discretionary powers and interprets the law of Parliament, in which he is assisted by the Clerks at the Table.

There is also a Chairman of Ways and Means and a Deputy Chairman, selected from among Members of the House. The former presides when the House is in Committee, replacing the Speaker but at the Table of the House and not in the Speaker's Chair. He also acts as Deputy Speaker in emergency when he actually does take the Chair. When necessary the Deputy Chairman may act for the Chairman of Ways and Means in both capacities.

The officials of the House of Commons are organized in three separate departments: namely, the Department of the Clerk of the House, the Department of the Speaker, and the Department of the Serjeant-at-Arms. Senior among the officials is the Clerk of the House, whose office goes back at least to 1363, when Robert de Melton was appointed to the office by letters patent.[1] The office developed over the years out of its mediaeval form until, by 1850, it had become a department in the modern style, divided into a series of functional offices very much in its present shape. As in the case of the State Departments it had passed through its fee-motivated and patronage phase and the position was still so fluid that the staffs of the two Houses were listed among the 'Principal Departments of the Civil Service in Great Britain' in the statistical appendix to the Trevelyan–Northcote papers published in 1855.[2] The total staffs for 1851 were shown therein as 74 for the House of Lords and 98 for the House of Commons.

The Clerk of the House is appointed by letters patent for life on the advice of the Prime Minister.[3] He is assisted at the Table by the Clerk Assistant and the Second Clerk Assistant who are both

[1] See O. C. Williams's *The Clerical Organization of the House of Commons, 1661–1850* (Oxford, 1954), and Philip Marsden's *The Officers of the Commons, 1363–1965* (Barrie and Rockcliff, 1966).

[2] *Papers relating to the Re-organization of the Civil Service* (Eyre and Spottiswoode for H.M.S.O., 1855).

[3] *Report from the Select Committee on House of Commons Accommodation, etc.* (H.C. 184, 1954) pp. ix-xiii.

appointed by Her Majesty, by warrant under the royal sign manual and are removable by her only on address of the House of Commons. Since 1953 a Fourth Clerk at the Table has been appointed by the Speaker on the advice of the Clerk of the House, with the special task of assisting legislatures of the Commonwealth in procedural and administrative matters. The remaining Clerks in the department are appointed by the Clerk of the House, who today insists upon similar academic qualifications to those required for the Administrative Class and nominates candidates to the Civil Service Commission to undergo the usual Method I or Method II examination tests. Salaries and other conditions are similar to those of the Civil Service but the Clerks remain a separate body, servants of the House and confined to the Department of the Clerk.

The Clerk of the House of Commons has a similar status to that of a Permanent Secretary, though his executive control is confined to his own department. As Accounting Officer to the House he has a general oversight of financial matters in the usual way. His department is organized in a number of offices: namely the Table Office, the Public Bill Office, the Journal Office, the Committee Office, and the Private Bill Office, whose titles indicate generally the sphere of their main activities. The Table Office, which is situated just outside the House behind the Speaker's Chair, is concerned not only with the immediate business of the chamber but also with advising Members on matters of procedure and dealing with communications from the public.

The Speaker has his own department, which consists of the Speaker's Office, the Library, the Fees Office, the Official Report staffs, and the Vote and Sale Offices. For senior posts the Speaker makes appointments from among persons with suitable experience, for which nominations may be invited, but for the junior posts appointments are made upon the recommendation of a Staff Board, which consists of the Clerk Assistant, the Deputy Serjeant and the Speaker's Secretary, namely representatives of the three departments. Reporters and sub-editors of the Official Report are selected on the recommendation of the Editor of Official Report of Debates, and special qualifications are required of candidates for junior library clerkships.

The Serjeant-at-Arms in Ordinary to Her Majesty holds an office which goes back to the reign of Richard II. His duties are partly ceremonial, in his attendance upon the Speaker as custodian of the Mace, but also administrative, for he is responsible for the maintenance of law and order throughout the precincts of the House of Commons. This includes the control of the admission of strangers to the building and supervision of the police. He holds his appointment from the Crown under warrant from the Lord Chamberlain and by patent under the Great Seal and officiates as housekeeper of the House under the House of Commons (Offices) Act, 1812. Nevertheless on appointment he becomes the servant of the House, by which he may be dismissed for a breach of conduct.

The Serjeant-at-Arms appoints the staff of his own department under the authority of the 1812 statute just mentioned. The Speaker's approval is invariably obtained for appointment of the Deputy and Assistant Serjeants-at-Arms, and in the case of all office staff the recommendations of the Staff Board are sought. The department needs a number of doorkeepers and attendants, whose posts are eminently suitable for ex-servicemen. Vacancies are therefore notified to the interested associations, to the employment exchanges, and to the press, questions of character and personal reference being of primary importance in making the final selections.

There are a number of other interesting officials, such as the Speaker's Counsel, his Chaplain and his Trainbearers, to whom more attention would properly be devoted in a comprehensive survey, but some mention must be made here to the Comptroller and Auditor General, as a most important officer of Parliament whose special position has already been touched upon.[1] He holds a special appointment and is not a civil servant, although he has usually had an extensive Civil Service career. He differs from the officers mentioned here in having control of a Civil Service staff organized as the Exchequer and Audit Department, which operates outside the precincts of Parliament.

*     *     *

The staffs of the Houses of Parliament are of considerable interest to students of the public services and deserve more attention than has normally been given them. Their organization and regulation go back to the pre-competitive era and to some extent demonstrate what might well have happened to the Government Departments had they continued very much on the same scale as at the time of the mid-century reforms.

These staffs serve directly the Queen's high officers and Parliament; their seniors are appointed by the older means and appointments at lower levels are still nominally on a patronage basis. But the Select Committee on Accommodation etc. of 1954 considered

[1] See page 175 above.

'that the present methods of appointment and the required qualifications for the various posts should be clearly stated, on the general principle that every vacancy should be made available to anyone of the necessary competence to fill it'.[1] Step by step the general conditions applied to the Home Civil Service have been accepted as appropriate in settling conditions of service for the Parliamentary staffs. Further developments in this direction are taking place in accordance with the Select Committee's recommendations.

In a way these Parliamentary departments and their staffs represent something of a compromise between the old and the new Civil Services, making the best of both worlds. It is largely a matter of scale, which of course is the fundamental problem of the modern Civil Service. It may well be that entrants to the service of Parliament are offered a somewhat limited career compared with their opposite numbers in the Departments, but they have the advantage of greater intimacy in their working relations. They become experts in an interesting and important field and are better able to understand the outcome of their activities than is often the case with members of the larger organizations of Whitehall. Instead of serving a Minister, whom many of them will never meet and who is likely in any case to be very much a bird of passage, they operate as the direct servants of the people's representatives or of active members of the peerage, in whose proximity they work during sessions and with whom as a matter of course they experience numerous personal contacts. It is an individual rather than a bureaucratic job, whose participants have the enviable experience of being at the very hub of the nation's affairs. The more important officials, particularly the Clerks of the departments of the Clerk of the Parliaments and the Clerk of the House of Commons, acquire an expertise which is not only of great interest in itself but must create in them the sense of constituting a small but important professional group with a particular niche inside the public sphere.

### THE LOCAL GOVERNMENT SERVICE

Local government officials are sometimes referred to erroneously as civil servants, but as employees of the several Local Authorities they are the servants of these authorities and not servants of the Crown. The confusion is to some extent understandable in the light of the increasing number of civil servants employed in the localities by several Government Departments more or less alongside the Local Authorities. Moreover, despite some important differences between the structure and conditions of employment of the two

[1] *Op cit*, para. 24, p. ix.

services, both are devoted to the service of the community, have similar attitudes to their work, and belong to much the same occupational groups. There is some prospect too, and substantial reason, that the two services will move closer together, and it is not out of place therefore in our present context to include a brief summary of the Local Government Service as it is at the present time.

With the exception of certain small Parishes, which have to make do with a Parish Meeting of the electors, Local Authorities consist of a Council mainly elected by the people, but in the case of Boroughs and Counties they have a number of Aldermen who are selected by the Councillors.[1] The Council is only to a minor extent a legislatory body, its work being mainly executive and its scope for policy-making strictly delimited by the statutes from which it derives its powers and by the legal doctrine of *ultra vires* which prevents it from undertaking activities in default of precise statutory authority.[2] Councils may, and in some matters must, appoint committees to which most functions may be delegated. These committees, with the exception of a Finance Committee, may, and in some cases must, co-opt outside persons, with appropriate experience and knowledge of their sphere of operations, to serve with them. These committees have a similar relationship to the departments among which the Council's work is distributed, as the Minister to his Department. It is through its committees that the Council becomes administrative and supervises the work of the officials who staff the departments.

Each Council appoints, pays, conditions, disciplines and may discharge its own staff. Its discretion in making such appointments is limited only by certain minimal requirements under various statutes. Thus a County Council must appoint a Clerk, a Medical Officer, and a Surveyor: the Councils of a Borough, an Urban District or a Rural District must appoint a Town Clerk or Clerk, a Treasurer, a Medical Officer and a Public Health Inspector, while a Borough or Urban District must also have a Surveyor. Specific appointments are also prescribed for those authorities responsible for certain services, such as a Chief Education Officer under the Education Act, 1944, and a Children's Officer under the Children's Act, 1948. In both these instances a short list of suitable candidates has to be submitted to the appropriate Minister (who may veto any person considered not suitable) before the

---

[1] To the extent of one-third of their own numbers, except in London where it is one-sixth.

[2] This is not strictly true of the Boroughs, which are incorporated by Royal Charter, although in practice there does not appear to be a deal of difference.

Council makes the final decision. Generally speaking the appointing Council specifies the qualifications required of candidates, but of course a general pattern has emerged to which they are bound to conform if they are to recruit competent officers. It is often difficult for a smaller and therefore poorer Local Authority to offer a sufficiently attractive salary to ensure this. In some cases—for example, Medical Officers, Weights and Measures Inspectors and Public Health Inspectors—minimum qualifications are laid down by statute. Professional appointees are expected to hold the normal qualifications of their profession.

In September, 1965, the total number of persons employed in Local Government was 764,000, divided broadly between officers and manual workers. The former, ranging from the higher appointments down to the clerical staffs, constitute the Local Government Service as generally understood. The occupational range is very wide, especially in the professional field. Below the senior appointments the service is divided into broad bands: a General Division at the base, a Clerical Division, and an Administrative, Professional and Technical (usually shortened to A.P.T.) Division, to each of which various salary scales are allocated.[1] The imposition of this general pattern of gradings upon what was formerly a diversity of staff groups was largely the outcome of the establishment in 1944 of national Whitley machinery, in place of the previous system of provincial Whitley councils which dated back to 1920 but had only achieved a limited success.

A Local Authority's work is organized in separate functional departments, under the control normally of professionally qualified experts. Their work is often highly technical and is essentially executive rather than administrative in type. The chief administrative official is the Clerk or Town Clerk[2], who is responsible for the Council's secretarial services and as a lawyer—by convention and not by law—for its legal business. He is co-ordinator of the administrative work but not director of all the Council's work on a par with the Permanent Secretary of a Government Department. He does not intervene in the technical activities of the several departments or override committee decisions, his position depending upon influence rather than power. At best he is *primus inter pares* in relation to the other departmental heads.

There is no administrative class in local government in any

[1] See J. H. Warren, *The Local Government Service* (Allen & Unwin, 1952).
[2] See T. E. Headrick, *The Town Clerk in English Local Government* (Allen & Unwin, 1962).

sense comparable to that of the Civil Service. As we have seen administrative, professional and technical officers are graded in one A.P.T. Division, and the senior administrative posts are usually occupied by officers with a professional background. The technician is on top, not merely on tap!

Many ways have been suggested for strengthening the Local Authorities' administrative direction and cohesion, possibly the most favoured being the separation of legal work from the Town Clerk's office and raising his status and administrative responsibilities in comparison with those of the other chief officers. Alternatively, introduction of the American city manager system has been advocated. Under this arrangement the Council would appoint a professional Chief Executive to manage the entire administration. Varying patterns could emerge, depending upon the actual powers given to the professional manager, and the result could very well be to modify radically the committee system which is such a characteristic of the British pattern of local government. The making of such an appointment during 1965 by the City Council of Newcastle upon Tyne will be followed with interest.

Promotion generally is in the hands of the employing Council, although vacancies are normally advertised and the field is thrown open to all officials with the right sort of experience. This means that local government officials are not tied to one authority or confined within a particular locality. This arrangement is particularly important to officers in small authorities, where career prospects are bound to be restricted. The consequent cross-flow of staff gives a flexibility to the Local Government Service which the Civil Service lacks. On the other hand the strict functional division of the work means that this movement takes place between departments concerned with the same functions, and movements between different departments of the same authority are less practicable. In this respect the Civil Service has the advantage.

Each Local Authority is responsible for the training of its own staff, but the insistence upon professional qualifications in so many branches of the work means that such professional training has to be acquired in the normal way, either before appointment or subsequently by day release or spare time study. Local government has been ahead of the Civil Service in assisting such studies but in the actual provision of internal training on the work the disparate nature of local government structure has rendered it less easy, except perhaps in the largest authorities, for adequate training to be provided.

Promotion in the professional and technical fields has depended upon the holding of the appropriate qualifications, but with the clerical staffs the position has been much less settled. In order both to improve the qualifications and status of such staffs and to establish comparable promotion standards as between the many Local Authorities a system of examinations has been sponsored by the National Whitley Council, with particular support from the National and Local Government Officers Association (NALGO), the body representing many staff groups in this field. The examinations are administered on behalf of that council, which of course is representative of both employer and staff interests, by the Local Government Examinations Board.[1] These examinations set promotion standards for both clerical and administrative grades and lead to the professional Diploma in Municipal Administration. Passing the appropriate examination does not guarantee promotion, but most Local Authorities accept such a qualification as a necessary condition of advancement.

The Local Government Service, despite improvements in remuneration and conditions of service, has run into difficulties similar to those of the Civil Service, particularly in recruitment and the maintenance of quality. The situation is aggravated by wide variations in capacity to offer adequate terms, due to the great disparity between the resources of the small and the large Local Authorities. Numerous attempts made since 1945 to revise the present system of Local Government have proved abortive, but there is now reasonable hope that essential modifications will be introduced as a result of enquiries being made by the Royal Commissions set up in 1966 separately for England with Wales and for Scotland to review the whole position. Their recommendations, on the personnel side, will no doubt be aided by findings of two committees appointed in 1964: the first under Sir John Maud on the Management of Local Government, which is concerned with the elected councillors and chief officers, and the second under Sir George Mallaby on the Staffing of Local Government, which is dealing with staffing in general.

[1] See page 100 above.

# CHAPTER XII

## CIVIL SERVICES OVERSEAS

Some Departments have overseas commitments and it is not un-usual for members of the Home Civil Service to serve for periods abroad, either for their own Departments, or on loan or second-ment to other bodies. With the growth of international administra-tion under the United Nations Organization and its Specialized Agencies the number of officials so detached tends to increase. A Great Empire, whose unpremeditated dissolution we are witnessing, had a need for officials permanently stationed abroad.

The American Colonies were first in the field and despite their revolutionary break during the eighteenth century their new form of government embodied much of the old, although in due time their Civil Service was to be moulded upon a democratic rather than an aristocratic tradition, not with entirely happy results. It was left to India to be first in organizing a comprehensive public ser-vice, and other territories followed suit.

A Colonial Service was built up gradually out of diverse ele-ments to serve the Governors appointed by the Crown to administer these territories. During the nineteenth century, with the spreading of self-government to the more developed colonies, the respective branches of the Colonial Service were replaced by the permanant services of the new governments. While modifications were wisely introduced to meet conditions on the spot these new Civil Services were constructed on the British model, so that much that has been written in this book would apply in many ways to them also. Thus the Civil Service of the Irish Republic, which has embodied some interesting variations, is very much a growth from the original plant that developed in Ireland equally with Great Britain during the formative Victorian years. Latterly there has been a hectic speeding up of this process, notably with the creation of many new African states calling for a veritable administrative explosion.[1] The Representative Services of several Departments centred upon Lon-don are now the most important surviving sector of the British Civil Service Overseas.

[1] See particularly A. L. Adu, *The Civil Service in New African States* (Allen & Unwin, 1965).

## THE INDIAN CIVIL SERVICE

The Indian Civil Service had its origins in the private commercial activities of the East India Company, chartered by Queen Elizabeth I in 1600. By 1675 a definite grading pattern had begun to take shape, under the influence of the Dutch East India Company which had been first in the field. It was for these commercial agents that the term 'civil servant' was first used to distinguish them from the Company's military functionaries.

With the accumulation by the Company of governmental responsibilities in India, Parliament found it necessary to pass a Regulation Act in 1773 creating a Governor-General, a Council of five and a Supreme Court in Calcutta with Judges appointed by the Crown. The Act also made it illegal for officials concerned with the collection of revenues to participate in trade. It vetoed the general Indian custom of accepting presents which served to mask many a scandalous transaction. Further legislation in 1784 and 1793 established a Board of Control in Britain to supervise the Company's non-commercial affairs, and laid down conditions of service for the Company's servants. Minimum salaries were established and the sale of nominations by the Company's Directors was abolished. In these eventful decades a great public service was being moulded and a remarkable pattern laid down for the Civil Service at home, which was still a chaos of privileges based upon patronage.

Moving with the times Lord Wellesley, in 1800, founded the College of Fort William to undertake the instruction of civilian recruits upon their arrival in India, but he was too far ahead of the Directors, who restricted the use of the College to the study of Oriental Languages, which was certainly better than nothing! In this they were foreshadowing the typical reactions of authority to the expensiveness of a training whose necessity it does not recognize! It was not long before an important advance in this field was made with the founding, in 1806, of a college in England to provide a comprehensive three-year course for youths of 15 nominated as suitable for service with the Company in India. Three years later the school was established at Haileybury in Hertfordshire, England.

The new method lasted until the East India Company lost its commercial functions under the India Act of 1833 and became a full-blown governing institution. Under the influence of Lord Macauley, its enthusiastic sponsor in the House of Commons, the new statute had embodied the principle of selection by competitive examination, with the object of eliminating patronage and ensuring the selection of highly competent recruits. In other words Parliament was prepared to apply to distant India a remedy they were not to accept fully for their own immediate field for another 37 years! The Directors, however, still had sufficient power to fight a successful rearguard action and to suspend the new regulations until 1853, although Haileybury continued to function and the qualifying examination had a certain beneficial effect.

In 1853 Parliament at last decreed that appointments in the I.C.S. should be thrown open to competition and that all British subjects, who met certain conditions with regard to age, health and character, should be eligible. The new examinations were designed to select candidates with educational attainments of the type and standard of a good Arts degree at Oxford or Cambridge. At first the age limits were between 18 and 23 but these were modified at various times until they were finally changed in 1921 to 21 and 24. There was provision for a year's probation, followed by an examination in specialized Indian subjects, but these arrangements were varied from time to time. Haileybury College, no longer needed, was shortly closed down and the first of the 'competition wallahs', as they were facetiously dubbed, took up their posts in India. In 1858, following the Mutiny, the East India Company was superseded by the Crown and control of the I.C.S. passed from the Directors to the Secretary of State.

Thus the Indian Civil Service had shown the way ahead to the Home Civil Service. Its subsequent development was to be truly a success story, but its detailed examination would be out of place here.[1] The principle of Indianization had been accepted under the Act of 1833, although here again the obstruction of the Directors impeded its operation, which also continued to be limited by the slowness of educational development in India and the need for would-be candidates to have access to sufficient funds to enable them to travel to Britain for the education necessary to enable them to qualify. However, well in advance of 1947 when the India Independence Act transferred control of the I.C.S. from the Secretary of State to the new Governments of India and Pakistan, a trained corps of Indian officials had grown up to carry over the traditions and methods of the I.C.S. into the Civil Services of the independent states.

### THE COLONIAL SERVICE

The Colonial Service became the responsibility of the Secretary of State for the Colonies, through the Colonial Office. He advised the Queen on the appointment of Governors and took responsibility

[1] See, for example, L. S. S. O'Malley *The Indian Civil Service* (Murray, 1931) and Sir Edward Blunt, *The I.C.S.* (Faber & Faber, 1937).

for other selections, with the help of the Colonial Service Appointments Board, on which the Civil Service Commissioners were represented, although actual appointment remained with the Governors. The general rules were similar to those applied to the Home Civil Service except that the Colonial Secretary retained considerable patronage, stemming from the Royal Prerogative. The more junior appointments were made locally by the Governor of the Colony.

As a consequence of the separateness of the individual colonies and territories the Colonial Service continued as a collection of separate services until as late as 1930 when unification was decided upon. Even then, since many of the posts had specific professional requirements which precluded an easy interchange of staffs, the new consolidated Service was really made up of a range of separate functional branches or services spreading horizontally across the many territories. Thus an agricultural specialist in one colony would look for advancement to a technical post in the agricultural branch of another colony. 'Unification' was officially defined as the harmonization of two ideas, mainly:

> 'that Colonies are separate political units, each with its own public service organized according to its particular needs and based on the principle of encouraging people to take a full part in the government of their own country; and the idea of the single Colonial Service at the disposal of the Colonial Empire as a whole organized and centrally directed with a view to securing the maximum effectiveness in the use of the available manpower'.[1]

The first real step in unification was taken with the formation of the Colonial Administrative Service in 1932. Subsequently, other specialist groups were formed until, with the creation of the Colonial Aviation Service and the Colonial Research Service after the Second World War, there existed as many as twenty separate technical services within the Colonial Service. The staffs of the Colonial Office continued to form part of the Home Civil Service.

The consolidation of these several unified branches was destined to be short-lived, for it became evident that their scope would be considerably restricted with the coming of independence to many of the territories. To extend the availability of members of the several branches serving in countries attaining independence the Colonial Secretary, on 1st October 1954, introduced a new grouping under the title 'Her Majesty's Oversea Civil Service' to absorb members

[1] Cmnd. 6023, p. 8.

who were willing to transfer elsewhere, while for the time being continuing to serve in their current posts.[1]

These many changes have inevitably restricted the scope of the Colonial Service, which has been dwindling fast. Special arrangements have had to be made to compensate many whose posts have become redundant and to find them jobs in other directions. Some have been absorbed into the Home Civil and Diplomatic Services, while others have found jobs similar to their old assignments on a contract basis with the new States, which have an even greater need than ever for the sort of expertise that the Colonial Service was well equipped to supply, though many have been unwilling to continue under the new conditions.

### THE FOREIGN SERVICE

It is in the diplomatic field that Britain's oversea services survive today. According to the MacDonnell Commission[2] an organized Diplomatic Service dates back to the seventeenth century 'when Ambassadors and residents were for the first time permanently accredited to foreign countries,' although the true beginnings go back at least to the time of Henry III and the first Edwards who were all actively involved in Continental affairs. A graded career service in the modern sense had not emerged before the early part of the last century when the Foreign Service existed as a number of separate groups dealing broadly with either diplomatic or consular work. It was to take a hundred years to bring the various sectors of the profession together and it will be helpful first to look at the two main groups separately.

First to be considered is the Diplomatic Service. Up till 1830 Ambassadors had been in the habit of selecting their staffs from among members of good families personally known or recommended to them. These attachés were treated more or less as members of the family. Hitherto they had usually been unpaid, but now salaries were introduced, subject to a period of probation being successfully accomplished. Nevertheless, changes were still slow in materializing. Diplomacy had always been a personal service, its practitioners the close representatives of the sovereign, its practices depending upon intimate acquaintance with the members of the ruling house. The servants of diplomacy needed to be *persona grata* at the foreign court. To serve was an honour eagerly sought by the unoccupied sons of the gentry. Thus it was necessary that

---

[1] *Reorganization of the Colonial Service* (Colonial No. 306, 1954) and *Her Majesty's Oversea Civil Service*, Cmnd. 9768 (1956).

[2] *Fifth Report* Cd. 7748 (1914), para. 2.

junior members of the service should have private means. Even when salaries were introduced this requirement continued, and it was not until the First World War that the new entrant ceased to be required to possess a private income of at least £400—a goodly sum at that period! With the tumbling of so many thrones as a result of that great catastrophe, the arrival of the era of the New Diplomacy can at last be discerned.

Examinations were introduced shortly after the setting up of the Civil Service Commission in 1855, but they were of a qualifying nature and not "of a character calculated materially to raise the efficiency of the service or to widen the area from which candidates were drawn"[1] Patronage continued and although considerable changes were introduced in December, 1872, there was no enthusiasm for the adoption of open competition. It is interesting to note that, under these new regulations, the holder of a university degree was exempted from further examination except in hand-writing, précis and French! In 1877 a resolution in the House of Commons, that the principle of open competition should be introduced into both the Foreign Office and the Diplomatic Service, was opposed by the Government and defeated.

The Ridley Commission (1886–90), which made a separate inquiry into the Foreign Service, recommended that the Foreign Office and Diplomatic staffs should be combined, but that selective competition should be limited in view of the special circumstances. They wanted to place upon the Secretary of State responsibility for securing that there should be real and effective competition for each vacancy, and 'that every competitor should be, as far as could possibly be ascertained, a person of such antecedents and character as to render him prima facie a fit and proper person to be entrusted with the affairs, often delicate and confidential of the British Foreign Office'. They recommended that training should include service in the Foreign Office in both commercial and diplomatic business, but they aimed at equality of opportunity in promotion and condemned the prescription of an income qualification. The Commissioners were ahead of their generation. The only immediate outcome of their recommendations was the assimilation of the examinations of the Diplomatic Service and the Foreign Office in 1892.

Until 1907 a specialized examination was prescribed for selection from among candidates nominated by the Secretary of State. Such candidates found it more profitable to place themselves under a crammer than to follow through a normal university degree course. Now important changes were introduced. The Secretary of State

[1] *MacDonnell Report*, para. 5.

for Foreign Affairs continued to exercise his patronage, but a Board of Selection was established to recommend the most likely candidates. At the same time the examination was brought closer to the Class I competition for the general Civil Service (equivalent at that time to the later Administrative Class examination). This not only reduced the advantage of the crammer but also, by removing the need to specialize at this stage, ensured that the unsuccessful candidate had a wider field of employment open to him.

The new Board of Selection was really a pre-selection body. The candidate's first step was to obtain the Secretary of State's permission to appear before the Board, which was under the presidency of the Permanant Under Secretary of State. This was given only to those who possessed the prescribed private income and were either known to the Secretary of State or recommended by men of standing and position. Nominated candidates could present themselves to the board and if acceptable were then free, subject to the usual conditions as to age and fitness, to sit the examination set by the Civil Service Commission. This was the same as for the Class I posts[1] except that a higher standard was needed for French and German and the optional subjects were restricted. Such was the position in 1914. The MacDonnell Commission held that the preliminary permission was undesirable, since it considerably reduced the usefulness of the Board. The composition of the latter was considered too departmental and it was recommended that membership should in future include the First Civil Service Commissioner and also an independent non-official member.

Let us now turn to the Consular Service which was concerned with commercial business in foreign countries. The office of Consul can be traced back to the fifteenth century, when such officials were arbiters of commercial differences and regulators of the mercantile marine in the ports of Spain and Italy. With the growing importance to Britain of commercial matters abroad and in particular the difficulty of regulating such interests in parts of the world where local government was weak, it became the practice to appoint officials to look after the interests of British nationals. The Levant Company had established in the Turkish Dominions, under the recognition of the Sultan, a complete system of consular administration. This was inherited by the British Government when the Company was abolished in 1825. Following upon the cessation in 1834 of the East India Company's trade monopoly with China a separate Consular Service emerged in the Far East, which, largely because of the language difficulty, remained a closed service. It was in fact the first to be organized. All its members were salaried and

[1] Equivalent to the present Administrative Class.

excluded from trade. It was at a later stage recruited by limited competition, and open competition was introduced early in 1872. Besides these Levant and Far Eastern Services there was also a General Consular Service.

In both the Levant and the General Services appointment was by patronage, organization hardly existed, and there was no promotional ladder. Persons selected as Consuls derived much of their incomes from trade. Vice-consuls were usually selected from among foreign merchants resident in the district. While, in theory, they were selected by the Secretary of State, in practice they were usually selected by the Consul and frequently paid by him.

Changes came slowly. A qualifying examination for admission to the General Consular Service was adopted in 1856. Following the investigations of two Select Committees of 1858 and 1870–72 open competition was introduced into the Levant Service and some organizational changes were made in the General Service, but it was not until the Walrond Committee of 1903[1] that any radical changes were introduced in the latter. It was then decided, in accordance with the Committee's proposals, that the General Consular Service should be graded[2] and recruited by limited competition following nomination by the Secretary of State. A proportion of nominees were to have had a business training, the examinations to have a commercial bias[3] and successful candidates to be attached for some months to the Commercial Intelligence Branch of the Board of Trade before taking up their appointments. Limited competitions were extended to the Far Eastern Service.

The MacDonnell Commission were satisfied that differences in languages, government and national customs in the various areas rendered the continuance of the three separate services unavoidable. They recommended the application of open competition and decided that the plans of the Walrond Committee to introduce young men with business experience had not been a success. Suitable candidates were not in practice forthcoming from the business field, where opportunities were so much more attractive. It was considered therefore that normal recruits of the right quality should be afforded an opportunity to acquire the necessary experience after selection.

After the First World War the administrative sectors of the Foreign Office in London were amalgamated with the Diplomatic

[1] A Departmental Committee appointed by the Secretary of State.

[2] *I.e.* Consul General (First and Second Grades), Consul (First and Second Grades) and Vice-Consul.

[3] The subjects included Foreign Languages, Commercial Geography, General Principle of Political Economy, and British Mercantile and Commercial Law.

Service, but absorption of the Consular Services was not completed until the mid-thirties. The entrance examinations were assimilated to those of the Home Admiinstrative and Indian Civil Service, with special provision in regard to languages. Open competition was not, however, finally achieved since candidates for the Foreign Service had still to satisfy a Board of Selection before they could compete in the written examinations. On the other hand the need to have a private income was at last abolished.

During the succeeding decades great changes came upon the world of diplomacy. The elimination of so many of the royal houses of Europe and the growing interest of the democracies in foreign affairs rapidly altered the whole outlook of the diplomat who also came to need the assistance of experts from other fields. The leisurely ways of the old regime disappeared under the impact of the aeroplane and the perfecting of electrical communications. It was not, however, until the Second World War that serious steps were taken to bring the personnel structure into gear with the needs of the world situation.

In 1943 the Foreign Secretary presented to Parliament a comprehensive scheme of reform.[1] The main proposal, covering the amalgamation of the Foreign Office and the Diplomatic Service, the Commercial Diplomatic Service and the Consular Service, was directed to the formation of a combined Foreign Service entirely separated from the Home Civil Service and treated as a self-contained and distinct Service of the Crown. It was considered that such a service, capable of dealing with the whole range of international affairs—political, economic and social—would provide a more effective instrument for the conduct of foreign relations in the modern world. While it was recognized that diplomatic and consular duties called for different knowledge and experience and that specialization would continue, hard and fast barriers would no longer exist and there would need to be a flow of staff, not only between the two wings of the Service, but also between the oversea and home posts. The latter were to be considered henceforth as steps in the normal Foreign Service career and not to be permanently held by stay-at-homes.

The new Foreign Service would require a more broadly based system of recruitment, which would need to accommodate a period of preliminary training. The Foreign Office Selection Board was to be abolished and the Secretary of State's age-long powers of patronage were thus to be greatly restricted. A most interesting proposal was that the Foreign Secretary should be given power to retire on

---

[1] *Proposals for the Reform of the Foreign Service* Cmd. 6420 (H.M.S.O., 1943).

pension higher officers who, though they had not committed any fault to merit dismissal, were no longer considered suitable to hold posts of highest responsibility in the Service.

The amalgamation of the Foreign Service was legalized without delay by Order in Council.[1] Changes in superannuation were approved in the Foreign Service Act, 1943, under which the Foreign Secretary could retire before 60 and pay superannuation benefits to an officer of a grade not lower than Second Secretary on the grounds that 'the termination of his employment is desirable in the public interest, having regard to his qualifications and the conditions existing in the Service.'

The new combined Foreign Service included for the first time the Executive, Clerical and other subordinate ranks of the Foreign Office, who had previously been excluded and remained part of the Home Civil Service, There can be little doubt that to realise this vertical amalgamation presented much greater difficulties than those arising from the horizontal amalgamation of the Administrative Class and the Diplomatic Corps. Even after the radical Reorganization of 1920 the separateness of the different strata of the Civil Service tended to be emphasized, and the gap between the lower ranks and the members of the Diplomatic Corps had been correspondingly greater. Such radical changes as were now being introduced were bound to take time. The new Foreign Service, as it now emerged, was classified into four branches, as follows:

*Branch A* comprising the top layers in nine grades, ranging from Third Secretaries and Vice Consuls, in Grade 9, up to Permanent Under-Secretary of State, in Grade 1.

*Branch B* comprising:

(a) Executive and Clerical Officers in the Foreign Service recruited through the ordinary Civil Service examinations, and higher grade members of the two classes.

(b) established accountants, archivists, cypher officers and clerks serving abroad, and

(c) unestablished employees of equivalent grades at diplomatic and consular posts, whose establishment is approved by the Treasury.

*Branch C* comprising the Shorthand and Typing grades.

*Branch D* comprising the Messengerial grades.

### OTHER REPRESENTATIONAL SERVICES

With the growth of the self-governing Dominions in the Commonwealth, the need arose for the provision of representational posts in these new countries to undertake similar duties to those performed elsewhere by the Foreign Service. To meet this new need

[1] The Foreign Service Order, 1943.

Trade Commissioners were first appointed by the Board of Trade in 1908. The Commercial Diplomatic Service, with duties in foreign countries similar to those of the Trade Commissioners developed under the Department of Overseas Trade which was set up in 1917 under the joint control of the Foreign Office and the Board of Trade. The Department also took over the Trade Commissioner Service and the arrangement continued until 1946. With the absorption at this time of the Department of Overseas Trade by the Board of Trade, the latter again took responsibility for the Trade Commissioners, while commercial representation in foreign countries went over to the Foreign Office. The Trade Commissioner Service, which operated in Commonwealth countries only, did not develop a separate staff structure but continued to be staffed by volunteers from the Board's normal staff, who served overseas for varying terms.

A separate development had begun in 1928 when members of the Dominions Office came to be posted to Missions in the Dominions, and out of this a formal Commonwealth Service was shaped in 1947, when the Dominions Office and India Office formed the new Commonwealth Relations Office. Although the duties of these officers were akin to those of the Foreign Service they also continued to belong to the Home Civil Service.

### H.M. DIPLOMATIC SERVICE

In view of the great changes which had occurred during the immediate post-war period, completely altering Britain's place in the world, in 1962 the Government decided to set up a small committee under the chairmanship of Lord Plowden:

> 'To review the purpose, structure and operation of the services responsible for representing the interests of the United Kingdom Government overseas, both in Commonwealth and foreign countries; and to make recommendations, having regard to changes in political, social and economic circumstances in this country and overseas.'[1]

The Plowden Committee carried out a detailed examination of the overseas services whose duties they summarized, in an informative Report,[2] as:

    (a) *Advice,* or 'the function of advising Her Majesty's Government on every aspect of foreign policy.'

[1] *Report of the Committee on Representational Services Overseas,* 1962–63, Cmnd. 2276 (1964), p. vi.

[2] *Op cit,* pp. 7–8.

(b) *Negotiation*, or 'the art of trying to persuade other independent powers to our point of view without effective sanction.'

(c) *Cultivation of Friendly Relations*, or representing 'the image of Britain abroad.'

(d) *Trade Promotion*, which 'includes assistance to exporters by the provision of market and tariff information, reports and advice on sales opportunities and help in finding agents.'

(e) *Information*, which means 'to explain, support and gain acceptance for British policies.'

(f) *Protection of British Persons and Interests*, or looking after and supporting 'the many-sided interests of British subjects and communities abroad.'

(g) *Aid and Technical Assistance*, meaning 'duties in connection with the giving of British aid and administration of technical assistance abroad.'

The great variety and considerable importance of these activities are evident from this listing of their objectives and it was clear to the Committee that the several services, as they had independently developed, did not provide the best arrangement for coping adequately with the changing situation. They recommended, therefore, the consolidation of the three services into one combined organization under the title 'Her Majesty's Diplomatic Service', and also the amalgamation of the Foreign Office and the Commonwealth Relations Office, although for the time being the two Departments were to remain separate. The principle of consolidation under the new title was accepted by the Government.

The real problem was to bring together existing staffs organized on both the Foreign Service and the Home Service patterns, each of which embodied the Treasury three-class structure under different titles, with over-lapping spheres of responsibility. A complete consolidation into a single branch was not considered suitable, mainly because it would disturb the relationships existing between the two systems and render transfers and secondments from one to the other more difficult. Nevertheless, the new structure was required to remove from the minds of the public the impression of differences in status and authority, induced by the employment of members of both Branch A and Branch B on the same or similar posts. Although the Committee did not say so, Treasury influence must have been against any complete assimilation, since the successful replacement of the three-class system abroad would inevitably provide the thin end of the wedge for the application of a similar solution at home, probably at no distant date!

In solving the problem separate recruitment of the three classes was to be maintained, but the two systems would be interleaved so that in some cases officials from more or less equivalent levels of the two classes or branches would be included in the same grade of the new structure and thus hold similar titles, although still receiving salaries appropriate to their existing class. The result of this idea is shown in Table IV on page 241 reproduced from the Report. From this it will be seen that this method of doubling up was incorporated in the new Grades 4, 5 and 7.

Obviously, although ingenious, this was very much a makeshift arrangement which could hardly constitute a permanent solution. It was important as marking the acceptance by an authoritative committee of the proposition, long advanced in staff circles, that there was no fundamental distinction to be drawn between work classified as 'administrative' and work classified as 'executive' in the Civil Service sense. It pointed the way to the future, but the equity of having different salary scales attached to work of equal status cannot easily be substantiated.

In conclusion, the Committee recommended their proposal on the grounds that it would 'avoid the extremes of integration and of fragmentation', 'give proper opportunities and status to members of all branches of the Foreign, Commonwealth and Trade Commission Services', 'acknowledge true differences of function and ability', 'preserve present links with the salary structure of the Home Civil Service', and 'meet the special needs of a representational Diplomatic Service.'[1]

H.M. Diplomatic Service, whose total strength on 1st April 1966 was 6233, is now being reshaped on the lines laid down by the Plowden Committee. Staffs of both the Foreign and the Commonwealth Relations Offices[2] have been consolidated in an Administration, under a Chief of Administration (ranking as Grade 2) appointed by agreement between the two Secretaries of State for Foreign Affairs and Commonwealth Relations respectively. Each Department retains its own Permanent Under Secretary of State (ranking as Grade 1), the senior of whom is designated Head of the Diplomatic Service. (In 1966 he is the Permanent Under-Secretary of State for Commonwealth Relations.) Under this new control the new Service will prove itself. It rests with the future to adjudge the perspicacity of the Plowden Committee's solution.

[1] See *Report*, para. 101, p. 29.
[2] Including former Trade Commissioners from the Board of Trade.

TABLE III[3]

## PROPOSED STRUCTURE OF 'H.M. DIPLOMATIC SERVICE'

| New Grade | Classes included in New Grades | Existing Foreign Service Grades and [2] Salaries Embraced | Corresponding Home Civil Service Grades |
|---|---|---|---|
| 1. | Administrative only | A 1 (£8,265) | Permanent Secretary |
| 2. | Administrative only | A 2 (£5,865) | Deputy Secretary |
| 3. | Administrative only | A 4 (£4,765) | Under Secretary |
| 4. | Administrative and Executive | A 6 (£3,115–£3,965) | Assistant Secretary |
|  | Administrative and Executive | B 1 (£3,540) | Principal Executive Officer |
| 5. | Administrative and Executive | A 7 (£1,959–£2,711) | Principal |
|  |  | B 2 (£2,237–£2,572) | Chief Executive Officer |
| 6. | Executive only | B 3 (£1,680–£2,126) | Senior Executive Officer |
| 7. | Administrative and Executive | A 8 (£1,498–£1,837) | Assistant Principal |
|  |  | B 4 (£1,369–£1,597) | Higher Executive Officer |
| 8. | Administrative | [1]A 9 (£846–£1,369) | Assistant Principal |
| 9. | Executive | [1]B 5 (£535–£1,296) | Executive Officer |
| 10. | Clerical | [1]B 6 (£345–£934) | Clerical Officer |

[1] These are the entry points to the three classes.

[2] The salaries, quoted from the Report, are included to illustrate the scheme in its application: they have been subject to subsequent wage adjustments applied to the Civil Service and do not represent the current figures, although the relativities remain substantially as before.

[3] See *Report*, p. 29.

# CHAPTER XIII

# WIND OF ADMINISTRATIVE CHANGE

During the period of scientific and industrial development the system of Cabinet Government in Britain has, in its flexible capacity to modify itself to the changing situation, provided a remarkable example of political stability. The Civil Service, emerging in its present form at a later phase of this political development but at a time of acceleration in communications and records reproduction, had to cope with the first revolutionary change in the techniques of administrtion since the discovery of the art of writing. It is therefore a great tribute to the foresight of the authors of the Trevelyan–Northcote Report that they were able to determine a pattern for the new Civil Service which would remain valid for over a hundred years and provide a stabilizing institution in the British system which has been largely ignored by historians and taken for granted by social reformers, who have too frequently considered themselves quite justified in drawing up their programmes without ascertaining the existence of the necessary administrative means.

In the past advocates of Civil Service reform, among whom one must prominently include the series of official investigatory committees to which reference has been made, have been able to assume that the changes they were to envisage would be required to serve a system which was reasonably settled in its principles and form. Today, in the face of an expanding technological revolution and the impact of a thinly disguised world upheaval, the investigator and reformer cannot take the social and political environment for granted. At least two terms of the equation are in question.

The Cabinet system itself is no longer as secure as it was. Presidential overtones – or should one state undertones? – could be creeping in, although one would have thought that this particular system's operation elsewhere left plenty of room for apprehension! More experts are wanted in the Departments and seem to be as difficult as ever to prevent from wasting their rare talents in doubtful administrative experiments. The Ombudsman threatens to invade us from its Scandinavian lair, while more influential parliamentary committees are promised on the pattern of foreign systems in which they constitute for differing reasons a basic need.

A system of regional devolution begins to emerge to grapple with social and economic situations which may already be on the point of passing away, while over all the spirit of Automation broods, whose modest fulfilment to date is a quite inadequate indicator of what is surely to come. The Civil Service reformer to-day would be unwise to take anything for granted, even the institution he aims to improve!

## LEADERSHIP

Leadership is of primary importance in any institution, and nowhere more than in public administration where there are special problems of initiative and control to be faced, not least the political limitations within which such leadership has to operate. Leadership is best when it is free and untrammelled, yet both the nature of public service and the inherent limitations of administering predispose civil service leadership towards mediocrity. No attack can justly be made upon the British Administrative Class on the score of incompetence, or failure to produce a leadership image effective in inducing the support of the rest of the Service. In fact in this latter capacity the class have been so successful as to still the most decisive criticism of their stewardship which, to have been sufficiently well informed, would have had to come from inside. As in the old-time Army they left the imposition of their most onerous instructions to those 'sergeant-majors' of the middle ranks whom they had chosen as the most competent for this burdensome office. So long as this was what the situation required the system worked.

The question to be asked is why, in the Civil Service of all institutions, should this particular arrangement still be considered appropriate. Apart from anything else ones inclination would have been to doubt whether an arrangement introduced to cope with the peculiar administrative needs of mid-Victorian government could possibly continue to be suitable in the greatly changed situation of today. The wonder is that it stood up so long with such little amendment, and our admiration of its original sponsors, especially of Sir Charles Trevelyan, is proportionately enhanced.

The first thing to be noted is that the leaders continue to be recruited direct from the universities. As clever, sophisticated schoolboys they enter into their profession at a level where competition from within, even if it existed in any measure, would already be too late to have much impact, except in rare cases. Certainly these late recruits have usually been conditioned to leadership, as were the sons of kings and princes in the past, but little attempt has been made to brief them in the particular type of statecraft that the

S

scientific age has brought upon us. In Victorian times, when administering still retained such characteristics as had endeared it, as long before as the beginning of the second millenium B.C. to the servants of Hammurabi in Babylon, there was little that could not be picked up on the job. Today few of them would ever get the feel of the working tasks of administering at ground level, i.e. at the point where such experience is best acquired. It would be too late to expect them to do so, for, apart from finding their way about a highly responsible job in a pretty complex organization, they still have much to learn in the realm of economics and sociology and may also be too deficient in modest arithmetic and basic science to be able to grapple with the administrative complexities of our new age. They will not even have been asked to brief themselves on the structure of government, although some of course may have done so. One of the consequences of all this is that they would for ever depend upon the reports of others for an interpretation of what goes on lower down the administrative line. The trouble is that headquarter types thereafter find neither the time nor the inclination to go out and see for themselves. It is to be hoped that the need to do this will be one of the lessons which the new interest in management will disseminate.

Even when the sheer quality of the Administrative Class has been accepted it still has to be asked whether it is the right kind of quality and why the Civil Service should differ from all other fields of activity in our democratic age in not being able to produce at least the larger proportion of its leaders, as, of course, is done in most public services elsewhere. It has to be remembered that once the original prototype had been delineated before 1853, by Macaulay, Trevelyan and others, it was left to the administrators themselves to determine the standards to be applied in the future and to promulgate the rules of their application. The politicians, who had the authority and power to do so, had not the competence, and were so well served by their administrative aides that they had not the slightest inclination to intervene or to consider whether there might not be some better alternative. As the Head of the Civil Service in 1965 assured the Estimates Committee of the House of Commons: 'The qualities which make a potential member of the administrative class are very scare'.[1] This may well be true, though its proving may raise some doubts when it is remembered that the tests devised to discover these scarce qualities come from the class itself, who quite naturally find it difficult to discover persons in their own meritorious image outside their own group. It is surely not surprising that the measure they apply for promotions from the

[1] See Report, qn. 816.

Executive and Professional Classes is disappointing in drawing out persons in quite their own image from these fields! They often decide to make do, and too many of those who are raised in this way must feel from the outset that they are receiving a sort of second-class membership. Of course the scene is changing rapidly, but it is always difficult to catch up without some radical leap forward. It is only since the war that a junior with a competent knowledge of economics could have been preferred to one who exuded an addiction to the spirit of Cicero or Jane Austen!

## POLICY OR MANAGEMENT?

The image of the higher civil servant as policy-maker has changed considerably since mid-Victorian times, when political minister and professional administrator could consult together about legislation that was still easily comprehensible and the Department's problems were well within the scope of one or two men, who spoke the same language in the quietude of office or club. Policy-making itself had hardly yet been subjected to the division of labour and it would often have been difficult to decide whether it was politician or official who had the better of the argument, although if the official's name happened to be Chadwick or Cole[1] one could have made a pretty safe guess!

Broad political decisions could still have been reached by the Cabinet before they came to the Departments, but with the growing complexity of government administration the process of policy-making itself became more complex, depending less and less upon the hunches of well-placed individuals and more and more upon a maze of technical factors which had to be assembled, often in statistical form, before the problem could be adequately tackled. The civil servant found himself more and more concerned with perfecting the means by which this information was prepared for the Minister's briefing than with the actual decision. His main task now, as expert adviser on how the Government's plans could best be administered, was sufficient to involve a much expanded team at the top, assembled in and about the Minister's Private Office, in which the Department, emerging from its purely secretarial phase, evolved its own secretariat, very much as the Privy Council years before had evolved the Cabinet, and the latter much later its Cabinet Office.

The Permanent Secretary, as head of this professional group and the Minister's interpreter of his own administration, had become a

[1] Sir Edwin Chadwick (1800/1890) and Sir Henry Taylor Cole (1807/1882) both eminent public officials of the Victorian era.

very busy man. But this was merely the beginning! Shortly new responsibilities fell upon his shoulders with the appointment in each Department by the Treasury of an Accounting Officer to take personal responsibility for the Department's financial activities and the extending practice of assigning this particular office to the Permanent Secretary himself. Furthermore, with the growing complexity of the departmental organization and the extension of the realm of public finance this duty in itself came to place a major burden on the shoulders of the official concerned. Nor was this all, for the mere expansion in the scale of administration called for an increasing degree of management for which the Permanent Secretary was responsible, even if the actual managing had to be left to others. Left it usually was, often with the minimum of provision, for as large-scale management realms the Departments just grew by extending the existing Civil Service structure to new uses. In the many executive offices, with which some of the Departments had to sprinkle the land in order to carry out their new functions, the existence of management had long been recognized and members of both the general and departmental Executive Classes were there to fill the bill.

At the Department's headquarters management tended to be taken for granted, so that it remained for the Plowden Committee[1], as late as 1961, to draw attention to the importance of improving Civil Service management practices, as though this was a major discovery. In fact the Administrative Class had been managers for some time without knowing it, but the advancement of their managerial skills in proportion to the size of the commitment had been retarded through lack of conscious thought on the subject, which is probably British public administration's major sin in entering the modern world.

The question that immediately arises from a mere exposition of the facts is whether such a heavy and varied load can possibly be borne by one man or group, and indeed whether the same skill is called for in the several areas of activity. Is the agility of mind required of the policy adviser the same sort of expertise as that required by the comprehensively methodical manager? Moreover the advisory area has been vastly broadened by equipping the Departments at various levels with advisory councils and committees consisting of outside representatives, and constant contacts are maintained with the numerous interest groups whose objects are associated with the Departments' functional spheres and which have

---

[1] See page 95 above.

grown into such important links between the public and private sectors of the community.[1]

Proposals have been made to extend the Minister's scope with outside appointments to his staff, but were these to approximate to the introduction of a personal cabinet as appears in certain other governmental systems or even to extending in depth the levels of political appointments at the top of the Department, an expansion of patronage would be involved, a development which all experience challenges on efficiency grounds. There are of course many outsiders who would welcome the innovation! In fact there is no difficulty in appointing experts from outside the Service under the existing rules. The Civil Service Commissioners have powers under the Order in Council to issue certificates of permanency in special cases where the required skills or qualifications are not available inside the Service and appointments of this type are listed each year in their Annual Reports; while temporary appointments can be made by the individual Departments. There is in any case good reason for the appointment of experts to be made on a short-term basis, at proportionately favourable remuneration, and this is a principle that could be fairly widely applied. It is important that members of the professions and other expert groups should have had recent experience in their own spheres when they come into the Service, and should not be left so long inside as to get out of touch with their own professional fields and to acquire the official viewpoint, which is not what is wanted of them.

While the Civil Service's participation in policy-making is still important it is clear that the area of policy-making has been substantially widened so that the civil servant is only one of a number of participants: on the other hand the task of departmental management, on which the effectiveness of the execution of the policy so much depends, has not only vastly expanded but remains firmly within the province of the Civil Service.

### FUNCTIONAL RE-GROUPING?

Before considering a reshaping of the Civil Service to meet the needs of the future it is necessary to decide how far the present organizational principles still apply. The continuance of the Department as the administrative arm of the Minister and the need to extend recruitment to obtain whatever experts may be required to fulfil the Central Government's aims and functions have been

---

[1] See, for example, P E P 's *Advisory Committees in British Government*, (Allen & Unwin, 1960) and Allen Potter's *Organized Groups in British National Politics* (Faber, 1961).

accepted, but two other questions arise: (1) is the broad staffing of the administrative–clerical sectors on a generalist basis still the most effective and desirable? and (2) is some form of regionalization of the Civil Service now needed?

(1) The basis of the generalist idea, as adumbrated by Macaulay and Trevelyan, was the obvious suitability at the time of the products of a literary type of education to be efficient office workers in the Ministers' secretariats. The homogenity of such administrative work up to as late as a half-century ago rendered the generalist approach in most cases admirably suitable for the Civil Service, while the example of those services in which there is a much closer definition of individual posts, on the basis of scientific job analyses, does not suggest that there is enough to be gained in principle from the adoption of such a system, to offset the undoubted flexibility of the British system. Any manager who has had the responsibility of keeping the work moving in an office subject to great pressures of work from the public or sudden staff shortages possibly through illness—maybe both factors working together—knows how important to the fulfilment of his task is the flexibility derived from maximum staff interchangeability within his unit. The more closely defined and limited in scope an official's job is the less easy it is to make changes, or even to prepare the staff in advance for such changes.

In the higher levels, where administration and management become the major responsibilities, the need for a high degree of generalization has long been recognized. It is at the basis of the theory of industrial administration—where in fact the technical factors are much more insistent than in government—so incisively formulated by Henri Fayol in his *Administration, Industrielle et Générale* published in France in 1916.

And yet there are good arguments for not pressing the generalist doctrine to extremes. So wide is the range of governmental business today that to expect an official to be the complete generalist is to ask for the talents of an Isaac Newton, who found little difficulty in his day in combining high competence in science with skill in administration. Administration today is something ever so much more complex, calling for a wide range of talents: literary and scientific, considerative and organizational, instructional and inspectorial, all long-standing ingredients of administration, it is true, but now grown into a series of full-time activities within the larger field. Some degree of specialization is unavoidable, and not merely the degree which was recognized by the division of the administrative sphere into the three generalist classes.

We have an interesting example of the type of specialization, that has actually taken place, in the Information Class which has emerged in the Executive Class sphere since the war—a class within a class, as it were. This was introduced to deal with the peculiarities of information and public relations work and to facilitate the recruitment of experienced experts from outside.[1] There are also the Welfare Officers who fall into much the same category.[2] The idea could be extended to cover, for example, such activities as establishments, staff training, organization and methods, and so on, although we have seen that this would have the drawback of sacrificing the advantages arising from the permeation of such skills within the generalist ranks.

On the other hand the generalist classes have in practice been divided up, for constitutional reasons, into practically self-contained departmental areas for staffing purposes, and some Departments have even managed to retain their own staff structures, so that the idea of a unitary Civil Service has in practice been substantially modified by the basic requirements of the departmental structure. Yet a compromise between the generalist and specialist principles could no doubt be achieved with some advantage by reconstituting the Home Civil Service into a number of specialist Services organized vertically to cover groups of Departments with associated functions. As we have already seen this principle has now been applied to the Oversea Representational Services which have been separated from the Home Civil Service,[3] while the Post Office, still staffed on a Civil Service basis despite its financial autonomy, may if current proposals materialize, leave the larger fold and become a separate service. It has become the practice inside the Service to group the Departments for certain purposes: thus in staff training the following groupings have been used: (i) Economic and Revenue, (ii) Social Services, (iii) Defence and Scientific.[4] Within such administrative groupings it would be easier to offer more closely defined careers, a better co-ordinated promotions system, improved opportunities to get out of the cul-de-sac in which some unfortunates at present find themselves. Such a reorganization would of course cut across the present lines of ministerial responsibility and a new principle would have to be introduced with regard to the deployment of staff, but it should not be impossible to ensure that the new arrangements did not affect the Ministers' individual functional

[1] See page 37 above.
[2] See page 60 above.
[3] See page 238 above.
[4] A fourth grouping under this heading, namely 'Smaller Departments' is not appropriate for our purpose, but as another example there are the several headings for statistical purposes used in Table II on page 6).

responsibilities, any more than the Treasury's overall establishments control does at present.

(2) Alternatively the Civil Service could be reorganized upon a regional basis. This would have certain advantages connected with the localization of recruitment, which is at present taking place over wide areas, and would encourage the dissemination of administrative posts throughout the country as a counter to the present concentration in Whitehall. Better careers in the regions could be offered if staff could move freely across the Departments while such management services as public relations, staff training, organization and methods, accounting and audit, office machinery could be much better co-ordinated in the areas than they are under the present arrangements. The way might even be opened to the creation of a series of new Regional Civil Services which would staff both central and local government offices in the regions!

Such a change could hardly be accommodated effectively within the present ministerial set up. It would be desirable to replace some of the functional ministers by a series of regional ministers, similar to those already existing for Scotland and Wales, and possibly to introduce Regional Administrative Commissioners rather on the lines of the French Prefect. While there are indications of some moves in this direction, particularly in the increasing interest in both economic and social planning in the regions, it is to be wondered whether this may not be one of those organizational changes introduced when the need has already passed its peak, as in the case of the recent appointment of a Commonwealth Secretariat, and whether, in such a small country as Britain scientific advances, notably in the sphere of automation, may not already be rendering such developments somewhat behind the times. Here certainly is a situation which the Civil Service must face up to and be prepared to produce the administrative answer to the politician's decision on whatever basis it may be made.

### RECRUITMENT

Much has been said in this book on the massive problems that have arisen in recruiting an adequately competent Civil Service since the Second World War, although with somewhat varying emphasis. The attention given in 1965 to the subject by the Estimates Committee[1] of the House of Commons is of particular significance. It has been strongly argued that the essential requirement here is that recruitment should be carried out by an independent and impartial selection body acting quasi-judicially. There should be no

[1] See page 79 above.

serious problem here except perhaps our national proclivity of taking things for granted. The independence of the Civil Service Commission must be unchallengeable and any idea that as a community we are now immune from the threat of patronage emphatically rejected.

In considering the broad cause for the breakdown of recruitment, though the reasons are various, it is clear that it rests in the greater demand for administrative and equivalent talents, despite its offsetting by an expanding supply, and the concurrent decrease in the relative attractiveness of the Civil Service as an occupation. The position up to 1939 was that the Civil Service, despite a widespread disposition on the part of its critics to talk nonsense about red-tape, was held in high esteem and there was no difficulty in its recruitment. Educational standards for candidates in all ranges were maintained at a somewhat higher level than was strictly necessary for satisfactory performance. Conditions of employment were generally above average compared with outside occupations. Remuneration in the lower ranges was certainly higher, although on the whole career prospects were unattractive, due to the restrictionist policies of the Government at the time, which applied in all spheres. On the other hand in the upper ranges the opposite was the case. Salaries were lower than for equivalent positions outside but an appreciable vocational pull and the availability of many more competent officials in the lower ranks than could possibly be promoted, meant that plenty of talent was forthcoming at the modest rates offered.

Quite apart from the considerable advance in working class status and rewards, which was generally considered overdue and a just outcome of the war, the civil servant's conditions tended to be dragged down much further than the changes appeared to justify. Wartime restrictions on annual leave and increased hours were continued, under pressure from the Treasury who seemed to welcome the imposition of such conditions which militant Whitleyism had managed to prevent even during the days of deep depression! After the war the staff associations seemed to suffer from a sort of guilt-complex which prevented them from quickly getting back into their old stride. Perhaps a predominance of left-wing sympathizers in controlling positions, naturally in evidence among staff representatives at all times, also had a slowing down effect at a time when a new Labour Government was showing its paces! Concurrently there was a resurgence of press criticism of a type calculated to spoil the image of the civil servant, who was characterized as the most blatant of bureaucrats. If such criticism had been confined to the rightward press it could have been interpreted as just another weapon for use against the great social and administrative advances then in progress, but in truth this does not seem to have been the case. Even left-wing journalists seemed to feel that, in challenging the competence of the public official, they were striking a blow for individual freedom. Moreover it was a popular, therefore an easy, line. What in fact ill-considered criticism was calculated to do was to reduce the potential efficiency of the public service and render the adequate execution of public business less easy in the future.

If it were desired to restore the high standards of the Civil Service in the new situation it is obvious that something positive had to be done about it. Yet it was not before the Priestley Commission issued its report in 1955 that anything much was done about it. The quick acceptance of the recommendation to extend the five-day week as widely as possible in the Departments, to counter a similar advance well under way in industry, effected an immediate improvement in the attractiveness of the Civil Service as a career. Due provision was made for handling essential public business on Saturdays but the shorter week was rapidly extended over large parts of the Service with much less dislocation and inconvenience to the public than had been anticipated.

The upward adjustment of salaries following acceptance of the Priestley principle of settling pay rates on the basis of fair comparisons[1] also had a good effect in restoring some degree of competetiveness between the Civil Service and its rivals, although the improvement was strictly relative to the previous adverse situation. The new system would in fact ensure that Civil Service remuneration should follow and not lead the market, and the problem of maintaining Civil Service standards was by no means solved. At the same time, in a package deal with the staffs, the Treasury managed to include a reduction in annual leave for future entrants, no doubt on the assumption that fair comparisons cut both ways! Whether it was wise at this juncture to worsen the Civil Service's attractiveness by this means is doubtful. It is only recently that steps have been taken to reduce the working day to more reasonable terms, and this only as a result of an arbitration award, to 41 hours weekly in London and 42 hours elsewhere, inclusive of the lunch break in each case. The Civil Service's hours had continued to be too prolonged for too long. It is doubtful whether long hours, with or without overtime, other than for emergency periods, are ever worthwhile, except to the underpaid who have little alternative, and ones impression is that the Departments worked much more effectively and economically under the 7-hour day of the pre-1939

[1] See page 50 above.

era. All these factors have an important effect upon recruitment, especially in a sellers' market.

Another problem of recent recruitment has been the steady erosion of the efficiency of the open competition tests, except at the highest levels, where Methods I and II still effectively achieve the ·older aims. But the introduction of the General Certificate of Education as a suitable test of competence for selection at the Clerical and Executive levels has practically effaced the competitive element and reduced the need for the candidate to make any special effort to enter the Service at these levels. Once this system was adopted it became almost inevitable that it would drive out any written test which called for active participation on the part of the candidate. The result has been to throw open the Civil Service at these levels to the type of person who does not really care whether he enters or not. Unless this trend is reversed by restoring the Service's competitiveness the Civil Service of the future will never again measure up to the Service of the past. All depends on the weight of the offer that is made to the school-leaver: not 'how cheap' according to the older Treasury philosophy, with thanks to Jeremy Bentham, but what price must be paid for the sort of product that the Service absolutely needs to cope with the tasks of the new administration. It is true that the GCE test falls in very effectively with the generalist approach, but the competence of the new recruits for their important profession is challenged by this easy-money method and the couldn't-care-less attitude of many of them to their new career. Certainly much more will have to be done in the future than in the past to ensure that after selection the newcomers are properly trained to meet the demands of their profession. Public administration in its growing complexity is surely not the only activity that, in our changing world, can be picked up without effort and almost in a state of absence of mind!

## STRUCTURE

The new Civil Service structure must depend upon the degree of generalism that is to be maintained and the extent of specialization that is to be introduced. Obviously a complete breakaway from the present system of broad classes is not to be recommended and could hardly be introduced at a stroke if it were. The Trevelyan–Northcote principles may need bringing up-to-date but they have not been superseded by a long way. It is desirable from a practical point of view to reduce the tall heirarchy of the present Treasury class pattern and this could in fact be achieved by returning to the original two-class scheme. It has long been evident that in practice the distinction between administrative and executive work, in the present Civil Service sense, is no longer tenable and an amalgamation of the two top classes is desirable. bringing a large part of the present executive field back into the sphere of true competition. This would not therefore mean the absorption of the entire Executive Class, as at present constituted, since those at Executive Officer level would not all qualify by the importance of their work to join the new managerial class. Part of it would be merged with the present Higher Clerical Officers to form a new Supervisory Clerical grade, which would at the same time constitute a suitable training grade for examination recruits and inside aspirants to the new enlarged Administrative Class.

Normal recruitment to the basic grade of the new Administrative Class would be at two levels, equivalent to the present Higher and Senior Executive Officer grades (but the latter would not continue as a separate grade or promotion step but constitute a range of allowance posts for officers assigned to special duties). The new hierarchy would scale up from Administrative Officer (present HEO and SEO), through Higher Administrative Officer (present CEO and Principal), Senior Administrative Officer (present Assistant Secretary) and then, as at present, Under Secretary, Deputy Secretary to Permanent Secretary, although I should prefer to substitute new titles with the term 'Secretary' superseded as being inappropriate at this level, interesting only as one of those administrative fossils of which we are not in short supply!

No longer would the new entrant to the Administrative Class go straight to Whitehall there to remain for the rest of his official career. Following a normal training period he would start out in the field and quickly occupy posts of responsibility which would give him basic managerial experience at an early date. Thus he would get front line administrative experience which under the present system the so-called flyers manage to escape altogether. This would help him to acquire that practical touch whose lack often leads to a degree of unrealism in the most brilliant administrative concepts: in addition he would have that healthy respect for the man who has to cope with the grass-roots problems of management that are only simple to those who haven't a clue as to what in practice they entail. The honours recruit would have the advantage of starting with an allowance post which, provided he made the grade, would open the way to headquarters appointments, as at present. His initial advantage would not however release him from the normal competition of other members of his grade. It is not likely that many would fall by the wayside, but the fact that at last the Civil Service had become a field really open to the talents would encourage more candidates of high quality and, one hopes, of energy and enterprise, to come in at the ground floor, whom today, if they really understand the position, one can hardly blame for sheering off, or leaving soon, before they get rooted. The present Method I and Method II style examinations would be maintained, with the adoption at the lower level of the modified examinations at present employed for the Special Departmental Classes.

The Clerical Class would need to be reconstructed as a series of shorter grades, with improved salary offers at lower levels and no limit to the possibility of advancement to the Administrative Class for those who prove themselves on their work and set out, with proper encouragement, to equip themselves for such advancement. Apart from normal promotion from supervisory levels it should be possible for junior officials, through the achievement of appropriate professional qualifications, to claim the right to probationary trial on Administrative Class duties without intervention of their Department. The new structure of the Clerical Class should facilitate the advancement of younger members to supervisory posts where they demonstrate the right qualities.

### ADMINISTRATORS VERSUS TECHNICIANS ?

The question of the proper relationship between administrators and members of other professions, especially scientists, has been widely debated, not only in the public service but wherever problems of power in a scientific age have been under consideration. In this sense it is a problem of politics and only new insofar as the rise of science is new. After all, among the early socialists Claude Henri Saint-Simon (1760/1825) seriously advocated the application of science to government and the division of power between a House of Invention to consist of civil engineers, poets, painters, architects and musicians, a House of Examination, to consist of physicists and mathematicians, and a House of Execution to consist of captain of industry, a sufficiently catholic solution which significantly ignores politicians and administrators as such. Ideas of this sort are endemic, appearing and reappearing in different forms as society changes and new interests become ascendant. For example, there were the strong advocates of government by technocrats in the United States during the inter-war depression and the recent somewhat artificial discussion over here of the division between the two worlds of culture and science. The whole concept has recently received its most creative examination, in relation particularly to the presidential system of government which embodies a basic separation of power, by Don K. Price in *The Scientific Estate*.[1] According to this interesting exposition the governing powers in society are now distributed between four distinct estates—the scientific, the professional, the administrative and the political—and the urgent problem is to strike a balance of power in which each contributes to the extent most effective for achieving the wellbeing of society.

The impact of science and technology is too great to require substantiating and is bound to effect the Civil Service in many ways. The need for a new awareness of science on the part of individual civil servants has already been accepted, but we are particularly concerned here with the relationships between administrators and scientists, including other specialists, inside the Central Administration. This must vary widely between those Departments on the one hand that are predominantly administrative and regulatory or providers of social services esssentially administrative in form, and on the other hand those that are concerned with research and production functions.

Naturally, discussion has hinged around the relationship between the Administrative Class and the Professional Classes, the latter reacting as a matter of course to the elite assumptions of the former and being less willing, in light of their own equally high academic experience at the universities, to accept the position, as have the other Civil Service classes who have started off with inferior academic equipment. However, this particular grievance has been considerably weakened by the introduction of gradings at the top of the several professional hierarchies which have practically the same status and remuneration as the Administrative Class and ensuring that members of the Professional Classes shall have access by promotion to the senior Administrative posts in the specialist branches of the Service.

The grievance formerly so widely canvassed that the administrators decided what professional advice should be communicated to the minister, has also been countered by improving the access of the Departments' professional experts to the minister. Obviously this must depend upon the relative importance of the advice which is being sought, and at lower levels experts must resign themselves to being confined to the appropriate levels of decision. If the expert has a right to expect a proper understanding of his position on the part of the administrator he on his side must be prepared to acquire the necessary understanding of administration to appreciate the administrator's position. Some Departments have introduced special machinery for the purpose. For example, the Defence Departments had long since set up councils to bring together poli-

[1] Belknap, Harvard, 1965.

ticians, professionals and administrators at the top while the Post Office, following the Bridgeman Report of 1932,[1] had introduced, as an integral part of the reorganized Department, a board under the chairmanship of the Postmaster General (the Minister) in which the deputy Postmaster General (his Parliamentary Secretary), the Director General (Permanent Secretary) and the senior heads of the internal departments dealing with engineering, finance, other technical, and regional matters come together in day-to-day management. The complaint that technical advice is sidetracked by the administrator, never perhaps convincingly substantiated, seems no longer to be well-founded.

But there is still the problem of the administrator occupying the seats of power, a natural outcome of past history when the King delegated executive powers to Great Officers of the Realm responsible for carrying out his policy. One of the virtues of the Parliamentary system is that, while ensuring that the power rests in the hands of the responsible Minister, the professional administrator provides the necessary skills and experience to do the administering. The administrative task today is no longer a chore which can be farmed out to deputies as formerly while the principal returns to his estates. It is a complicated technique to be laboriously acquired as any other professional technique and its exercise is becoming more and more the sphere of the expert.

However, it is still possible for the pompous and self-important to sit in the administrator's seat, wield a certain amount of power and a greater amount of influence and get away with it by leaving the actual job of work to competent subordinates, who will probably get the blame for any failure without receiving their due for the organization's success. It is important to the efficiency of an organization that other experts shall not be allowed to get into this position. Yet there is no reason why anyone with the right experience should not demonstrate a flair for administration, for this is not easy to define in advance. There is still a high degree of chance in getting the right people into the right places and there is no reason why competence in one field should be accepted as proof of competence in another. Yet many people fancy themselves as administrators and some may be right about this. It is possible for a scientist, a medical man, a teacher and so forth also to be, or to have the potentialities of, a good administrator, although normally the more deeply he is involved in his own specialism the less likely he will be to want to expend his talents in another. It is human

[1] *Report of Committee of Enquiry on the Post Office* (1932) Cmnd. 4149.

nature that the less competent in one line should turn to administration for salvation if the way is open to them, but the less figurehead inefficiency we have in the public services the better!

Having said so much it would be wrong to suggest that experts coming into the Civil Service in one line should not have every opportunity to move over to administration if they really do have the flair and inclination. Much will depend upon the extent to which their own specialisms will be of value in the administrative post, for few will want to sacrifice the hardly earned knowledge and skill which practice of a profession entails.

In the long run this particular problem will be solved as soon as (1) we get it into our heads that in the new world the administrator is not a power wielder but a highly skilled operator in his own field, and (2) better means have been devised for testing administrative performance.

In the acutal staffing of the professional Civil Service the solution may well be found in the direction of cutting the number of permanent posts to a minimum, but being prepared to pay the highest market rates for the services of the expert, who should be encouraged to take his services elsewhere after a reasonable period of public service. There is much to be said for such professionals keeping up-to-date and not acquiring a typically public service outlook. Of course this idea can hardly apply to those numerous experts whose main occupation is found mainly in the Civil Service, notably in the Communications and Defence Departments.

### PROFESSIONAL QUALIFICATIONS

Our national faith in the liberal arts as providing the last word in the education of an administrator dies hard. Traditionalist Britain is finding more difficulty than most in acclimatizing itself to the new scientific world and the idea that administration is as much a science as an art, still not universally accepted, although this was already clearly grasped by such outstanding administrators as Haldane, Beveridge and Stamp way back at the beginning of the century. It is to America that we have to turn for perceptive treatises in the subject—and of course to Germany, if we can find adequate translations. In Britain we prefer Professor Parkinson to Max Weber!

Despite encouragement given by a few universities to the study of public administration and the efforts of the Royal Institute of Public Administration, supported by a few of the staff associations, the growth of such studies and their acceptance have been very limited. The time has surely come to insist that career civil servants should acquire suitable qualifications in the subject.

Every civil servant surely needs a good basic knowledge in such subjects as are called for in degree courses in political science, economics and sociology, in university diplomas in public administration, and in the, so far not very successful, Civil Service Diploma in Government Administration. Apart from public administration these subjects include machinery of government (under whatever label it may be defined), constitutional history, constitutional law, economics, statistics, social studies and the several branches of general administration. The Civil Service must throw aside its prejudice, which is not, by the way, shared by the professional and technical sectors, and decide to give due credit to the holding of accepted professional qualifications in public administration in all internal selections of staff.

More weight should also be given to such subjects in the entrance examinations. Where recruits continue to come in on a general educational basis, such as the holding of GCE qualifications, they should be expected, and of course assisted, to undertake the studies required to obtain a professional qualification. The staff training authorities should assist in this, since the acquirement of the essential background knowledge must be a vital factor in the scheme of continuous training which it is to be hoped will in future be developed. To this end there must be close co-operation between the public service and the educational establishments. Instruction in public administration is a practical matter calling for close co-operation between inside trainer and outside teacher. It is not a subject that can be effectively dealt with by either field alone. Theory and practice must be meshed at all levels. This suggests the need, if not for a staff college of the older type, for a Public Administration Studies Centre where facilities can be found by all branches of the public service and the educational authorities for the conduct of staff training, public administration studies and suitable evening classes, in close co-ordination. Such a Centre, which might well develop into a new type of University in Administration, with only a servicing staff would no doubt be first developed in London, near to the largest number of public offices, but the aim should be to establish a network of such centres throughout the country. It would cost money but would be a sound investment which could bring substantial efficiency returns. It could also provide common service facilities for existing training branches and accommodation for inter-departmental meetings, conferences and seminars, and so forth.

The truth is that instruction in public administration has been

T

concentrated too much at the top, as though public administration were different from other subjects in calling for such treatment. The proper place to start is at the grass roots, like English, arithmetic, geography and history: the foundations should be laid in primary school. In modern democracies the study of civics is a primary citizenship need. Life has become too complicated for the ordinary voter to spring fully equipped from an ordinary school course to cope effectively in the democratic type of government about which we boast so much. It is heartening that there has been a new drive since the war to teach civics in the schools and a steady expansion which should certainly have the blessing of the public service authorities, will bring continuous improvement in methods of teaching and the supply of suitable text-books. Only in this way can public administration throw down the roots whereby it can hope to prosper and expand, and eventually support much more extensive faculties in the subject than the universities at present feel justified in developing, paving the way to the future General Administration Studies which will provide the universal co-ordinating subject to enable all the diverse specialisms, which inevitably tend to proliferate, to be seen for what they are, convenient informational atoms of Human Knowledge as a whole.

## ACHIEVEMENT OF MAXIMUM INITIATIVE

An undoubted advantage of the elite system has been to preserve in at least one sector of the Civil Service an area of high individual initiative. But this has been offset elsewhere by the development of strict rules, in the interests of fairness and against favouritism, for the control of selection, which has had the effect of turning the individual official into little more than a cog. The civil servant who presumes to show initiative, except along closely defined channels, is looked upon with suspicion both by his chiefs and by his peers. Those who do not conform to a widely accepted pattern do not get promotion, however excellent their reports may otherwise be. On the other hand some extraordinarily unenterprising individuals get along very nicely just because—whether by astute foresight, but usually quite by accident—they have known how to dress the shop-window to advantage with a quite modest stock of talents.

In the closely regulated service mediocrity is not so much protected as ignored. The individual's career is not much influenced by the good work he may do. His best policy is to do nothing to earn him the reputation of being different. In any case chance will figure prominently in his career. Much will depend upon his being of the right age, at the right place, at the right time. Only general trends outside or changes in official policy will radically modify the regimented system. It is not possible to favour an individual, but advantage can be given to a group or a class in the name of administrative necessity. To rectify past mistakes in staffing policy the authorities can suddenly decide that special emphasis shall be given to youth. Then those who have had to await promotion because hitherto strict weight has been given to experience or seniority will suddenly find themselves stranded on a rapidly dwindling island amidst the promotion stream, missing the current as well as the boat. Under pressures from the staff, selections in a large Department have to be distributed more or less evenly according to branch, region or sex. Added to all these administrative exigencies there are the unavoidable variations in opportunity due to outside changes and pressures, the expansibility or compressibility of the particular Department, and so on, and so forth. The individual could do little about it, even if he were clever enough to be able to diagnose what was happening. Such a situation which is a hazard of all large-scale organizations, is liable to encourge a fatalistic attitude, particularly among the middle and older age-groups of the staff.

It is necessary to look at the position afresh. Has the protective element in the Civil Service personnel system been over-developed? Should not the individual be given some means of breaking out of the hidebound staff strait-jacket? For example, could there not be instituted an overriding authority to which any official, who feels that he has capacities that are not being used to the full, could apply for consideration? Should not the civil servant, instead of being departmentally bound have the privilege of belonging to a career service which extends beyond the confines of his own Department? Should not promotion be placed under an all-Service authority, and the individual have a right of appeal to an impartial body? Should not entitlement to his salary and pension be a matter of legal right no longer depending upon the grace of the Crown— however good in practice that grace may be—and capable of being tested in the courts? Will anyone in future be inclined to belong to a profession which is so chary of granting its members the normal freedoms and rights? These are some of the leading questions which the immediate reformer must answer.

Furthermore, in this new administrative world where ideas are at at a premium and new inventions open out untold territories for experiment and advance, is it desirable to continue to nurture the image of the unenterprising bureaucrat, doing as he is told, tempering his words to his leaders' hunches, living by the regulations alone and asking, as some seniors still do, for everything to be spelled out in detailed black and white? Administration, if it still, by nature, has an important element of routine, is also an adventure calling for the probing mind. The trouble is that the slowcoach can always get the right answer given the time, and when the file has been completed and put away his work will stand upon its meticulous correctness and not upon the expedition with which the results were achieved. It is more often than not that speed with relative accuracy is more effective in achieving the required results than the slowness imposed by absolute acuracy. Too often in the past the unenterprising has got away with the prize. But automation has come to alter all that!

### THE IMPACT OF AUTOMATION

In little more than a decade the electronic computer has come to revolutionize the whole sphere of administration by ruthlessly telescoping the routine stages in large-scale operations, speeding up the production of basic information, and broadening vastly the field over which such information can be made rapidly available to the administrator and the policy-maker. All this depends upon the simple possibility of representing the basic facts in terms of arithmetic (usually reduced to the binary system), storing it for future use, adding new or amending details at any stage, and extracting it as and when required, all at quite fantastic speeds. Initially devised for working out research mathematics of great complexity, the computer was first found most helpful in administration when applied to the production of weekly or monthly pay rolls or the keeping of stock records. Instead of having to deploy large clerical staffs, often under a regular hierarchy of supervisors, almost continuously to keep the payroll documents up-to-date from one pay-out to the next, the new method, which meant the serving into the computer details of variations in pay for many causes to amend data in the already existing store, made it possible to reduce the staff occupied in this work to a mere handful and to cut out much of the laborious cross-checking usually needed under the old system. In fact a large proportion of the previous soul-destroying clerical donkey-work was made to vanish as effectively as by Aladdin's lamp.

This was only the beginning. The manipulators of the new machinery have to feel their way. Certainly the first steps take time. It may be some years before the programme to deal with a particular problem or use has been devised and the necessary machine designed and manufactured. There is an inevitable gap before the new system supersedes the old, plenty of time to plan the useful deployment of redundant staff when the moment arrives! But results henceforth are likely to be cumulative; with increasing experience even more complicated processes are being reduced to the essential arithmetical ingredients; multi-purpose and therefore more flexible computers are beginning to appear. The revolution is manifold: saving in staff, abolition of a good deal of routine work, speeding up the administrative process, and greatly increased accuracy; for self-checking routines can be built into the programme.

The question has to be asked whether the abolition of much routine clerical work may not deprive of his livelihood a certain type of worker who has not the capacity to do much else, just as the development of the mechanical digger and bulldozer has reduced critically the need for the ordinary navvy in the world of manual labour. Public administration in the future is certainly likely to need a smaller proportion of routine clerical workers, but it would be foolish to regard such work as a good in itself. In future the State, through the Civil Service, will find it less practicable to earmark a substantial proportion of its lower jobs for the nation's lame ducks. However lame, and deserving, it should be possible under conditions of full employment to find them a niche elsewhere.

Although in the long run there should be a net saving of labour, immediate experience, in America particularly where to date the greatest uses of automation have been made and in the public service itself, suggests that the saving on specific jobs is offset by the expanding field which the new facilities bring within the range of practicability. The long run result should be an overall increase in the effectiveness of the Administration, and apart from the net staff saving a switch over from routine to more intrinsically interesting and responsible work.

This is not a treatise on automation, or more precisely in our particular field on Automatic Data Processing (ADP), but we are much concerned with the probable impact of the new processes on the Civil Service. The actual production of the new electronic equipment calls for scientists, engineers, mathematicians and other specialists, and of course the Civil Service must contain experts in these fields, although in the main the actual production of the machines is being left in private hands. The Civil Service's job is to determine the objectives it wants the computer to reach and to use it economically when it has been produced. Even the normal servicing may continue to be carried out by the suppliers' own engineers. Civil servants have to produce the required data, prepare it for the machine in appropriate form—punched cards, magnetic tapes, etc.—which requires the services of expert machinists, often graded at Clerical Assistant level, but the most skilled part of the process is devising the programme to which the machine works to achieve the answers that are required. This is based upon a thorough knowledge of the job processes involved, a meticulous analysis of the work in detail, and working out what steps the computer will have to take to achieve the objectives set. The programmer does not have to be an engineer, but of course he must know how the machine works and must have a detailed knowledge of the administrative procedures, which he has to be able to rationalize. It all adds up to a certain sort of approach which calls for an aptitude to get the right answers. It also calls for abundant patience, for it takes time. It has been decided that the Civil Service shall not introduce a special class of programmers, but that the task can best be handled by the several grades of the Executive Class, who are the people with the right practical experience of the work processes, the right sort of education and abilities. Moreover, programming is another one of those jobs on which an official should not be employed permanently. Members of an existing grade can easily be switched elsewhere when the time comes, and their experience with computers will continue to be of value in their work.

Automation is bound to have a far-reaching effect upon the changes which we know are already called for in the Civil Service. It points to a simplification of the staff hierarchy by the elimination of many of the routine stages in the administrative process and the speeding up of activity in the higher reaches by the rapid supply of the complicated information required for reaching effective decisions. Its impact is still difficult to forecast but obviously no reform can hope to have much permanancy that does not attempt to take this into account.

### A NEW IMAGE?

The image of the public official as a slow-moving, tortuous-minded bureaucrat is a traditional one, based upon a natural dislike of official interference, especially by the tax-collector, shot with overtones from earlier societies. It is one in which publicists delight, although a little thought should tell their readers that the creative activities of the Welfare State could not have been carried out by drones and incompetents. Despite widespread advocacy of State activities in the direction of social reform and socialism this anti-bureaucratic idea is actively propagated. Even the equal-income socialism of George Bernard Shaw went into full retreat at the approach of the income tax man! The lucubrations of Professor Parkinson, now accepted as blind gospel by a large section of the intelligencia of Britain, gain their popularity neither from their originality nor from their verisimilitude, but because they give ready support to the half-baked prejudices against those servants of the people who devote their lives to the public welfare.

If it be thought that these strictures are unwarranted or grossly exaggerated the following quotation early in 1966 from a review in *The Times Literary Supplement* of a book that has nothing to do with the public service will open the reader's eyes:

'To assume that all ghastly people are stupid is something we all do. Alas, it is not true. The higher civil service has people with quite high IQs in it.'[1]

In the face of such prejudice it is hardly surprising that the Civil Service's image is not so attractive today as to improve the recruitment position. If the image were true, which emphatically it is not, something drastic would have to be done about it as a matter of national urgency, for the new society which is emerging—whether we like it or not—will continue to depend upon a high degree of devoted service from its public servants. Honest and constructive criticism, as vigorous as may be, is to be welcomed as an essential means to the sort of improvement to which all human institutions are amenable. The Civil Service will certainly benefit from more well-informed criticism but the propagation of the sort of anti-bureaucratic myth which issues often from the mouths of apparent authority is socially destructive and should be challenged at every step.

More information is needed about the working of the administrative sectors of government. There is some evidence of an unhealthy trend towards making such inside information even more difficult to come by, to cover with a shroud of secrecy matters which are not basically confidential and to strain arguments against publicity to the limits. More fresh air needs to be blown into the corridors of bureaucratic power. On the other hand certain developments referred to in this book indicate a movement in the right direction: e.g., the increasing interest in civics, government and public administration as subjects for study; the expanding interest in the techniques of public administration from a professional standpoint; and the introduction of new means of looking in from the outside through the proposed introduction of an Ombudsman and the setting up of permanent parliamentary committees to ensure the better informing of M.P.s—and of course of the people—on the way the Administration works.

The official's own secretiveness will have to go, and a widening of the scope of the Administrative Class, as proposed, should help

[1] 'Too Clever by Half' in the issue for March 31, 1966.

to bring this about. The notion that administering and policy-making are mysteries only to be operated by the elect is much out of place in a democratic society. By their works shall we know them, and could know them today if we recognized how much quite incredibly bad policy has been formulated since the beginning of the century, to go back no further. In future the hunches of the inspired will soon have to give way before the magic selections of the electronic computer.

We not only need better informed administrators but also a citizenship which is better informed about administration. The officials themselves will have to take a hand in countering slanderous propaganda and making a better job of explaining what they are about, for which end the rules may have to be made more flexible.

The Civil Service needs a professional body to do just this. Such an institution cannot be imposed from without, and is likely to emerge from within only when a forward-looking professional outlook has been born out of the new situation which is surely emerging. This book should have pointed at least one moral: there are still a lot of cobwebs to be blown away!

# SELECT BIBLIOGRAPHY

This list includes books and pamphlets dealing with the British Civil Service which have been published since 1939 together with selected titles of works dealing with the Central Government and the Departments which have a particular bearing upon the Civil Service. Other writings have been mentioned in footnotes to the text. References to the Civil Service and allied topics will also be found in works on the British Constitution, in books on public administration in a general sense and in the biographical writings of statesmen and officials. The files of *Public Administration,* published quarterly by the Royal Institute of Public Administration, and of the periodicals of the various Civil Service staff organizations also contain a store of basic information on the subject. The list is divided into Non-Official and Official sections and arranged generally according to the date of publication.

NON-OFFICIAL

1941  **The Growth of the British Civil Service,** 1780–1939, by Emmeline W. Cohen. 221 pp. (Allen & Unwin)
    *A brief history of the Civil Service; the only one so far available.*

1941  **The Higher Civil Service of Great Britain,** by H. E. Dale. xiv+232 pp. (Oxford University Press)
    *A valuable examination of the manners and quality of the highest ranks of the Civil Service between the wars.*

1942  **Passed to You Please,** by J. P. W. Mallalieu, 160 pp. (Victor Gollancz)
    *Mainly a polemic against officialdom to a popular recipe, with a characteristic 'Introduction' by the late Prof. H. J. Laski.*

1942  **Civil Service Reform,** by the Liberal Party. 16 pp. (Liberal Publication Dept.)
    *The interim report of a sub-committee on the Reform of the Civil Service appointed by the Party's Industrial and Social Reconstruction Committee.*

1943  **So Far . . . ,** by W. J. Brown. 295 pp. (Allen & Unwin)
    *The informative autobiography of a prominent Civil Service trade union leader.*

1943 **The Civil Service: Retrospect and Prospect,** by W. J. Brown. 80 pp. With a 'Foreword' by Sir N. F. Warren Fisher. (Published by the Author)
*A brief description of the Civil Service with reference to wartime developments.*

1943 **Civil Service Staff Relationships,** by E. N. Gladden. xi+184 pp. With a 'Foreword' by Sir Horace Wilson (William Hodge & Co.)
*Discusses the rise of staff associations and the Whitley system of joint consultation.*

1943 **The Personnel and Problems of the Higher Civil Service,** by H. E. Dale. 16 pp. (Oxford University Press)
*Text of the Sydney Ball lecture, to the Association of Barnett House, Oxford.*

1944 **Post-War Reconstruction,** by the Institution of Professional Civil Servants, 15 pp. (Published by the Institute)
*Deals with the professional, scientific and technical branches of the Civil Service.*

1944 **The Professional Civil Servant's Handbook,** by L. A. C. Herbert. 352 pp. (Institution of Professional Civil Servants)
*A later edition is available of this useful compendium which covers a wide range of Civil Service topics.*

1944 **Representative Bureaucracy,** by J. D. Kingsley. 324 pp. (Antioch Press, U.S.A.)
*A stimulating survey of the development of the British Civil Service which, nevertheless, loses by leaning too much on a preconceived class interpretation of administrative history.*

1945 **The Civil Service and the People,** by R. W. Rawlings. 162 pp. (Lawrence & Wishart)
*An interesting account based upon a class interpretation of Civil Service development.*

1945 **The Civil Service: Its Problems and Future,** by E. N. Gladden. 187 pp. (Staples Press)
*A survey of development, structure and internal problems, together with a proposed scheme of reform. A second edition appeared in 1948.*

1945 **Law and Orders,** C. K. Allen, xvi+385 pp. (Stevens & Sons)
*A general study of the relations between the Executive and other branches of government, with numerous references to the position of the Civil Service and the delegation of powers. Follows the tradition of Lord Hewart's famous polemical study, 'The New Despotism'.*

1945 **A Modern Guide to the Civil Service,** by L. C. White. 78 pp. With a 'Foreword' by the late Prof. H. J. Laski. (University of London Press)
*A practical description of the Civil Service at that time.*

1947 **Officials and the Public,** by Sir Henry Bunbury. 19 pp. (*Current Affairs*, issued by the Bureau of Current Affairs)
*A general survey of civil servants and their work, for discussion purposes.*

1947 **The Civil Service and the Changing State,** by H. R. G. Greaves. 240 pp. (G. Harrap & Co.)
*A controversial discussion of the higher Civil Service, supplemented by chapters on the public corporations and the machinery of government.*

1947 **The Crisis of the Bureaucracy,** by L. Skevington. 14 pp. (The Pilot Press)
*A stimulating essay by a wartime civil servant contributed to Pilot Papers, Vol. 2, No. 2.*

1947 **Recruiting Civil Servants,** in *Planning*, No. 266. 19 pp. (P.E.P.)
*Continues a discussion launched by P.E.P. during the war on the political aspects of the machinery of central government in Planning No. 173 'The Machinery of Government', and No. 214 'A Civil General Staff'.*

1947 **The Experience of a University Teacher in the Civil Service,** by Sir Oliver S. Franks. 17 pp. (Oxford University Press)
*Text of the Sydney Ball lecture to the Association of Barnett House, Oxford.*

1947 **The Reform of the Higher Civil Service.** 60 pp. (Fabian Society)
*For a Fabian report this document displays an ununsual degree of upper-class consciousness and a tendency to overstress the parallel between the Civil Service and the Armed Forces.*

1950 **Master of the Offices,** by H. Legge-Bourke. 41 pp. (Falcon Press)
*A polemic on the control of the Civil Service.*

1950 **Portrait of a Profession,** by Sir Edward Bridges. 33 pp. (Cambridge University Press)
*The Rede Lecture, 1950, by the Head of the Civil Service.*

1951 **Staff Reporting,** by I. E. P. Menzies and E. Anstey. 95 pp. (Allen & Unwin)
*A useful survey of Civil Service practice, which does not, however, presume to delve far below the surface. Has a Foreword by Sir Horace Wilson.*

1951 **The Civil Service Today,** by T. A. Critchley. 150 pp. (Victor Gollancz)
*Pays special attention to the work of civil servants of different grades.*

1952 **Le Civil Service Britannique,** by Paul-Marie Gaudemet. 172 pp. (Libraire Armand Colin, Paris)
*A comprehensive and detached survey on legalist lines by an eminent French scholar.*

1952 **How the Civil Service Works,** by Bosworth Monck. 258 pp. (Phoenix House)
> *A brief account not only of the Civil Service but of the Central Government. The second half of the book is devoted to a summary of the work of the individual departments.*

1952 **Modern Staff Training,** by F. J. Tickner. 159 pp. (University of London Press)
> *Although dealing with the wider aspects of its subject this book, by a former Director of Training and Education at H.M. Treasury, is undoubtedly based largely upon the author's experience of Civil Service training.*

1952 **The Fountains in Trafalgar Square,** by C. K. Munro. x+202 pp. (William Heinemann)
> *Personal recollections and opinions of a retired civil servant who is also well known as a dramatist.*

1952 **The C.S.C.S. Compendium.** xvi+556 pp. (Civil Service Clerical Association)
> *The latest edition of a work first compiled before the war, bringing together a budget of official information relevant to personnel management of the Civil Service.*

1952 **Whitehall to West Indies,** by F. A. Norman. 256 pp. (Bodley Head)
> *A senior Civil Servant's account of a varied career mainly in employment administration.*

1953 **Yours for Action,** by Bernard Newman. viii+196 pp. (Civil Service Clerical Association)
> *A well-illustrated commemorative volume describing the development of the largest staff association of office workers in the Civil Service.*

1953 **Whitleyism,** by James Callaghan. Fabian Research Series, No. 159. 40 pp. (Fabian Society)
> *A study of joint consultation in the Civil Service written from a Labour standpoint.*

1954 **The Civil Service in the Constitution,** by K. C. Wheare. 34 pp. (The Athlone Press)
> *A lecture delivered before the University of London to commemorate the centenary of the Trevelyan-Northcote Report.*

1954 **The Contracts of Public Authorities,** by J. D. B. Mitchell. xxxii+256 pp. (LSE/Geo. Bell)
> *A comparative study covering England, United States and France.*

1955 **The Battle of Crichel Down,** by R. Douglas Brown. 192 pp.
(The Bodley Head)
*A balanced survey of an occurrence that caused a considerable
stir at the time.*

1955 **Higher Civil Servants in Britain,** by R. K. Kelsall. xvi+233 pp.
(Routledge and Kegan Paul)
*A study of the origins and social background of members of
the higher ranks of the Civil Service from 1870 onwards.*

1955 **A History of Red Tape,** by Sir John Craig. ix+211 pp. (Mac-
donald & Evans)
*A broad general survey of the development of the central
departments, their officials and their work.*

1955 **The Civil Service in Great Britain,** by G. A. Campbell. 383 pp.
(Pelican)
*Covers the whole machinery of the central administration; a
readable and reliable if somewhat mixed up budget of information.*

1955 **The Real Rulers of Our Country,** by Elijah Wilkes. 16 pp.
(Routledge & Kegan Paul)
*A provocative essay in a pamphlet series entitled 'Passport to
Survival'.*

1955/6 **40 Years On,** by Douglas Houghton. 28+35+30 pp. (Inland
Revenue Staff Federation)
*Three remarkably interesting brochures tracing the careers of
Tax Clerks who were recruited to the Inland Revenue De-
partment in 1915 and 1916 (i.e. during the First World War)*

1956 **Civil Service or Bureaucracy?** by E. N. Gladden. xii+224 pp.
(Staples Press).
*Forerunner of the present book, containing a critical analysis
of the Civil Service at that time.*

1956 **The Civil Service; Some Human Aspects,** by Frank Dunnill.
vi+226 pp. (George Allen & Unwin).
*A valuable account of the Service which places the chief
emphasis on the human element.*

1956 **The Civil Service in Britain and France.** Edited by W. A. Rob-
son. vii+191 pp. (The Hogarth Press)
*A series of instructive essays by a number of well-known
experts on the subject, extended from a special issue of 'The
Political Quarterly', originally published at the end of 1954.*

1957 **Central Administration in Britain,** by W. J. M. Mackenzie and
J. W. Grove. xvi+487 pp. (Longmans)
*A comprehensive study for the student of Public Administra-
tion, Part I of which deals with 'The Civil Service'.*

1957   **The Growth of Public Employment in Great Britain,** by Moses Abranovitz and Vera F. Eliasberg. 151 pp. (Princeton, U.S.A.)
*A factual account covering the period 1890 to 1950.*

1957   **The Organization of British Central Government, 1914–1956,** by a Study Group of the R.I.P.A. Edited by D. N. Chester and written by F. M. Willson. 457 pp. (George Allen & Unwin)
*A detailed examination of the structure and activities of the Government Departments over the period, providing an invaluable background study to Civil Service problems.*

1957   **The Civil Service,** by Peter de Sautoy. 158 pp. (Oxford)
*A succinct discussion of Civil Service in its general aspects.*

1958   **Clerical Unions in the Civil Service,** by B. V. Humphreys. xiv + 254 pp. (Blackwell & Mott)
*Covers the development of the staff associations in the clerical field from a distinctly staff viewpoint.*

1959   **The Civil Service,** by Charles Dixon. 105 pp. ('Target for Careers' Series, Robert Hale)
*A current survey.*

1961   **British Public Service Administration,** by E. N. Gladden. 328 pp. (Staples Press)
*A detailed survey of the structure and functions of public administration in Britain which includes much information about the work of the Departments.*

1961   **Morale in the Civil Service,** by Nigel Walker. viii + 302 pp. (Edinburgh University Press)
*Subtitled 'a study of the desk worker' this massive investigation is interesting as an example of modern social research, but it does not go much further than any group of competent supervisors could have hazarded in informal discussion.*

1961   **The Ruling Servants,** by E. Strauss. 308 pp. (George Allen & Unwin)
*A stimulating comparison of the working of 'bureaucracy' in Russia, France and Britain, which touches upon the Civil Service in the modern phase.*

1962   **The I.P.C.S. Handbook, 1962** published by the Institution of Professional Civil Servants. viii + 466 pp.
*A valuable budget of information about the Civil Service in general.*

1962   **The Civil Service,** by Frank Dunnill. 94 pp. ('Sunday Times' Careers Books)
*A current survey which manages to avoid the deadly dullness of so many compilations of this type.*

1963   **Whitley Councils in the United Kingdom Civil Service,** by Richard Hayward. 20 pp. (C.S. National Whitley Council (Staff Side))
*An authorative summary by the Staff Side's Secretary General.*

1963   **Salaries in the Public Services of England and Wales,** by Hilda R. Kahn. 428 pp. (George Allen & Unwin)
*Covers a wide field and deals only to a small extent with the Civil Service. Based on details relating to 1951.*

1963   **Patronage in British Government,** by P. G. Richards. 284 pp. (George Allen & Unwin)
*An interesting study covering a much wider field than the Civil Service.*

1964   **British Government Observed,** by Brian Chapman. 64 pp. (George Allen & Unwin)
*Only partly concerned with the Civil Service. A fiery polemic obviously aimed at stimulating discussion rather than disclosing the truth.*

1964   **The Administrators: The Reform of the Civil Service,** by a Fabian Group. 45 pp. (Fabian Society)
*A stimulating discussion of a number of Civil Service problems and proposing inter alia the removal of Establishments from the Treasury to a reformed Civil Service Commission.*

1964   **The Civil Service and Local Government as a Career,** by Ronald Field. 132 pp. (Batsford)
*A current survey.*

1964   **The Treasury Under the Tories, 1951–1964,** by Samuel Brittan. 374 pp. (Penguin Books)
*While concerned mainly with finance and control this stimulating work gives some attention to Civil Service control.*

1965   **Not in the Public Interest,** by David Williams. 224 pp. (Hutchinson)
*A detailed examination of the scope and enforcement of executive security in which a good deal of attention is given to the Civil Service's position.*

1965   **Public Service Pensions** by Gerald Rhodes and a Study Group of the Royal Institute of Public Administration. 320 pp. (George Allen & Unwin)
*A massive and valuable survey going far beyond the bounds of the Civil Service.*

1965 **The Government Explains,** by Marjorie Ogilvy-Webb. 229 pp.
(George Allen & Unwin)
> Subtitled 'A Study of the Information Services' and spon-
> sored by the R.I.P.A. this is a comprehensive account of the
> and activities of the Information Officer Class.

1965 **La Funcion Publica en Inglaterra,** by G. Laso Vallejo. 403 pp.
(Centro de Formacion y Perfeccionamiento de Funcionarios).
> A competent and comprehensive synthesis in Spanish of
> writings on the British Civil Service.

1966 **The Civil Servant and His World,** by John Carswell. 144 pp.
(Victor Gollancz).
> A careers study which attempts with considerable success to
> project the Civil Service in depth.

For convenience the *New Whitehall Series* about the several
Departments, published on behalf of the Royal Institute of Public
Administration by George Allen & Unwin Ltd., are listed together.
Dealing primarily with the work and structure of the Departments
they are also in varying degree concerned with the civil servants
working in them.

**The Home Office,** by Sir Frank Newsam. (1954). 224 pp.

**The Foreign Office,** by Lord Strang. (1955). 226 pp.

**The Colonial Office,** by Sir Charles Jeffries. (1956). 222 pp.

**The Ministry of Works,** by Sir Harold Emmerson. (1956). 171 pp.

**The Scottish Office,** by Sir David Milne. (1957). 232 pp.

**The Ministry of Pensions and National Insurance,** by Sir Geoffrey
S. King. (1958). 162 pp.

**The Ministry of Transport and Civil Aviation,** by Sir Gilmour
Jenkins. (1959). 231 pp.

**The Ministry of Labour and National Service,** by Sir Godfrey Ince.
(1960). 215 pp.

**The Department of Scientific and Industrial Research,** by Sir Harry
Melville. (1962). 200 pp.

**Her Majesty's Customs and Excise,** by Sir James Crombie. (1962).
224 pp.

**The Ministry of Agriculture, Fisheries and Food,** by Sir John Winni-
frith. (1962). 271 pp.

**The Treasury,** by Lord Bridges. (1964). 248 pp.

**The Inland Revenue,** by Sir Alexander Johnston. (1965). 201 pp.

The above titles are arranged in order of appearance: in several instances
later editions have appeared. Further titles will be added to the series from
time to time.

OFFICIAL

1942 Report from the Select Committee on **Offices or Places of Profit under the Crown.** 55 pp.
*Deals 'inter alia' with the position of civil servants.*

1942 Sixteenth Report from the Select Committee on National Expenditure (session 1941–2) on **Organization and Control of the Civil Service.** 55 pp.
*This report led to the development of O & M and Staff Training in the central administration.*

1943 Proposals for the **Reform of the Foreign Service** (Cmd. 6420). 10 pp.
*Summary of the Government's proposals for reform following the Foreign Minister's statement in the House of Commons on June 11th, 1941.*

1944 Report of the Committee on the **Training of Civil Servants** (Cmd. 6525). 34 pp.
*The Assheton Report on which the present system of training is based.*

1944 **Recruitment to Established Posts in the Civil Service during the Reconstruction Period** (Cmd. 6567). 23 pp.
*A Statement of Government policy and Report by the Civil Service National Whitley Council.*

1945 **The Scientific Civil Service** (Cmd. 6679). 16 pp.
*A White Paper, stating the Government's plans for reorganization. Includes as Annexe, 'Report of the Barlow Committee on Scientific Staff'.*

1945 **Post-War Prospects for the Established Civil Servant.** 16 pp.
*A pamphlet addressed by H.M. Treasury to serving civil servants, especially members of H.M. Forces.*

1945 **The Administrative Class of the Civil Service** (Cmd. 6680). 2 pp.
*This briefest of all White Papers, covers an organizational change and announces revised salaries for the whole class.*

1945 **Appendices to Minutes of Evidence taken before the Royal Commission on Equal Pay.** 52 pp.
*Evidence covering the Civil Service.*

1946 Report of the **Royal Commission on Equal Pay, 1944–46** (Cmd. 6937). xi + 219 pp.
*Complete survey covering both public and private sectors including comprehensive information about U.S.A., Australia, France and the U.S.S.R.*

U

1946 **Marriage Bar in the Civil Service** (Cmd. 6886). 24 pp.
*Report of a Committee of the Civil Service National Whitley
Council.*

1947 Fifth Report from the Select Committee on Estimates (session
1946–7) on **Organization and Methods and its Effect on the
Staffing of Government Departments.** xxv+111 pp.
*Includes a brief appendix listing the functions of Treasury
and Departmental O & M.*

1947 **Working Conditions in the Civil Service.** 164 pp. and appendices.
*A comprehensive survey by a Study Group appointed by
H.M. Treasury.*

1947 **Suggestions Schemes in Government Departments** by Treasury
O. & M. (H.M.S.O.). pp. 28.
*An analysis of existing schemes.*

1948 Ninth Report from the Select Committee on Estimates (session
1947–8) on **The Civil Service Commission.** xiii+43 pp.
*Includes an examination of the work of the Civil Service
Selection Board.*

1949 **Staff Relations in the Civil Service.** 38 pp.
*A valuable survey issued by the Treasury; up-to-date editions
are published from time to time.*

1949 Report of the Tribunal to inquire into **Allegations reflecting on
the Official Conduct of Ministers of the Crown and other Public
Servants** (Cmd. 7616). 82 pp.
*Known as the Lynskey Report, it exonerates the Civil Ser-
vants involved in the Inquiry.*

1949 Report of the Committee on **Higher Civil Service Remuneration**
(Cmd. 7635). 14 pp.
*Known as the Chorley Report, it recommends improvement
for the higher posts.*

1949 Report of the Committee on the **Political Activities of Civil Servants** (Cmd. 7718). 42 pp.
*The Masterman Report.*

1950 Report of the Committee on **Intermediaries** (Cmd. 7904). 92 pp.
*An inquiry into 'how far persons are making a business of
acting as specialists in the submission of applications for
licences or permits, or otherwise as intermediaries between
Government Departments; and to report whether the activities
of such persons are liable to give rise to abuses; and to make
recommendations.*

1951  Seventh Report from the Select Committee on Estimates (session 1950–1) on **the Foreign Service.** xxx+284 pp.
*Contains useful information about the establishments abroad.*

1951  Memorandum by the Civil Service Commissioners on the **Use of the Civil Service Selection Board in the Reconstruction Competitions.** 46 pp.
*An authorative account of the 'house-party' experiment.*

1951  Report of the Committee on the **Organization, Structure and Remuneration of the Works Group of Professional Civil Servants.** 28 pp.
*An investigation carried out in accordance with recommendations of the Chorley Committee* (Cmd. 7635).

1952  **Digest of Pension Law and Regulations of the Civil Service.** 382 pp.
*A comprehensive collection of extracts, etc., from Superannuation Acts, and Rules, Regulations and Orders issued in connexion therewith, compiled by H.M. Treasury.*

1952  Report of the Committee on the **Organization, Structure and Remuneration of the Professional Accountant Class in the Civil Service.** 22 pp.
*Discusses 'inter alia' the question whether the scope of the class should be extended to cover accounting work habitually carried out by members of the Executive Class.*

1952  **Report of the Post Office (Departmental Classes) Recognition Committee** (Cmd. 8470) 24 pp.

1954  **Public Inquiry ordered by the Minister of Agriculture into the disposal of land at Crichel Down** (Cmd. 9176). 34 pp.

1954  Report of a **Committee appointed by the Prime Minister to consider whether certain Civil Servants should be transferred to other duties** (Cmd. 9220). 4 pp.
*A footnote to the Inquiry into the Crichel Down affair* (Cmd. 9176).

1954  **The British Civil Service, 1854–1954,** by Wyn Griffith, 32 pp.
*A brief history officially published on the occasion of the centenary of the publication of the Trevelyan-Northcote Report.*

1954  **Royal Commission on the Civil Service (1953).** Introductory Factual Memorandum on the Civil Service. 184 pp.
**Royal Commission on the Civil Service (1953):** Supplement to Introductory Factual Memorandum on the Civil Service (Medical and Legal Staffs). 13 pp.
*Information compiled by H.M. Treasury for the guidance of the Royal Commission.*

1954/55  **Royal Commission on the Civil Service:** Minutes of Evidence 1–28. 1, 176 pp. in twenty-four separate issues.

1954  **Royal Commission on the Civil Service:** Appendix I to Minutes of Evidence: First Selection of Supplementary Statements from Witnesses. 57 pp.

1955  **Royal Commission on the Civil Service:** Appendix II to Minutes of Evidence: Second Selection of Supplementary Statements from Witnesses. 89 pp.

1955  **Royal Comission on the Civil Service, 1953–5: Report.** 239 pp.
*The Report of the Priestly Commission on the Civil Service.*

1955  Report concerning the **Disappearance of Two Foreign Office Officials.** 8 pp.
*White Paper on the case of Burgess and Maclean who disappeared behind the Iron Curtain in 1951.*

1956  **Statement on the Findings of the Conference of Privy Councillors on Security.** 5 pp.
*A White Paper following an inquiry into the lessons of the Burgess-Maclean affair.*

1956  **Staffing and Organization of the Factory Inspectorate** (Cmd. 9879). 48 pp.
*Report of a Working Party set up by the Minister of Labour and National Service. Includes a useful summary of the Factory Inspectors's work.*

1957  **91st Report of Her Majesty's Civil Service Commissioners for** the period 1st April, 1956 to 31st March, 1957. 40 pp.
*Includes the text of the Civil Service Order in Council, 1956.*

1957  Inquiry into **Certain Allegations made by the Civil Service Union Relating to the Carlisle and District State Management Scheme** (Cmnd. 168). 18 pp.
*An impartial examination of alleged pressures upon certain of the Union's membership.*

1957  **Recruitment to the Administrative Class of the Home Civil Service and the Senior Branch of the Foreign Service** (Cmnd. 232). 32 pp.
*A statement of Government Policy and Report by the Civil Service Commission.*

1958  **Civil Service Pay Research Unit: First Annual Report, 1957.** 18 pp.
*The first of a series of regular reports by the Unit.*

1958  Report of the Committee on **Remuneration and Conditions of Service of Certain Grades in the Prison Service.** 52 pp.
*A survey of this specialized branch, with recommendations.*

1958 Report of an Enquiry into an **Allegation of Misuse of Official Facilities for the Circulation of Documents** (Cmnd. 583). 8 pp.
*An investigation by the Joint Permanant Secretary to the Treasury, as directed by the Prime Minister, which clears departmental officials of specific allegations by an M.P.*

1958 Sixth Report from the Select Committee on Estimates, Session 1957–58 on **Treasury Control of Expenditure.** xlii+414 pp.
*This important Report is not primarily concerned with establishments but is of interest here because of its outcome in the following entry.*

1961 **Control of Expenditure** (Cmnd. 1432). 33 pp.
*The Plowden Report, arising out of the preceding Estimates Committee Report, deals inter alia with the management aspects.*

1962 **Security Procedures in the Public Service** (Cmnd. 1681). 42 pp.
*Report of the Radcliffe Committee providing details of the working of the Security Services.*

1963 Report of the **Tribunal Appointed to Inquire into the Vassall Case and Related Matters** (Cmnd. 2009). 88 pp.
*A notorious case of espionage inside the central administration.*

1964 Fifth Report from the Estimates Committee, Session 1963–64 on **Treasury Control of Establishments.** xxxvi+172.
*An important inquiry aiming at the tightening of Treasury control in this sphere.*

1964 Report of the **Committee on Representational Services Overseas** appointed by the Prime Minister, under the chairmanship of Lord Plowden, 1962–63 (Cmnd. 2276). 176 pp.
*A review of these Services with recommendations for reorganization.*

1965 **The Organization of the Scientific Civil Service.** 28 pp.
*The Tennant Report, with recommendations.*

1965 Report of the **Standing Security Commission,** June 1965 (Cmnd. 2722).
*Examines the circumstances of the Bossard and Allen cases.*

1965 **Digest of Law and Regulations Affecting the Superannuation of Members of the Civil Service, Governors of Colonies and the Judiciary.** 715 pp.

1965 Sixth Report from the Estimates Committee, Session 1964–65, on **Recruitment of the Civil Service.** xxxviii+269 pp.
*A valuable preliminary survey of the problem which led to the appointment of the Fulton Committee on the Civil Service early in 1966.*

1965    Report of a **Board of Inquiry appointed by the Prime Minister following the Report of the Security Commission on the Bossard and Allen Cases** (Cmnd. 2773). 11 pp.
       *Examines the conduct of the civil servants referred to in Cmnd 2722.*

1965    **The Parliamentary Commissioner for Administration** (Cmnd. 2767). 7 pp.
       *Outlines of Government's proposals for the introduction of an Ombudsman.*

1966    National Board for Prices and Incomes: Report No. 11 **Pay of the Higher Civil Service** (Cmnd. 2882). 5 pp.

1966    National Board for Prices and Incomes: Report No. 18 **Pay of Industrial Civil Servants** (Cmnd. 3034). 29 pp.

# INDEX